Class Context
and
Family Relations
A Cross-National Study

Class Context
and
Family Relations

A Cross-National Study

LEONARD I. PEARLIN

National Institute of Mental Health

LITTLE, BROWN AND COMPANY
BOSTON

LIBRARY OF CONGRESS CATALOG CARD NUMBER: 74–134475

FIRST PRINTING

*Published simultaneously in Canada
by Little, Brown & Company (Canada) Limited*

PRINTED IN THE UNITED STATES OF AMERICA

The author thanks the following publishers for their
permission to adapt materials for inclusion in this book.

AMERICAN SOCIOLOGICAL ASSOCIATION. For "Social Class,
Occupation, and Parental Values: A Cross-National
Study" by Leonard I. Pearlin and Melvin L. Kohn, in
American Sociological Review 31 (1966): 466–479.
Adapted for Chapter IV.

UNIVERSITY OF CHICAGO PRESS. For "Unintended Effects
of Parental Aspirations: The Case of Children's Cheating"
by Leonard I. Pearlin, in *American Journal of Sociology*
73 (1967): 73–83. Adapted for Chapter V.

To Michele Leonard Ferrero

and

the Other Children of Turin

Preface

This monograph brings together several sociological themes and research strategies, and as a result it can be described with equal accuracy from a variety of perspectives. One description might emphasize the particular issue in family relations that the study examines, relations involving parents and children, husbands and wives, the nuclear and extended family systems. Another might stress the fact that the work was done in Turin, Italy, and provides an empirical view of the urban Italian family system, something that has been missing from the literature. But when I am called upon to describe this book, I tend to emphasize somewhat different features.

Most salient to me is that the study attempts to understand what goes on within the family by recognizing relevant social circumstances originating outside the family. Too often the family is treated in sociology as though its functioning is entirely independent of its surroundings. And too often family relations are conceptualized as acquiring their structure and character from the thrust of individuals' personalities. This study, in contrast, was designed to unravel some of the complex relationships that exist between the family and other social systems, especially social class and occupation. Thus an important focus of this book was to be on the interconnections of the family and its social contexts.

A second major feature of the study is the use of the very powerful analytic tool of cross-national comparisons. By conducting the work in Italy, and especially in the city of Turin, I was able to plan the study in a way that would permit me to see if similarities in social structure produce similarities in family relations in countries having very different cultural traditions. Thus the comparisons across nations were to be of the effects of social conditions on the family. To ensure that such comparisons would be possible, I borrowed heavily from research into the family that had been carried out in the United States by my colleague Melvin Kohn.

It would be grossly pretentious to suggest that I was drawn to Italy only — or even primarily — because of research considerations. For as long as I can remember, I entertained very attractive and fetching images of the country, its people, and its family life. Consequently when I had an opportunity in 1962 to work abroad, Italy had no serious competitor among the nations I considered. I should add that although I was to discover that most of my images were fanciful, the year was every bit as interesting as I anticipated.

It was much simpler to decide upon Italy than it was to choose the most suitable location within the country. Occupation and occupational conditions were factors that I was most interested in examining in relation to family issues. These interests had developed out of my previous studies in the mental hospital where I had found repeatedly that structured conditions of work influenced a host of feelings and actions. I saw the present study as an opportunity to ascertain if the effects of occupation transcend the occupational setting and reach as far as family relations. These interests dictated that the research be located in an industrial city. Whereas most previous studies of Italian families had been conducted in rural areas, especially of the south, this one was to have an urban setting.

Turin was an outstanding candidate. It is a modern city, a principal industrial center of Italy, encompassing a range of occupations. It is fairly large, but not so large that a foreign researcher would have to mobilize a large part of his efforts simply to learn his way around the city. Moreover, its modernity and industrialization would enhance the opportunity to compare what I learned about the family there with the findings of American studies, most of which had been done in urban areas. All in all, Turin seemed to satisfy the important requirements of my research interests.

Other reasons led me to select this city. Of extreme importance to the successful execution of the study were a number of logistical advantages resulting from the location of the work in Turin. The normal difficulties of launching a survey are compounded when the work is being done by an alien in a foreign culture. Gaining local institutional support, hiring and training interviewers and clerical staff, printing interview schedules — all the tasks that are ordinarily taken in stride become problematic. While such logistical requirements are somewhat extrinsic to the substance of research, they are nevertheless vital to it. For these reasons, the opportunity to have the collaboration of Dr. Pier Brunetti was a dominant consideration in the choice of Turin. Brunetti, an American-trained social psychiatrist, is a native of Turin and is thoroughly familiar with the city and its culture. He had the demanding role of being my collaborator in the field, my stern critic, and my friend. It is difficult to imagine that this study could have progressed very far without the knowledge and guidance it received from him.

But no matter how wise or considered preparations may be, the alien observer cannot possibly be ready for everything he has to cope with. Although many of his problems can be managed by established procedural prescriptions, he is likely to feel that the strange culture and the unfamiliar language conspire to keep understanding from his grasp. Fortunately, this does not last indefinitely; before he is aware of it, the capriciousness he observes early in his stay begins to give way to meaningful regularities. What saves the day for him are his concepts, not his intellect. Concepts enable him to organize his attentions and sensitivities and help him to see that many phenomena that appear to be disparate, unrelated, or chaotic actually fit together in ways that make sense. Indeed, without his concepts the sociologist would have difficulty in understanding the institutions of his own nation, much less those of a foreign culture.

Theories, concepts, and methodologies do not completely shield the sociologist from mistakes and misjudgments. Any research undertaking is necessarily incomplete and is host to inaccurate data and misleading interpretations. Perhaps this is especially true in research in foreign societies. I cannot be sure where or to what extent such problems entered into the present study. I can be certain, though, that they are entirely my responsibility and not that of the substantial number of people who have helped me in this research.

In particular, I have accumulated an extraordinary measure of indebtedness to my fellow scientists in the Laboratory of Socio-environmental Studies of the National Institute of Mental Health. They are Gordon Allen, Roger Burton, John Campbell, William Caudill, Melvin Kohn, Morris Rosenberg, Carmi Schooler, and Marian Radke Yarrow. I am beholden to them for their criticisms of the manuscript and for their intellectual companionship over the years. I wish to emphasize that the analytic acumen of Morris Rosenberg, which he has shared with me for two decades, is sprinkled throughout the following pages. The contributions of Melvin Kohn need to be especially underscored. He collaborated with me in most of the analysis presented in Chapter IV and generously provided data and materials from his American studies for comparison with my findings from Italy. With equal generosity, he made many additional contributions throughout the manuscript.

I would like further to acknowledge that I have drawn upon the perceptive criticisms of Bernard Barber, Stanley Coopersmith, Alex Inkeles, Richard Lieban, Roberta Simmons, and Yngvar Løchen of the University of Oslo.

Finally, I am indebted to the late Luciano Saffirio of the University of Turin for his wise help and warm support. Until his premature death I relied on his close friendship and his keen sociological judgment.

The Fondazione Adriano Olivetti was most generous in its sponsorship and its administrative support. Its director, Dr. Massino Fichera, and its staff members were unstinting in their help, a fact that aided the acceptance of the study by the Turinese.

It was my good fortune in Turin to have as my secretary Mrs. Ena Cabutti Velline. She assumed the major responsibility for administrative chores and for the organization of the interviewing. Her good sense saved me from more blunders than I am comfortable thinking about. Among the interviewers there are four who were particularly instrumental in setting the high standards and in maintaining the momentum of this critically important task: Mrs. Feretti, Mrs. Piotti, Miss Viara, and Miss Meriano. Here in Bethesda, I have enjoyed the assistance of Clarice Radabaugh, who possesses a rare combination of research skills and splendid human qualities.

Last, and most of all, I thank the fine and gracious people of Turin for an unforgettable experience.

Contents

52 II

51

99

123

xi

Tables

I

The Changing Social Contexts
of Family Relations

The family in many respects is different from any other human group. Its durability continues across generations, it is the main arena for the expression of intense and varied emotions, it confronts countless situations, and it is of utmost importance to its members. Because of these unusual qualities, it is understandable that studies often have approached the family as though it were self-contained, possessing a life generated entirely by conditions within its own boundaries.[1] The present work utilizes a different approach. It attempts to understand the transactions that occur within the family by looking at circumstances originating outside of it. It has as its major aim the exploration of the effects of social structure on the internal relations of the family.[2]

A second goal of this inquiry is to learn if social structural effects on family life are similar in nations having different cultures. The location of the study in Turin is particularly appropriate to this purpose, for it is a city that provides a very suitable vantage point from which meaningful cross-national comparisons can be made. Turin is set within a culture that is distinct from that of the United States,

[1]Winch points out that not only is the family unit often viewed as self-contained, but the mother-child relation is treated as a closed system. He goes on to say that a sociological approach considers the parent-child dyad as a sub-system of the family, and the family as a sub-system of the larger society. Robert F. Winch, *Identification and Its Familial Determinants* (New York: Bobbs-Merrill, 1962), pp. 31 – 32.

[2]Interest in the relationships between family and society far exceeds the empirical knowledge we possess. According to Goode, this is a principal reason for the absence of systematic propositions regarding the inter-relationships between the family and other institutions. William J. Goode, "The Sociology of the Family," in Robert K. Merton, Leonard Broom, and Leonard S. Cottrell, Jr. (eds.), *Sociology Today* (New York: Basic Books, 1959), pp. 178 – 196.

1

yet many of its social conditions, especially those associated with industrialization and urbanization, are comparable to those of American cities. The lack of uniqueness of elements in Turin's social system, together with the distinctiveness of its cultural environment, permit cross-national comparisons to be focused on a single central question: Do social conditions common to modern industrialized societies penetrate with similar effects families embedded in different cultural environments?

This study has a third purpose, somewhat subsidiary to the first two, but nonetheless important. Although it will emphasize elements of family life that generally prevail in modern nations, it is intended also to provide a picture of the distinguishing features of the urban Italian family. Considering how interested Americans are in the cities and monuments of Italy, we know surprisingly little that is authentic about the Italian people or their family life. We study their antiques and art, search for inspiration at their religious shrines, devour their food, and gaze at their women. But, except in journalistic accounts, we have made little effort at pulling back the curtain that divides this public panorama from their more intimate lives. What we have learned comes mainly from studies of rural villagers, and they are quite different from the large mass of their countrymen living in urban-industrial centers. Among the large cities of Italy, Turin and its residents are least well-known, particularly to Americans. It is off the main tourist trail and those with limited time by-pass it for Venice, Florence, and Rome. For this reason a descriptive overview of the city and its people will be useful to understanding more concretely the goals of this study and their implementation.

THE SETTING OF THE STUDY: TURIN (TORINO)

Turin rests in a valley directly under the Alps in the northwest section of the country, not far from the French border. On a clear day one can see and identify the various mountains, among them the imposing Mt. Blanc. The Turinese are fond of the mountains; either individually or as members of organized clubs they use their slopes for skiing or, in the warm months, for hiking and climbing. The climate in the area is between extremes; the temperature in the summer is occasionally uncomfortably high, but in the winter extreme cold is rare because of the protective barrier of the Alps.

Turin is one of the more prosperous cities in Italy; it supports a population of over 1 million and is economically vital to the entire country. Because of its proximity to the Alps it has access to ample sources of hydroelectric power, a resource generally lacking throughout Italy. This has been a very important factor in its economic development and population growth since World War II. Over 90 per cent of the automobiles manufactured in Italy are produced in Turin, and it is also the main center of Italian metallurgy, engineering and textile manufacture.

In addition to its industrial activities, the city serves as an important commercial center for the region. The Po River, which flows through the city, is lined by some highly fertile farm areas. Agriculture in the surrounding countryside is consequently considerably more productive than in many other parts of Italy, and this, too, contributes significantly to the level of the economy. The economic position of the area, which compared favorably to the rest of the country even during the nineteenth century, has led to a high degree of stability of its native population. Very few Turinese were among those who were part of the waves of immigration to the United States or, more recently, who provided migrant labor for other European countries.

Turin is the capital of the Piedmont region, which, before the unification of the country, constituted a major part of the Kingdom of Savoy. In addition to the local cultural patterns that differentiate virtually all of the regions from one another, the Piedmont was also subjected to considerable French influence. Lying as it does at the head of strategic Alpine passes below France, for many centuries it has been actively exposed to outside cultural influences. Its regional dialect, which is maintained as a second language, bears some resemblance to French. In recent years, with the large-scale migration from the South, this dialect has come into more prominent use as a differentiating and exclusion mechanism.

Turin has a prominent place in the political shaping of modern Italy. As the capital of the Kingdom of Savoy, it gave to unified Italy its first king, Victor Emmanuel II. Many of the leaders of the *Risorgimento* were Turinese, and, in fact, Turin was the capital of unified Italy before Rome. Its street names provide a constant reminder of this period of Italian history, for a number of its thoroughfares are named after the political and military heroes of the unification movement.

The visitor to present day Turin is immensely impressed by the city. He is struck by the broad boulevards and by the miles of graceful arcades that line the major streets. These arcades house countless shops, each vying with the next in the artful display of their goods. The city is dotted with *piazze*, each likely to have a monument to some hero of a glorious victory or defeat. Sidewalk cafes surround these squares where the Turinese take their *aperitivi* to stimulate their appetites and their *digestivi* to settle their stomachs. Parks are located throughout the city where people enjoy strolling, reading, holding political discussions, or boating.

Except during the long, mid-afternoon break between the hours of 12:30 and 3:00 P.M., the streets are crowded with automobiles and the sidewalks with very well-dressed pedestrians. The Turinese have a great fondness for their city and use it much more intensely than Americans use theirs. While there has been an upsurge in the construction of *ville* in the outskirts, people prefer to live directly in the city and the suburbs hold little attraction for them. Most of the industries and commercial establishments are located well within the city, so that work is often not far from home. Thus, the Turinese look to the city for their homes, their work and also their recreation. On Sundays there are crowds of strollers, many of them families who have come in from surrounding towns; the restaurants, movie houses and cafes are at capacity. The sight of the people peacefully walking arm-in-arm gives the picture of tranquility and satisfaction. I was to learn that alongside this peaceful air there exists a good deal of anxiety, worry and discontent.

A word is required concerning the representativeness of the Turinese as Italians. The newcomer to Italy is frequently warned by Italians that the particular place he happens to be at the time is not typical of Italy. Regardless of the location, all such warnings are justified. Because of natural physical barriers that lace the country, local differences are generated and perpetuated. The centuries of invasions, along with their cultural infusions, have contributed to these differences. Also a sense of loyalty and devotion to the nation and its centralized institutions is still associated in the minds of many Italians with fascism and, therefore, to be eschewed. A strong national identification, consequently, is not sufficiently extant to level local and regional variations. The upshot of this is that we can hardly speak of the Turinese as being typically Italian, for there are no typical Italians.[3] In fact, it is quite certain that if this study had been con-

[3]A similar caveat is leveled by Moss and Thompson who were interested in southern Italian families. They, too, are careful to point out regional variations and the consequent limitations on the generality of their statements. Leonard W. Moss and Walter H. Thompson, "The South Italian Family: Literature and Observations," *Human Organization*, 28 (1959), pp. 35–41. The lower-class Neapolitan families described by Anne Parsons, furthermore, are quite different from the working-class families in Turin. Anne Parsons, "Paternal and Maternal Authority in the Neopolitan Family," in Rose Laub Coser, *et al.*, (eds.), *Belief, Magic, and Anomie: Essays in Psychosocial Anthropology* (New York: The Free Press, 1969), pp. 67–97, published originally in Italian, "Autorità Patriarchale e Autorità Matriarchale Nella Famiglia Napoletana," in *Estratto dai Quaderni di Sociologia*, 11 (1962).

ducted in the South or in any rural area our results would not have been the same.

But the very characteristics of Turin that distinguish it from rural Italy make it an advantageous site from which to draw cross-national comparisons. Indeed, in many respects the Turinese may be engaged in a social structure more similar to that of Detroiters than to that in which Italians of the rural South participate. Throughout the course of the analyses I shall be searching for precisely those elements of social structure that do cut across nations and influence their family systems.

CLASS AND OCCUPATIONAL CONTEXTS
OF THE FAMILY

This study examines many elements of social structure in relationship to various aspects of family life. Most of these are derivatives of the class and occupational contexts of the family.

First consider class, whose importance to the family would be difficult to exaggerate. The reasons for its importance, nevertheless, are not always clear and direct. Essentially class is important because of its powerful regulatory functions on a host of social experiences. Many of these experiences are concomitants of one's "life chances" which, in turn, closely hinge on one's position in a class order. To cite but a few examples, a person finds that what is on his table, the medical care he receives, his schooling, his treatment under the law, the attention he receives from public bureaucracies, and the regularity with which he is superordinate or subordinate to others are tied to his class standing. The experiences embodied in life chances, therefore, have a remarkable consistency through time and space.

Class is also important because it significantly influences the group and institutional memberships of people and the social encounters that accompany these memberships. A person is likely to live in a neighborhood, work, marry, go to church, belong to a political party, join a club, and be friends with people of the same social class as his. The homology of his social contacts means that he finds in others a reinforcing confirmation of his own perspectives and feelings. He learns that his hopes and frustrations and his likes and dislikes are similar to those of his intimates. The pooled experiences of his membership groups provide the basis for the development of norms that he shares with others similar to him.

Because life chances and social participation depend so closely on class, there is a regularity in the experiences of individuals from one situation to another and from one time to another. The sheer regularity of class-linked experiences makes all the more powerful their

cumulative effects in creating ideologies and values, in shaping predilections and actions. By these processes an existential world distinctive of a given class stratum is developed, sustained and legitimized.
Class thus comes to constitute an encompassing basis on which the
lives of people are organized.[4]

This organization of life must have a direct and fundamental
bearing on family relations. What a person comes to understand of
his world cannot remain segregated from his actions and feelings in
the family domain. His relations with other family members will be
established partly on the basis of the realities he encounters while
engaged in social roles outside. The norms and orientations he acquires in his associations, the "knowledge" he gains from repeated
experiences, and the pattern of his successes and disappointments all
help to define his expectations of and actions toward other family
members. In this way, the structured conditions of class that impinge
on people reach deeply into the family to influence the form and
direction of its interpersonal relations. Although this assertion may
appear self-evident, it has surprisingly little empirical data to support
it. Much of the present work is aimed at filling this gap.

The second context that figures prominently in this study is occupation. Clearly the things that people do to earn a living are inseparable
components of their class standing: there are no upper-class street
cleaners and no lower-class investment brokers. *However, when I
speak of occupational context I refer to the constellation of experiences
a person has in his work, not to the class status his job provides him.*
There is sufficient independence between these two factors to allow
them to be treated separately. This will be evident in the course of
the analyses.

The effects of occupation reach into the family as a result of the
multiple roles of its members. In this respect it is not different from
the way other institutions may influence the family. Simply put, the
experiences an individual has in one institutional domain are expressed
in the ways he acts in other domains. The occupational experiences
that will have the most deep-seated effects are those that are structured and repetitive. These experiences may be anchored either to
the nature of the tasks one performs or to one's role vis-à-vis others
in the work setting. Of greatest relevance are experiences that reflect

---

[4]That class affects individuals in so many ways and with such consistency is
one reason why empirical indicators of class are highly interchangeable. Thus, patterns of association, styles of life, place of residence, church affiliation and many
other social characteristics are closely intercorrelated, and each is reflective of
economic position. See Bernard Barber, *Social Stratification* (New York: Harcourt, Brace and Company, 1957), pp. 96 – 186.

a regularity of action and of relations with others, for it is the patterned and enduring aspects of occupational experiences, rather than the happenstance or marginal events, that are likely to affect family relations.

Previous research is too limited and inconclusive to be of much help in hypothesizing with precision or confidence the relationships between occupation and family. Some earlier work, however, is useful in clarifying the conceptual issues involved in these relationships. A study by Aberle and Naegle, for example, while involving data that permitted only speculative results, yielded several fruitful ideas.[5] They were particularly interested in asking how fathers' occupations provided both the goals they set for their children and the benchmarks for judging children's progress toward these goals. It is a theoretically useful question, for it directs attention to the occupational sphere as a source of socializing values and standards. The same question is threaded through much of the exploration here.

In the work of Miller and Swanson, the main focus is on differences in child-training practices found between families where the father is an independent entrepreneur or a salaried employee in a bureaucracy.[6] The authors conceive of these occupational settings as creating different views of the individual in relation to his world, fostering different values and impelling parents to employ distinct modes of child rearing. They think that the entrepreneurial setting leads to training children eventually to be self-directed, while the bureaucratic setting results in training children to be accommodative. For methodological reasons it is difficult to assess how well their findings actually substantiate their propositions. Furthermore, "entrepreneurial" and "bureaucratic" are global occupational categories, encompassing many elements; consequently, a comparison of the two tells us very little empirically about the specific conditions of work or of the occupational experiences that may be contributing to child-rearing differences. Nevertheless, to the extent that their work calls attention to the structural properties of the occupational setting in relation to socializing practices, it is very congenial with the approach taken here.

A third study, by McKinley, is relevant mainly because of the contrasts it provides to the present work.[7] His work discusses aggressive

[5]David F. Aberle and Kaspar D. Naegle, "Middle-class Fathers' Occupational Role and Attitudes Toward Children," *American Journal of Orthopsychiatry*, 22 (1952), pp. 366–378.

[6]Daniel R. Miller and Guy E. Swanson, *The Changing American Parent* (New York: John Wiley & Sons, 1958).

[7]Donald Gilbert McKinley, *Social Class and Family Life* (Glencoe, Ill.: The Free Press, 1964), pp. 118–151.

elements in father-child relations, such as hostility and authoritarianism. He then traces these patterns to occupational frustrations, placing paternal attitudes squarely within a frustration-aggression framework. At several points the data of this study suggest that McKinley may misinterpret what actually takes place. Feelings aroused at work are expressed in the home, but more is involved than the mere displacement of feelings from one institution to another. Specifically, evidence suggests that constant subordination to the authority of others, which McKinley presumes produces frustration, may serve as a model for fathers. When they assert their own superordination to children, they are not reacting to frustration, but conforming to a model for interpersonal relations. What is carried into the family, in other words, is a structured experience that becomes a foundation for establishing relations with others.

From the flow of their occupational experiences, men — and indirectly, at least, women — acquire conceptions of what is desirable and what is necessary in relations between themselves and others. They learn what is mandatory and should be encouraged, what is harmful and should be forbidden. The occupational sphere, in which so much is invested and on which so much depends, thus serves as a source of standards for interpersonal obligations and expectations in the family. This is the general conceptual framework that is used in examining the associations between the occupational context and family relations.[8]

FAMILY RELATIONS

The family encompasses an extensive reservoir of human affairs, and without ignoring some and conceptually unifying others, proceeding in a useful way would be impossible. To describe fully the activities of a single ordinary family over a single day would alone require several volumes. The nuances and fine shades of feelings and their communication, the ebb and flow of actions and reactions constitute a boundless mosaic. But knowledge does not rest on taking separate account of all things — even if this were possible. It is both desirable and necessary to capture those phenomena that form describable patterns through time and space. In terms of the present study the task is to identify selectively broad currents in family relations rather than the vagaries of moment-to-moment family life.

The process of selection is bound closely to the major goals of this study. First, the search for relationships between the family and

[8]This position is very similar to that which was formulated by Kohn. See Melvin L. Kohn, "Social Class and Parent-Child Relationships: An Interpretation," *American Journal of Sociology*, 68 (1963), pp. 471 – 480.

structured elements of its social contexts ignores all those peculiarities that distinctly set one family off from all other families. My concern is with aspects of family life that are shared with a multiplicity of other families exposed to similar conditions of life, not with the customs and unspoken understandings that result in each family being a unique entity. It may be interesting to know the culinary secrets that make Signora Ferrero's spaghetti sauce different from all others, but it is more important to know that many families must eat spaghetti six days a week and meat only once.

Although each family within a society is a unique entity, the research strategy I have adopted stresses characteristics shared by a multiplicity of families. A parallel approach will be used in cross-national comparisons. I could emphasize those patterns that make the Italian family different from those of other nations. And many constellations of values and behavior, points of emphasis and modes of expression do make it unique in the world. But a more productive strategy is to search for those things that are problematic to families in all industrialized and changing societies, regardless of their cultural contexts. It is by focusing on issues not co-extensive with national boundaries that we can determine whether similar conditions of life produce similar patterns of action and sentiment in societies whose histories and cultures are divergent. Thus, in order to assess the effects of environmental circumstances, we must look for family patterns shared by collectivities rather than for the peculiar and idiosyncratic; and, to see if these effects exist in other societies, we must attend to those aspects of relations generally found in family systems of contemporary nations.

The family relations that I have selected for examination in this study are relevant to all industrialized nations. A detailed description of them, their specifications and measurements, will be deferred to the time when each is analyzed. At this point I wish only to present a "conceptual imagery" of them and to indicate generally how they serve the major aims of the study.

PARENTS AND CHILDREN. The largest part of this inquiry is addressed to sentiments and transactions involved in parent-child relations. Such an emphasis is deserved because the training and care of children is one of the principal functions of the family. Moreover, much of the structural character of the family can be revealed in the way it is mobilized for the performance of the vital tasks connected with raising children. When we learn how parents pattern their feelings and actions in dealing with their children, we are at the same time able to learn something about the total family.

Parent-child relations are of paramount importance for another reason, one that closely fits the goals of the present inquiry. Many of the transactions between parents and their children are best understood as part of the process of preparing the young for adult status, socialization. Socialization necessarily reveals some of the connections between family and society because it is oriented to the roles children will eventually assume in the larger social order. Four chapters deal with issues clearly relevant to the preparation of children for future roles and, consequently, they directly implicate elements of the surrounding society, its requirements and rewards.

The first of these, Chapter IV, is concerned with parental values and considers the kinds of people parents want their children to become. Specifically, parents were asked to indicate the characteristics they view as most important for their children to have and that, presumably, they attempt to inculcate. The hierarchical ordering of characteristics by their importance is more problematic to parents than might at first appear evident. Parents are scanning an array of desirable personal qualities, each potentially important for future roles, each competing with others for priority. The range of qualities parents would like their children to acquire is at least as varied as the surrounding social structure, the roles and statuses it offers and the expectations it sets forth. The social changes that are characteristic of contemporary societies also make the valuation of characteristics problematic, for the qualities deemed important in one generation may be obsolete in the following. Knowing the present becomes an increasingly uncertain guide to knowing the future as the pace and extent of change increases. A parent under these circumstances is unable to judge from his own experiences what his child faces and what he should be prepared for. Consequently, it can be difficult for parents to establish a stable order of priorities among the characteristics they want their children to acquire.

The cross-national comparison of parental values was built into this study by adapting questions from an investigation conducted earlier in Washington, D. C., by Melvin Kohn.[9] By using the same questions we can compare Turinese with Americans and see if the relationships of social class and occupational conditions to parental values are similar in the two societies.

In distinction to parental values are parental aspirations, a second issue in parent-child relations, discussed in Chapter V. Whereas values refer to characteristics and qualities that are stressed, aspirations concern the social statuses parents hope their children will achieve. Values

[9]Melvin L. Kohn, "Social Class and Parental Values," *American Journal of Sociology*, 64 (1959), pp. 337–351.

and aspirations are alike insofar as they both pertain to the future state of children in the social system. For this reason, again, it is expected that aspirations would be directly affected by parents' experiences in the system. One may think that aspirations are concentrated at the highest levels, since every parent "naturally" wants the very best for his child and the rewards that come with the best. But the goals parents envision for their children are closely associated with their own material positions and their experiences in an opportunity structure. What may represent the very best in one family may be considered demeaning in another, depending on their positions. Much of our interest in parental aspirations is in delineating such social structural sources. A rich body of theory and data already exists in the United States that is directly pertinent to our work in Turin. Consequently several cross-national comparisons can be made to see if similar aspirations evolve from similar conditions in the two countries.

Once formed, aspirations do not simply remain dormant in the minds and fantasies of parents. Direct observations of parents and their children were carried out in many homes, providing an unusual opportunity to follow through the analysis of parental aspirations to a point where it is possible to talk about their behavioral consequences. Aspirations were traced to the kinds of interactions parents establish with their children in the home settings; these interactions, in turn, affect the observed actions of children in dealing with achievement tasks. The analysis of parental aspirations thus ranges from some of their social roots to some of their concrete manifestations, particularly in behavior that is neither intended nor desired by parents.

The third issue in parent-child relations, considered in Chapter VI, is that of discipline. Its relationship to surrounding social circumstances is less readily apparent than in the case of parental values or aspirations. Physical punishment, especially, may be viewed simply as a spontaneous response to the eruptions that occur in interaction or as a manifestation of the personalities involved. However, when disciplinary practices are conceived as mechanisms for the long-range constraint and control of behavior toward desired goals, the significance of social factors becomes more readily apparent. The nature of parents' goals for children, the deferments they require, and the fear of failure to achieve them are among the conditions that will be shown to underlie parental discipline. Occupational experiences of fathers are relevant here, too. The nature of the authority system in which their work is set is especially pertinent, for fathers pattern their own disciplinary practices after the kinds of constraints they experience at work.

In Chapter VII we discuss affection, the final matter in parent-child relations. Affective relations between parents and children are more difficult to conceptualize and assess than any other issue entering into this study. Parental feeling states are intimately bound to self-images and role conceptions; feelings about children, therefore, cannot easily be probed without arousing a host of other feelings also important to individuals. Other complexities also make the study of parental feelings difficult: the ways feelings are manifested in interaction, their intensity, and the occasions that stimulate and dampen them.

We will avoid some of these complexities by confining the analyses to the ways parents express affection. Although it might appear that expressiveness is regulated by widely accepted cultural definitions of parenthood, there is in the demonstration of affection considerable variability that is associated with identifiable social circumstances. For example, affection may function as a subtle mechanism to maintain filial loyalty and family unity. This is an important function to those parents who see their rapidly changing world as a threat to family solidarity. Other evidence suggests that affection may be used to control and channel the behavior of children in a direction consistent with the distant goals parents hold for them. Finally, fathers' occupational experiences, particularly those reflecting frustrations at work, also influence patterns of affection. The effects of occupation are not what one is likely to predict, however, for they depend on the sex of the child and the socializing functions of the father.

HUSBANDS AND WIVES. The relations between husbands and wives, studied in Chapter VIII, undoubtedly affect the way they socialize their children and, indeed, the overall character and functioning of the entire family unit. They are important and interesting in their own right, too, especially in periods of social change where old bonds disintegrate and new ones evolve. An outstanding feature of the modern nuclear family is that its unity no longer depends on a joint economic struggle. A division of labor between spouses still exists, of course, but a tight interdependence of roles organized around economic functions is diminishing.

These changes are very much in evidence in Turin. Marriage there seems to be at a turbulent junction at which new elements flowing in are clashing with many remaining traditional patterns. Some of the old arrangements that were considered to be an expression of a natural order are being challenged, resulting in conflict, strain and disaffection. Yet, it would be grossly misleading to describe husband and wife relations in Turin as fragile. On the contrary, there is considerable unity, based now on *consensus* and *companionship*, issues crucial to the solidarity of modern marriage, which will be our major foci in looking at husband-wife relations. Consensus and companionship are elements that contribute to making marriage more intimate than any other interpersonal relation, one that is outstandingly enclosed in its own net of understanding and shared feelings. The social conditions that influence consensus and companionship between husband and wife, consequently, are reaching into the center of the modern family system.

KINSHIP RELATIONS. The extended family system has often been viewed as a victim of industrialization. Stripped of its economic functions, the kinship system is thought to have lost a principal sustaining bond to its smaller units. Urbanization, geographic and social mobility and occupational specialization are among the factors viewed as having had an erosive impact on the family network. Recent studies in the United States, however, have severely challenged any conception of the nuclear family as indifferent to the extended system. Despite the separation of households, considerable interdependence and social contact between relatives are still to be found. Turin is a particularly suitable site for observing the impact of modernization on kinship; though Turin is highly industrialized, kinship still can command strong loyalties and obligations. By cross-national comparisons, we can contrast societies each having a high level of industry, although in one the family is traditionally a more salient institution.

A comparison of the loyalty of Italians and Americans to the larger system is not the only purpose served by the examination of kinship. Loyalty is not self-supporting; it rises or falls with circumstances. The identification of these circumstances and the understanding of how they contribute to the maintenance or attenuation of kinship relations occupy most of Chapter IX.

This completes, then, an overview of the family patterns that will serve as the major dependent variables: parental values, parental aspirations, patterns of discipline, patterns of affection, husband-wife relations and kinship relations. These elements of family life differ in their *prima-facie* relationships to social circumstances surrounding the family. Parental values and aspirations, for example, have reference to the futures of children in the larger social system; we could expect, consequently, that they would be shaped and molded directly by parents' own experiences within the system. By contrast, the affection of parents for their children, or the closeness of their marriages, stand in a less clear relationship to conditions external to the family. It is more tempting to think of these aspects of family relations as arising entirely from the personal characteristics of the participants. But in each instance the social contexts to which the family is connected exert, in a myriad of ways, considerable influence. Judging by the comparisons we can make, furthermore, the effects of society on family are similar in the United States.

CROSS-NATIONAL ASPECTS
OF TURINESE FAMILY RELATIONS

It is a fair statement, I believe, that most comparative studies treat societies as internally uniform while emphasizing the differences between nations. This study does the opposite; it is concerned with the differentiation existing within societies and the cross-national similarity of these internal differences. The contrast in approaches is partly derived from the traditionally divergent perspectives of anthropology and sociology. The former focuses on culture, which is mirrored in the uniformities among people within a society, in the beliefs and modes of actions they share. Sociological analyses depend more on the location of differences between collectivities, for it is only by delineating patterned variations among groups that we can then identify the structural arrangements contributing to these variations. When the same arrangements are associated with similar differences in a plurality of nations, we are provided with evidence both more compelling and more general that the effects are not cultural artifacts, but result from the structured conditions. Cross-national comparisons can thus be employed as an extension of this established strategy of sociological analyses.

We must meet several requirements before we can realize this strategy. Some are methodological and these are discussed in the following chapter. Here I wish only to emphasize that to ascribe cross-national similarities in family relations to structural conditions, the same conditions must exist in each of the societies. Clearly, it makes no sense to compare societies whose social systems are different with respect to the very conditions whose effects are being compared. With regard to this inquiry, there is reason to believe that the social conditions studied in relationship to the Turinese family also prevail in the United States, for most of these conditions are associated with industralization and urbanization. Thus, Turin's system of stratification, the range of its occupations, the organization of its occupational settings, the nature of the goals toward which people strive and its opportunity structure are comparable with those of this country. By no means is there cross-national identicality in these conditions. They are sufficiently similar, however, to permit the assertion that what is learned in Turin about the effects of social structure on family life has a generality that extends far beyond Turin itself.

Nations need to be structurally similar in order to be compared sociologically, but they must also be culturally distinct. Were they similar *both* structurally and culturally, cross-national similarities could be just as well attributed to cultural as structural effects. Italy certainly possesses a cultural distinctiveness. As in the case of all nations, it has its own accumulated history, its own confluence of events and conditions that give to its people an identifiable and unique character. Indeed, one needs only to look at the Turinese family itself to find much that is culturally distinguishing. I shall document in Chapter III the meaning and importance of the family to its members, how it serves as a fortress against hostile elements in the outside world, how its members rely on it for many needs unsatisfied by other institutions and how its solidarity is nurtured and fiercely protected. If social conditions can permeate Turinese family relations whose walls are buttressed by these cultural traditions, similar conditions may penetrate even more easily in societies where the family is less dominant an institution. Thus the distinctive character of its culture, together with the non-uniqueness of many of its social conditions, makes Turin a most strategic site for a study searching for cross-national relationships between family and society.

Although the logic of cross-national comparisons suggests that it is possible to separate cultural from social structural effects on family relations, empirically they are not easily separable. In almost every comparative table I shall present, the effects of each can be observed. Cultural elements are reflected in the fact that Italians located in different positions in their social order are still more similar to each other than they are to Americans located in corresponding positions — and vice versa. To take a concrete example, there is a closer sharing of values by middle- and working-class Italian parents than by Italians and Americans of the same class position. The effects of social factors, on the other hand, can be detected in the fact that where class divisions create value differences between people in one culture, corresponding differences are likely to appear in the second culture where there are similar social divisions. Cross-national comparisons of structural conditions, therefore, establish only that social factors can influence family independently of culture; they do not deny that culture also has a powerful presence independent of social structure.

SOCIAL CHANGE

The social circumstances surrounding the family and affecting its internal relations are not static, unchanging through time. In Turin, as in many urban centers around the world, large-scale changes are underway. At several places in the analyses the sentiments and interactions observed in the family at one point in time are probably reflections of social changes that have already occurred or are in process. Yet, I shall not be able to relate empirically alterations in the larger society to those in the family. This would require accurate before-and-after descriptions of the family covering a considerable span of time. It would require also knowledge of where to look for relevant changes in society and how to assess them, how to follow their consequences into the family. This kind of knowledge is surprisingly limited in the sociological armory.[10] In the absence of concrete information there is a tendency to reconstruct the past, to put it together as we imagine it must have been, and this can result in a picture of earlier family life that exaggerates its differences from the present and idealizes its lost virtues.[11]

Though our knowledge of change and its inter-institutional consequences is imprecise, its presence is a fact and the Turinese family is very much a part of it. The specific concomitants of industrialization and urbanization may be obscure in relation to the family, but it is nonetheless evident that much of what we see in family relations represents a struggle to adapt to shifting conditions of life. Parents must prepare their children for a future they cannot foresee with clarity and of which they are afraid. Husbands and wives are no longer bound together by the same conditions, nor are they as willing to accept traditional marriage; so they, too, must find new bases of unity. And, of course, nuclear family units live in greater physical isolation from their kin, there are new demands that blunt their attentions and divert loyalties from the larger family system. Yet, kinship solidarity is something they also want and work to maintain.

I do not wish to present the Turinese family as in danger of collapse; it is very much a going institution. Nor is it serenely following an unwavering course. It is under challenge to adapt to changes occurring in all quarters, and many of the interpretations threaded through this study are necessarily formulated in these terms. There are stable elements in the environment of the family, but it should be emphasized that much that is observed of its internal relations rep-

[10]Moore provides a brief but incisive discussion of some of the problems in the conceptualization and study of social change. Wilbert E. Moore, *Order and Change* (New York: John Wiley & Sons, 1967), pp. 3 – 29.

[11]Goode suggests that our picture of the American family of the past is more a product of nostalgia than historical reality. William J. Goode, *World Revolution and Family Patterns* (New York: The Free Press, 1963), pp. 6 – 7. Through the use of diaries, books and other accounts by foreign visitors of life in the United States, Furstenberg concludes that a number of features of family thought to represent recent changes actually existed a century ago. Frank F. Furstenberg, Jr., "Industrialization and the American Family: A Look Backward," *American Sociological Review*, 31 (1966), pp. 326 – 337.

resents a continuing effort to cope with a world that is not standing still.

It would be well to end this introduction by reaffirming what is generally recognized: The complexity of all societies far exceeds our knowledge of them. This, perhaps, is especially the case when our knowledge rests on limited direct contact. In Italian social life, many currents appear contradictory and are difficult to understand. It is, of course, unimaginable that any contemporary society could be integrated to the extent that it is free of conflicts and inconsistencies, and the observer is soon struck and puzzled by some of these in Italy. He discovers that Italians are warm and outgoing, yet distant and preoccupied. They can involve themselves in a sincere search for the essence of man and, at the same time, engage in much face work and show. They are both worldly and provincial, magnanimous and petty, democratic and subservient to status, tolerant and prejudiced. But, while these contradictions are confounding, they enable the sociologist to learn much about a society. Its points of friction help to reveal its structure, values and aspirations. If, therefore, I dwell on these areas, it is not because that is all there is to the life of the Turinese, but because these areas can be so revealing.

II

The Research Milieu
and the Research Procedures

Most of the data of this study come from a survey of Turinese parents. The methodological problems that arose are essentially similar to those a researcher encounters in planning a survey in his own society. Even familiar problems, however, are more difficult to resolve in an unfamiliar setting. The native researcher is able at the outset to plan and adapt his procedures to the extensive knowledge that he already possesses of his society. The alien's understanding is likely to be more limited; he knows less of the people he is studying, their institutions and their culture. Consequently, the methodological decisions he is able to make may depend on what he is able to learn about the society in a relatively short time. The quality of his decisions are often no better than the understanding he acquires of the research milieu.[1] This study had the enormous advantages provided by the collaboration and advice of people thoroughly familiar with Turin and its citizens.

The major methodological tasks that entered into the planning of the survey and the procedures adopted to deal with them fall into four areas: the preparation of the interview schedule; defining and drawing an appropriate sample; gaining acceptance by interviewees; and establishing the bases for cross-national comparisons.

PREPARATION OF THE INTERVIEW SCHEDULE

Much of the content and character of the interview schedule was dictated by the substantive goals of the study. Some questions in-

[1] For an excellent treatment of the problems met by the alien researcher see Robert E. Ward (ed.), *Studying Politics Abroad* (Boston: Little, Brown and Company, 1964). Articles especially pertinent in this volume are Ward, "Common Problems in Field Research"; Frank Bonilla, "Survey Techniques"; and Herbert H. Hyman, " Research Design."

quired into past, present and anticipated social conditions of the lives of the participants; others were designed to reveal feelings and behavior involved in the various family relations. The substance of the questions, therefore, was largely determined by my interest in the effects of social circumstances on family life. The specific areas covered by the interview and the concrete questions that were asked are found in the Appendix, which reproduces the original Italian as well as an English translation.

Deciding *what* questions should be asked in the interviews was much simpler than discovering *how* they should be asked. It is necessary to formulate questions so that they convey the intended meaning; otherwise the responses they evoke can only mislead us. It is always a challenging and difficult task to arouse the desired frame of reference. Even when working with a single language, the same words are capable of communicating different meaning to different people. This study faced the additional job of translation at every stage of the development of the interview schedule. Because of my interests in cross-national comparisons, many questions were borrowed directly from studies previously conducted in the United States, particularly from Kohn's Washington study. Even those items originating in Turin had their first formulations in English. Clearly, then, the translation of items into Italian was a long and difficult task of utmost importance. It is difficult because to translate successfully requires much more than bilingualism; it every bit as much demands biculturalism, for only in this way can translation be tailored to capture the intended meaning of the questions.[2]

It is not possible to create a satisfactory instrument at one's desk no matter how much care and pain one takes. We arrived at the final form and content of the interview schedules only after considerable interviewing, testing, revising and retesting blocks of questions. Twelve interviewers participated in this study; all were Turinese women, most had had previous experience in social research, and most were bilingual. As part of their training for this study as well as for the development of the questionnaire, they conducted many trial interviews intended to test for the format and understandability of items and to determine the meaning with which they were interpreted by respondents. The trial interviews were critically reviewed by the entire staff and on this basis successive revisions were made. The schedule that was finally constructed took from one to one and a half hours to administer.

[2]The demanding problem of maintaining meaning in translation was handled by Pier Brunetti who, as a result of his own bicultural experiences and his training in psychiatry, is very sensitive to these issues.

The trial interviews served one other purpose. We wanted to identify values, aspirations and practices that are important to the Turinese, but which we possibly had overlooked in the initial planning. Social scientists are captives of their societies and can easily fall into the trap of thinking that their own culture embraces all important problems and perspectives. To guard against this we conducted several unstructured interviews that enabled us to make some revisions, substitutions and new inclusions, though the last were surprisingly few in number. We also made post-tests of the schedules. A group of parents who had previously been interviewed by schedule was reinterviewed by more unstructured means in order to establish their frames of reference in dealing with several questions. The unstructured interviews both preceding and following the survey provide a body of qualitative data whose use I will describe later.

None of the steps taken in the preparation of the interview are unusual in survey research, although the alien researcher experiences them as more difficult and problematic and more critical to the ultimate outcome of the study. Some interviewing problems, however, were somewhat special to this study. These are more appropriately discussed in the context of the sample.

DEFINING AND DRAWING
AN APPROPRIATE SAMPLE

Using a sample representative of the adult population of Turin was not suited to the goals of this study. First, family relationships, especially those involving children, probably shift systematically with age; to take account of these shifts would require a sample much larger than our resources allowed. To control this problem, I decided to limit the sample to parents having children of the same age. Parents were selected with a child in the fifth grade, from 10 to 12 years old. This is the last year of elementary school and a very critical year, for parents must make irreversible decisions about future schooling. If they select vocational school, the child is prepared for a blue collar or clerical career; if they choose the middle school, the child in effect passes the gates to all higher educational routes. It is a year, consequently, in which parents are likely to focus their attentions and reflections on the child. This suited the interests of our study.[3] To maintain this focus during the interviews, virtually all

[3]Kohn selected the same age group in his study of parental values. This enhances the comparability of Turinese parental values with those he found among Americans. Melvin L. Kohn, "Social Class and Parental Values," *American Journal of Sociology*, 64 (1959), pp. 337 – 351.

questions regarding children were asked specifically with reference to the fifth grader, using the child's given name wherever appropriate.

Second, the sample does not represent completely the class distribution existing in Turin. Simple class comparisons are only a beginning step in analyzing the various dimensions of family relations. Once we determine class relationships, we can introduce additional variables that help explain the relationships or that indicate conditions under which relationships vary. We could predict that a sample representative of class would produce too few middle- and upper-middle-class families to allow this type of analysis. For this reason, we decided to draw our sample in such a way as to give us approximately equal numbers of middle- and working-class respondents. To avoid the potentially biasing results of this sampling procedure, all tables will take class into account.

Finally, the recent influx of southern migrants into Turin created a sampling problem. They bring with them different cultural patterns, even different dialects. They are concentrated, furthermore, at the bottom of the economic ladder since, typically, they possess no special industrial skills or experience. In a representative sample, their characteristics would result in a fusion of region of origin with economic position, clouding interpretations of class differences. This is something I wanted to avoid.

We needed procedures, then, to locate a sample of parents of fifth graders that would over-represent the middle class and under-represent recent southern migrants. Following discussions with the school authorities and their review of the research proposals, we were given permission to compile from school records the rosters and home addresses of all the fifth-grade children in the city. These records also included fathers' occupations. Thus, the rosters automatically provided the age group we wanted and also gave a fairly accurate indication of occupational status. We then selected names from the school rosters at random. As could be expected, this procedure left us with too few names from middle-class families; in order to achieve the desired balance, we over-sampled from two schools known to have a concentration of middle-class children. With regard to concentrations of migrant families, we were able to eliminate those schools serving neighborhoods in which there are large pockets of southerners. This did not systematically screen out all such families, but it did minimize effects that would have been grossly distorting. Our final sample, then, consisted of families of fifth-grade children who are typically natives of Turin or long-term residents from surrounding regions. The families do not reflect fully the social and economic divisions of the entire population, but they are reasonably representative of established middle- and working-class families engaged in raising children.

It is not quite accurate to say that we drew a sample of families. It would be more consistent with actual procedures to state that we drew a sample of mothers and fathers, for these are the family members who participated in the survey. For two important reasons we intended wherever possible to conduct independent interviews with the mother and with the father in each household. One reason is my interest in occupational experiences in relation to fathers' family roles; obviously, if there are connections between these institutional areas, they are best identified from information asked directly of fathers. Second, independent interviews are desirable for assessing some of the internal structural properties of the family, such as those bearing on consensus. For these reasons, we constructed two schedules, one for use with fathers and the other for use with mothers. Most of their content is identical; the main difference is that the fathers' interviews contained a section dealing with their occupations, while the mothers' interviews contained a section that is concerned, among other things, with their relations with the larger kinship system.

We sent a letter to all households in the sample describing the study and advising parents that they would be telephoned or called upon for an appointment. Where feasible, we arranged for mothers and fathers to be interviewed simultaneously by assigning two interviewers to the family, one to talk with the mother and one with the father. In many cases, however, we could not do this, usually because the father was not at home. In such instances, an interviewer returned to question the father at a later time. On other occasions both parents were at home but there was only one interviewer. In these cases the interviewer would conduct the interviews one after the other and would ask that the nonparticipating spouse leave the room. In a few instances the spouse was unable or unwilling to do this and the interviewer simply directed her questions to one of the spouses. Although actual multiple participation occurred but rarely, there is some lack of uniformity in the conditions under which the interviews were conducted. An examination of responses to selected questions, however, revealed no consistent difference in the nature of the responses given when interviews were conducted under different conditions. The chances of agreement in spouses' responses seemed to be about the same whether they were interviewed simultaneously, whether one was away from home, whether both were at home but in different rooms, or even whether both were present in the same room.

The distributions of most of the relevant characteristics of our sample are subsumed by tables presented throughout the text, but some of them should be enumerated here. We conducted 861 useable interviews; of these 628 were husband-wife pairs. There were 206 interviews with mothers whose husbands could not be reached, and, similarly, there were 27 interviews with fathers whose wives were not available.

I shall have more to say shortly of the indicator employed for determining social class. Here I will just point out that in accordance with the aims of the study, there are approximately equal numbers of middle- and working-class respondents, with some gradation within these classes. The sampling procedures also were such as to produce approximately equal numbers of parents of fifth-grade boys and girls; in fact, 52 per cent are parents of boys, 48 per cent of girls.

Certain features of the sample reflect the pressures for change that urban life exerts on traditional practices, even those supported by institutional edicts. Contrary to what we might imagine it to be, family size was quite small. Thus, 80 per cent of the families in the study had no more than three children and almost 30 per cent had only a single child. The largest families were disproportionately found among the most recent southern migrants. Gini and Caranti give several reasons why Italians are limiting the size of their families.[4] The modern woman, first of all, does not want a large brood. Three-fourths of the women, they report, consider two or three children ideal, though very few wish to have none. The laws of the nation notwithstanding, there is evidence of widespread use of contraceptives and the termination of pregnancies. Family size is also limited by age at marriage; for the entire country it is 29 and 25 years for men and women, respectively, and Gini and Caranti report that it is actually higher in the North than elsewhere. This is consistent with the average age of our respondents, which is about 44 for fathers and 40 for mothers. It is probable that they were somewhat older than American parents having a child in the fifth grade. Finally, out of 547 households represented by our respondents, only 81 have in residence a relative who is not a member of the nuclear family.

Once we drew our sample we could not assume that those chosen would automatically welcome the study. Much preparation went into maximizing our acceptance and stimulating an interested participation by respondents.

---

[4]Corrado Gini and Elio Caranti, "The Family in Italy," *Marriage and Family Living* (November 1954), pp. 350 – 361.

GAINING ACCEPTANCE BY INTERVIEWEES

In the United States a certain cultural license for survey research opens homes to strangers. Perhaps this comes about from an ethos asserting that one's opinions in a democracy really matter to the course of events, that opinions must be expressed freely to have full impact, and that one man's opinion is no less valid than the next fellow's. The way one thinks and feels on any issue is of importance, therefore, and it is quite understandable that the thoughts and feelings of individuals should be solicited by those having a legitimate interest. Even where the expression of opinion serves no visible end, gaining knowledge of it for its own sake may be a perfectly acceptable goal to many Americans.

We were not confident that Italians, in the absence of such traditions, would accord us the liberty of entering their homes. Several well-informed people expressed serious doubt that enough Turinese would open their doors to make the study possible. They have an overlay of suspicion of the motives of strangers and a rather prevalent view that an individual's opinions have no influence on his society or even the course of his own life — except, perhaps, adversely. These attitudes could block the success of a survey. A few things were in our favor, however.

Primary among these is the content of the inquiry, dealing as it does with the family. This is an area of great affective involvement and, unlike politics, for example, it is neutral and above suspicion. The letter that was sent to each family in the sample explaining our purposes emphasized the prominent place of the family in the feelings of Italians and gave this as one of the reasons we wanted to learn more about it.

The letter also stressed the auspices of the study. We benefited greatly from the material support, encouragement and sponsorship of the *Fondazione Adriano Olivetti*. The Foundation is well known in the Piedmont and highly respected by the Turinese. They associate it with an industry that employs progressive labor policies and is concerned with social problems. The contribution of any single measure we took is difficult to evaluate, but I think that the general trust and confidence of people in the Foundation aided the acceptance of our study.

This was not the only sponsorship of the study. I made a point of my own American affiliation, the National Institute of Mental Health, and its support of the research. Again it is difficult to assess what effects this had, but there is reason to believe that they were in the direction of enhancing participation. My nationality seemed to stimulate curiosity; it led people to wonder just what kind of questions about Italian family life American social scientists would ask. More important, it identified the investigator as an alien, a stranger. This endows a person, at least in Italy, with certain privileges. It explained and made more permissible to Italians behavior that otherwise would be interpreted as outrageous, stupid or arrogant. While we are all familiar with literature stressing how important it is for the observer to know the observed, even immersing himself in their ways, we can also argue that being an outsider can be of value to research. Exchanges that ordinarily would be unthinkable can be quite natural between strangers. Although I interacted face-to-face with only very few of the participants, the interviewers made clear that the study was directed by a foreigner. This helped to expand the roles of interviewers and subjects by bringing to the interview elements of a situation where Italians could talk to Americans through the medium of an interviewer. It was a kind of symbolic interaction between representatives of different nations that seemed to enlarge the areas of acceptable discourse, perhaps to a greater degree than if the study had been conceived and directed by Italians.

I do not want to give the impression that doors were open to us in every instance or that we were met only with enthusiasm. Of all the households we attempted to contact, we were unable to administer interviews in about 25 per cent. Somewhat less than half of these simply could not be reached because of recent moves or incorrect addresses in the school records. But close to 15 per cent of those contacted refused to participate.[5] Among those who were interviewed, the vast majority gave some indication of being interested and pleased, but not all. A few began with an air of hostility or indifference and remained so throughout the course of the interview; others began this way and warmed up as it went along. Some were anxious and uncertain, and so on. In short, the study was received in Turin very much as it would have been in an American city.

ESTABLISHING THE BASES
FOR CROSS-NATIONAL COMPARISONS

Since one of the principal aims of this study was to observe the transnational generality of social structural effects on family life, it had

[5]It is interesting that our rate of non-response in Turin is within the range for interviewing reported by Nye in his review of American family studies. According to him, this varies between 10 and 15 per cent. F. Ivan Nye, "Field Research," in Harold T. Christensen (ed.), *Handbook of Marriage and the Family* (Chicago: Rand McNally and Company, 1964), pp. 247 – 274.

to face the methodological issues in comparative studies. Sociological analysis is typically comparative. The rich are contrasted with the poor, urban with rural dwellers, black with white, the highly educated with the lowly, males with females, and so on. These comparisons correspond to the structural divisions of society and consequently are basic to the study of social organization and its consequences. Some of the very methodological issues involved in cross-national comparisons parallel those found in intra-national research. In both instances language must be found that communicates the same meaning and indices must be formed that reflect the same phenomena among all elements taken for study. As in other areas, the problems presented by cross-national comparisons differ more in difficulty than in kind.

But cross-national comparisons are worth the difficulties they entail; they make it possible to distinguish structural imperatives from cultural directives, something that intra-national studies do not allow.[6] If we find, for example, that middle-class parents value extended education more than do working-class parents, we cannot be certain whether this difference arises inexorably from their relative positions in the society or whether unique sub-cultural systems are operating to produce it. If it is the latter, similar class differences would not necessarily be found in societies where different cultural patterns exist. Cross-national comparisons, in effect, enable us to apply a kind of quasi-experimental reasoning to our findings: If the variation of parental aspirations with class structure is the same in two societies of different culture, then it is structure rather than culture that best explains the variations. Looking across two nations thus expands and takes advantage of natural "laboratory" conditions. Unlike replication, which attempts to reproduce relationships under the same conditions, cross-national comparison endeavors to see if the same relationships appear under different conditions. Cross-national comparisons can thus be used as a stringent test of relationships and this, perhaps, is one factor underlying an impressive resurgence of interest in systematic cross-national research.[7]

The cross-national comparisons that can be made here are neither as extensive nor as systematic as I would like. Partly this is because the relationships being sought in this study have not been dealt with

[6]This terminology is used by Walter Goldschmidt in "Values and the Field of Comparative Sociology," *American Sociological Review*, 18 (1953), pp. 287 – 293.

[7]For a discussion of the present interest in cross-national social science research and its history see Stein Rokkan, "Comparative Cross-national Research: The Context of Current Efforts," in Richard L. Merritt and Stein Rokkan (eds.), *Comparing Nations* (New Haven: Yale University Press, 1966), pp. 3 – 25.

in other studies. Consequently, once an analysis passes beyond a certain point, usually involving a simple class comparison, nothing is left that is comparable. It is most easy to find opportunities for comparison when the question is one of identifying *who* thinks or acts in a particular way; these opportunities diminish when the question becomes one of *why*. This is less problematic when the research in two or more nations is planned and executed by the same investigator, but these circumstances are rarely found.[8]

In some respects, the limitations on comparative analyses most difficult to deal with stem from the generic problem of equivalence. At the risk of being tautological, we may say that before things may be compared they must be comparable. They are most directly comparable when they are equivalent, but this is not often the case. Problems of equivalence arise in this study in at least three areas: equivalence of *meaning*, of *relevance* and of *indices*.

I have already touched on the most important points concerning equivalence of meaning when I discussed the task of translation, and the matter need not be belabored. The real difficulty of translation is not in finding counterpart words, but in discovering language that conveys the same meaning in the two cultures and that is equivalently evocative.[9]

The second problem of equivalence has to do with the relevance in the two cultures of the issues to which interview questions are directed. At a gross level, it is easy to see how disparate relevance can preclude equivalence. A comparative study of voting behavior, for example, could not attain equivalence unless the societies being compared each have a range of institutionalized options that may be behaviorally expressed by similar mechanisms. But differential relevance interferes with equivalence in more subtle ways, I believe. For example, the observer has the impression that the concerns of

---

[8]Though it is unusual, in a few instances the same investigator has been responsible for the design and content of multi-nation comparative research involving the collection of primary data. Some of these are identified by Hill in his survey of cross-national research into family life. In his classification of comparative studies, these would fall into "Type II." Reuben Hill, "Cross-national Family Research: Attempts and Prospects," *International Social Science Journal*, 14 (1962), pp. 425 – 451.

[9]While much literature deals with problems of equivalence, no aspect of it has received more attention than this. For examples, see Susan Ervin and Robert T. Banner, "Translation Problems in International Surveys," *The Public Opinion Quarterly*, 16 (1953), pp. 595 – 604; Bradford B. Hudson, Mohamed K. Babakat and Rolfe LaForge, "Problems and Methods of Cross-cultural Research," *Journal of Social Issues*, 15 (1959), pp. 5 – 19; R. Bruce W. Anderson, "On the Comparability of Meaningful Stimuli in Cross-cultural Research," *Sociometry*, 30 (1967), pp. 124 – 136.

many American parents, such as those involving the personality development of children, are either not understood or considered trivial in societies where parents are preoccupied with satisfying basic needs. The problems that may worry some societies could be viewed as luxury problems by others. With regard to our study, it is most difficult to be certain of the extent to which we have reached equivalence of relevance. From the sifting and screening process in our pretesting and from the general responsiveness and interest of the interviewers, I would judge that the questions were as relevant to Turinese as to Americans, though there are probably differences of degree. But overall, equivalence of relevance is maximized in this study simply because it deals with an institution of unquestioned importance in contemporary societies.

The third barrier to equivalence pertains to indices. In the behavioral sciences it is characteristic that the very things that are of greatest interest are those that are also hidden from direct observation. No one has ever seen a social class, an authority system, a value, an aspiration. We can only make inferences about these phenomena on the basis of deeds and words which reflect their presence, their intensity and their scope. To learn about feelings toward children, we asked parents selected questions; from their answers we constructed an index which mirrors the direction, intensity, stability or other properties of the feelings in which we were interested. Or, perhaps, we could make similar assessments from the observation of interaction between parent and child. In either case, we use information which is observable to tell us about something not observable.

The problem this poses for comparative research can be stated simply: identical information does not necessarily yield equivalent indices in different societies. I shall discuss social class in this context; it provides both an excellent example of the general problem of equivalence of indices and an opportunity to specify how this important concept is indexed throughout most of the study.

A number of criteria are commonly employed to determine how people stand relative to one another in a class order. They include such objective characteristics as education, place of residence, style of life, income or occupation. It is no more difficult to get information on each of these characteristics in Turin than in the United States. And they are about as discriminating of position in that country as here. The possible exception is neighborhood, since this is likely to be more economically heterogeneous than in most American cities. Generally, though, these data, which are probably highly intercorrelated, can reveal the existence of stratified systems in both countries. The difficulty is that the systems are not necessarily equatable. Educational attainment may be taken as a case in point. The extent of one's formal schooling is a good indicator of social class in Italy just as it is in the United States. However, far fewer Italians than Americans have university training and it is less of a requirement for some jobs there than here. In terms of cross-national equivalence, this means that a secondary education in Italy may be roughly equivalent to our university degree. Thus, education is a useful indicator of class in each country, but the strata it indexes are not easily comparable across countries.

The same is even more true of income. This, of course, is an indicator of economic class that easily provides an objective ordering of people. The size of income that realistically would signal an upper-middle-class position in Italy, though, would reflect a lower position in the United States. As in the case of education, it is the distribution of income throughout a given population that may make it a suitable indicator of the stratification of that population. But the same income does not indicate the same relative position in another population.

The one datum that comes closer than any other to serving as an equivalent indicator of class is occupational status. All industrialized societies, apparently, use occupation as a criterion to place people in the hierarchical order. Beginning with the work of Inkeles and Rossi, considerable evidence has been accumulated that occupationally stratified orders are remarkably similar in such societies, regardless of culture.[10] My impression is that occupational status in Turin is distributed in much the same way as in the United States and other industrialized nations.

We decided on these grounds to adopt an eight-fold categorization of social class based on the occupation of the head of the household. From highest to lowest in status, these are: (1) those trained for and engaged in the professions; (2) proprietors, managers and others having major administrative and technical responsibility; (3) clerks, tech-

[10]Alex Inkeles and Peter H. Rossi, "National Comparisons of Occupational Prestige," *American Journal of Sociology,* 61 (1956), pp. 329 – 339; Edward A. Teryakian, "The Prestige Evaluation of Occupations in an Underdeveloped Country: the Philippines," *American Journal of Sociology,* 63 (1958), pp. 390 – 399; Kaare Svalastoga, *Prestige, Class and Mobility* (Copenhagen: Gyldendal, 1959); R. Murray Thomas, "Reinspecting a Structural Position on Occupational Prestige," *American Journal of Sociology,* 67 (1962), pp. 561 – 565; A. O. Haller and David M. Lewis, "The Hypothesis of Inter-societal Similarity in Occupational Prestige Hierarchies," *American Journal of Sociology,* 72 (1966), pp. 210 – 216, and Robert W. Hodge *et al.,* "A Comparative Study of Occupational Prestige," in Reinhard Bendix and Seymour Martin Lipset (eds.), *Class, Status, and Power: Social Stratification in Comparative Perspective,* 2nd ed. (New York: Free Press, 1966), pp. 309 – 321.

nicians and office staff; (4) sales personnel; (5) foremen; (6) skilled workers; (7) semi-skilled workers; and (8) unskilled workers. Largely because of the dissipation of cases that occurred, I did not use all eight categories in the analyses. Depending upon the issue I am presenting, I simply distinguish middle (first four categories) and working class (last four categories) or upper-middle, middle, upper-working and lower-working, in which the categories are combined by twos. In Chapter V, dealing with parental aspirations, I use income in place of occupational class because economic resources are more pertinent to the particular problems analyzed.

Adopting occupational status as the indicator of social class did not solve the issue of equivalence. I am confident that using occupational status *approaches* equivalence more than any other single criterion or composite index of class. It is still not possible to be certain, however, whether the "status distance" between skilled and semi-skilled workers in Italy, for example, is identical to that in the United States, or if an Italian and an American physician stand at precisely equal heights. We have a situation of close comparability, I believe, but one whose cross-national fit is somewhat ambiguous. This uncertainty is not limited to social class, for it is doubtful if we have *complete* equivalence among any of the indicators that will be used comparatively.

The uncertainty of equivalence need not be as limiting as it may appear. Although perfect equivalence is most difficult to achieve — perhaps impossible — there is a way to sidestep this obstacle. Our cross-national comparisons will not be directly of Italians and Americans bearing the same labels. Instead, we will first observe differences intra-nationally and then the cross-national comparisons will be made of the direction and magnitude of these differences. Such cross-national comparisons of intra-national variations minimize the need to make assumptions about equivalence across nations. This is the accommodation to the problem also arrived at by Almond and Verba in their comparative study of politics:[11]

> By phrasing the comparison *between* nations in terms of the similarities and differences in the *patterns* of relations *among* variables *within* each country, one controls somewhat for the differences in meaning that these variables have from one nation to another.

This completes the overview of the major methodological issues that confronted the development of the interview schedule and the

[11]Gabriel A. Almond and Sidney Verba, *The Civic Culture* (Princeton: Princeton University Press, 1963), p. 70. This statement is drawn from a more extensive and excellent treatment of the problem of equivalence in comparative research.

planning of the survey. In addition to the main body of data that comes from the survey of parents, two other sets of data are employed. One comes from observations of parent-child interactions in the homes of 79 families all of whom had earlier been interviewed. There were two observational sessions in each household, one with the father and the child and the other with mother and child. Some of these observed interactions are presented in conjunction with parental aspirations (Chapter V) and the very special methodological problems they present are discussed at that time.

Finally, we used qualitative data, mentioned earlier, from unstructured interviews conducted both before and following the survey. Many of the themes that emerged from these interviews cut across the issues that are treated quantitatively in subsequent chapters. They provide, therefore, an excellent opportunity to look behind the numbers and statistics to gain a different view of Turinese family life and the surrounding world. The views that are presented are essentially those seen through the eyes of Turinese parents themselves. It is fitting that the first substantive chapter present these subjective perspectives, for they set a stage for much that will follow.

III

Parental Views
of Family and Society

The Turinese are uneasy about the world in which they live. They communicate this even in casual conversation; in the unstructured interviews they talked about it most pointedly and forcefully. Many of their feelings of anxiety are dominated by the vast and rapid changes that are under way in Turin. Perhaps these changes are no more pervasive than those occurring in the urban centers of other nations. However, they have a particularly unsettling effect on Turinese parents, for they see many of the changes as threats to something dearly prized and desperately wanted: family solidarity. Much of the content of this chapter is an account of the reasons why family solidarity is so important, how it is being challenged by change and what Turinese parents do to protect it. These issues are consistent with the central concern of this study in exploring the effects of social circumstances on the family. The materials presented here examine such effects, but from the perspectives and with the language of those engaged in the system.

Twenty-seven people participated in the unstructured interviews: 10 men and 17 women, 16 from the middle class and the remainder from the working class. Approximately one-half of the interviews were conducted prior to the initiation of the survey, the others following its completion. We used the first group to help us in the preparation of the interview schedule employed in the survey in a last effort to identify important areas that we may have overlooked. The post-survey interviews were intended to provide us with information concerning the subjective frameworks from which some of the scheduled items were perceived by respondents. Hence, this latter group of respondents was composed entirely of those who had previously participated in the survey.

Because they were intended to serve definite purposes, the unstructured interviews were not completely without structure. The limits imposed by the information we wanted were quite broad, however. We gave respondents considerable latitude in setting the direction of their discussions and in bringing in issues, regardless of how pertinent the interviewer thought they might be to the main purposes. Consequently, many of the themes running through the interviews are not specific answers to specific questions, but reflect sentiments that are subjectively salient and spontaneously voiced.

The interview materials presented here are intended to provide a qualitative view of issues that reappear in different form throughout the following chapters. They will also provide for the reader some more direct contact with the people of Turin than is afforded by quantified data. Both to enhance this contact and to impart some of the flavor of the thinking and styles of communicating, direct quotations from the interviews are used wherever they are appropriate.

THE BACKGROUND OF FAMILY SOLIDARITY

A widespread element in the images held by foreigners of Italians is the paramount place of the family in their affections, thoughts and loyalties. This is one national stereotype, at least, that has some basis in fact, and it is certainly confirmed by the tone and substance of the interviews. As an institution, it is prominent in the hearts and minds of most Italians.

Many factors contribute to the dominance of the family and to its solidarity, some from the past and others very much from the present. The history of Italy is marked by numerous invasions and by many wars between the various city-states. This turbulence continued for centuries and few generations and few regions escaped its consequences. Military actions not only endangered the physical well-being of people, but probably made the fabric of social institutions highly fragile and unreliable. For the forefathers of contemporary Italians, most likely the family stood foremost as a dependable source of welfare, security and continuity. Nor did a lasting change come about with unification, for fascism again taught Italians that they lived in a society where true concern for their welfare could be found only in the family.

To this day Italians are closely bound and intensely committed to their families. In extreme form, found especially in the rural South, individuals' actions may be predominantly organized around family expectations and obligations. This is the condition that Banfield refers to as "amoral familism" in order to emphasize how family considerations preempt a concern with social problems and interfere with the ability to take collective action.[1] Though it cannot be characterized as amorally familistic, the modern family of industrial Turin is still marked by intense loyalties and identifications.

Much more than the momentum of historical forces is required to sustain family cohesion. It is also supported in part by a view of the surrounding society as essentially unconcerned with or malevolent toward its members. This is not a normative paranoia without foundation it is substantiated by everyday experiences with a number of social institutions, including public bureaucracies. In encounters with these institutions there is little to inspire the belief that the individual can count on fair and impartial treatment, that his welfare will be protected regardless of who he is. On the contrary, his ordinary experiences confirm the *particularism* of the society.[2] He learns that what really matters to one's welfare is what he represents, the "connections" he can invoke, the status he possesses, the power he has or appears to have. Only the family accepts him for himself and offers him security; here there is unconditional faith and trust, here his needs are recognized and met. To many Italians, then, the family is a place of refuge.[3] This attitude is articulately expressed in the words of a middle-class female respondent who, in talking about what the family means to her, said, "It is a group of people who struggle to collaborate at a maximum in order to create an oasis in the chaos which surrounds them." Few of our respondents could put the matter in this way, but it echoes a prevailing sentiment.

Closely akin to the particularism of their social institutions is a widespread resignation among Italians to extant conditions. If, as some Turinese have argued with me, Americans are engaging in delusions when they see themselves as masters of their environment, Italians are at the other extreme, sweeping aside any idea that they can alter important conditions of life.[4] They may have strong negative feelings about some of these conditions, but they are also likely to be imbued

[1]Edward C. Banfield, *The Moral Basis of Backward Society* (Glencoe, Ill.: The Free Press), 1958.

[2]In a five-nation comparative study of politics, Italians were next to lowest in their expectations of fair treatment by government bureaucracies and police. Gabriel A. Almond and Sidney Verba, *The Civic Culture* (Princeton: Princeton University Press, 1963), pp. 106 – 114.

[3]This attitude emerges in many of the observations made by Anne Parsons in her work with Neapolitan families. Rose Laub Coser *et al.* (eds.), *Belief, Magic, and Anomie: Essays in Psychosocial Anthropology* (New York: The Free Press, 1969).

[4]It is interesting that on almost every indicator used by Almond to assess an individual's sense of political engagement and potency, Italy is lowest of the five nations studied. See Almond and Verba, *Civic Culture*, pp. 180 – 229.

with a sense of futility — or fatalism — about them. This, I submit, also contributes to familism, for it is mainly within this institutional domain that the Italian is able to feel some mastery. In the home men and women are able to know that the things they want, their words and their actions will have a meaningful impact.

Finally, for many Italians economic insecurity is a major force for family solidarity. Despite the real advances of recent years — what the mass media describe as the "economic miracle" — earning a living is a serious struggle for a large segment of the population. As one respondent put it, it is difficult "to dock the boat at the end of the month." While there are national programs organized for social and economic welfare, there is a feeling among people, particularly in the working class, that they are at the economic brink. It is expressed in the worries of men and women about such things as sudden illness, accidents, the loss of jobs in advanced age or other misfortunes that can topple them into economic disaster. Such worries, of course, are not simply products of the imagination; they are deeply rooted in the events to which people have been witness throughout the course of their lives.

Those caught up in hardship and uncertainty look to the family for the economic support and security that is not provided elsewhere. A network of expectations and plans are formed that have economic considerations at their center. Here, for example, is a quotation from a blue-collar worker that points up both the importance of the economic role of young children and how their contributions may affect the future of family members:

> When we were young, if someone studied he was considered as a "white fly" [an oddity]. At that time it was possible to make a living without study; nowadays one cannot do anything without at least three years of vocational. I would like her [his daughter] to have at least three years after elementary [a total of eight years of education]. The main trouble is that it is costly. If we had more sons, it would be possible. . . . With only one working, it is tough going.

The economic dependence of the family on its members is something that may continue indefinitely in poor families. Old age is anticipated with some anxiety because of its economic uncertainties and adult children are expected to maintain an obligation for the care of their parents. This obligation isn't solely moral; it can assume the nature of a calculated exchange:

> If tomorrow [after marriage] she should be in financial trouble or in the dumps because she doesn't get along with her husband, we could help her. In addition, we would also like to have that trust and

security that when we are old she will behave toward us as we behaved toward our parents.

Of course, this working-class parent would prefer not to lay claim to his child's help nor, for that matter, to be called upon by his child for aid. These patterns of expectation flourish under circumstances of adversity and anticipatory calamity. Economic insecurity makes family solidarity something to nurture and protect.

I have emphasized the salience of the family and some of the elements contributing to its solidarity: a history of exploitation, the particularism of Italian institutions, the absence of feelings of mastery and economic insecurity.[5] It is difficult to weigh the role of each of these; but together they make the family a sanctuary to which people can escape from an outside world that is hostile, unresponsive to their needs and potentially harmful. It is the major buttress against abuse and calamity. Thus, the importance of the family derives from the range of needs it is called upon to satisfy, from the critical functions it performs for its members and from its unsubstitutability. *It can function in these ways, however, only as long as its members identify with it and remain bound to it in their loyalties and actions.* Too many consequences hinge on family solidarity for parents to take it for granted. Instead, they are fiercely protective of it, and, in recent years at least, they have had some reason to feel that family solidarity is being threatened.

SOCIAL CHANGE AND FAMILY SOLIDARITY

The threat to the Italian family is stimulated by the changes taking place throughout the society. For several years Italy has been experiencing a period of marked social and economic change. The pace of change is particularly accelerated in the industrial centers of the country, located in the North. The main thrust of economic development is in these cities, and it has had as an immediate consequence a rather profound expansion of population in Turin and other urban areas. In the decade between 1951 and 1961, the population within the immediate city grew by almost 50 per cent.[6] The bulk of this increase

[5]Family solidarity and the social elements supporting it, while very evident in the North, are even more pronounced and intense in the rural South. For a powerful description and keen sociological analysis of their presence in the life of a small southern village, see Joseph Lopreato, *Peasants No More* (San Francisco: Chandler Publishing Company, 1967).

[6]This is calculated from a comparison of the 1951 and 1961 census. *IX Censimento Generale della Popolazione* (Roma: Instituto Centrale di Statistica, 1955), pp. 88 – 89, and *X Censimento Generale della Popolazione* (Roma Instituto Centrale di Statistica, 1966), pp. 100 – 101.

is attributable to migration by people attracted to opportunities for steady employment, especially southerners who saw a rare chance to remove themselves from a life of poverty. One very visible result of these changes at the time of this study was the severe strain placed on public facilities. To the discomfort of the population, transportation, schools, hospitals and housing were all inadequate to the new demands placed upon them.

Inevitably, perhaps, the Turinese were inclined to feel that these problems were visited upon them by the deficiencies of the southerners. In talking about the problems of their city, the natives placed the brunt of the blame on the migrants and on their social and characterological inferiority. Prejudice and scapegoating were prevalent, and the customs and dialects of the southerners were common subjects of derisive remarks.

Along with the dislocations and inconveniences of population growth, other changes have been taking place; they are less apparent but probably have a more deeply disquieting effect on parents. These are the new values, goals and morals that have edged into daily life. Changes of these kinds are seen as having a potentially divisive effect on the family, mainly separating the young from the old. The most casual conversations would contain apprehensive references to the disastrous ends toward which the society was headed, particularly its youth. And in the interviews there are many worry laden comments about the disruption of everyday social relations, the breakdown of precepts and of family ties.

One mother undoubtedly spoke for many Turinese as she reflected on changes separating the generations: "We are very different from our parents and our children are even more different from us. . . . Things changed with a certain rhythm for us, but for our children change is more rapid." She completed her observation by indicating that she still has some hope: "On the other hand, there is a return to a liking for old things, particularly in good families."

The sense of loss that so many Turinese experience with social change is occasionally focused on what they view as burgeoning aspirations for the acquisition of material goods. These aspirations are identified as essentially unappeasable and as a result they are a source of disaffection and even shame. One woman put it this way: "I think everything has changed. In our times, no one had a car; today they feel ashamed if they don't have one. It is a different way of life." Another pointed out that people are no longer made happy with what they have; instead they are only distressed by what they would like but don't possess:

Life was more calm [when I was a child]. Today we are all in turmoil because the pace has changed, and there are more difficulties and obstacles. Everything has changed since the war. Before there was a more easy acceptance and now no one is contented with what he has. Everyone wants to have more.

Some parents didn't see material aspirations and discontent as a general problem as much as one that affects young people in particular. This is apparent in the discussion by a working-class man of how young people approach marriage: "At the start they want their wives to work so that they can buy a car, and they expect their fathers to buy flats for them. We are far from the times when they are contented with a card game."

There is, then, a keen awareness of the changes taking place in Turin, and the people to whom we spoke were far from complacent about the alterations that were occurring. Even the improvement in the standard of living is, by their thinking, a source of discontent and unhappiness. And they may very well be correct in this assessment. It was also my impression that at the same time people would speak of the real improvement in living conditions, they would be dispirited by the problems they encountered in pursuing their aspirations and by the many hopes that remained unfulfilled. For large numbers of Turinese, there is a vast disparity between what they want, both for themselves and for their children, and what they feel they will be able to realize.

Thus, the Turinese are worried that material aspirations will result in an endless and unhappy quest by their children. Some feel also that an excessive concern with material gain is antagonistic to and erosive of the moral order. This is implicit in the following statement made by a deeply religious woman who is the wife of a highly placed industrial executive:

What should be taught to a child in the first place are moral values. They should not be taught to value money; the less one is attached to money the better it is. This view is not shared by many in Italy. For most people what counts is the career; to make a lot of money, to arrive by any means, to become important. Even the workers want to become bourgeois. They act as though money could make one happy. There are so many rich people who commit suicide.

To strive after prestige and material aggrandizement is incompatible with the loftier values of this woman. While her concern for workers is somewhat patronizing, similar sentiments were voiced by working-class parents themselves. A semi-skilled worker, for example, said, "In my economic category one should not want more than he can get.

We shouldn't compromise ourselves to get what we want." The compromise he referred to is a moral one, and he thought that young people, especially, are susceptible to forsaking moral values for economic gain. He called them "burned youth."

In addition to the moral erosion that results directly from materialistic striving, there is a more over-arching concern that children are moving away from proper conceptions of right and wrong. A working-class father put it simply: "One should have a precise knowledge of what is good and what is bad. Today the young people take serious things lightly." He then went on to discuss an event that was being given wide coverage in the press. It concerned a popular singer who was made pregnant by a well-known married actor. With considerable feeling, he related how young friends of his daughter defended the singer, though "she is a sinner." He concluded by saying: "They [children] take things like this lightly. The old way of looking at things is the right way." Perhaps this is a sentiment held to by older generations everywhere, but it could be no more salient than it is among present-day Turinese parents.

If parents are concerned that there is a loss of morality involved in the changes that are taking place, they are equally concerned that there is a loss of *gemeinschaft* and family cohesion. The retrospective remarks of a worker convey this poignantly:

> When we were young we were content with very little. It was a pleasure to wait for family picnics in the woods. Today there are other ways of amusing one's self and workers don't even take food along with them on Sunday, but go to little restaurants. They don't talk any more about taking their bicycles into the country; they want autos. There used to be more togetherness in the family as a result of this.

Social change has brought new opportunities, new appetites, new styles of life and, perhaps, a new morality. These alterations are worrisome, for they are seen as creating a gulf between the young and the old, between parents and children. They challenge the solidarity of the family.

Reactions to these changes were not exclusively negative, however. Parents spoke with considerable pleasure of opportunities available to their children that were completely out of reach a generation ago. Since these opportunities are, for the most part, attainable only through extended education, this was stressed by several parents. We find statements such as the following sprinkled throughout these materials: "My mother worked like a beast and did not follow us in our studies. I'm much more concerned about school and help my children all the time." Another also spoke of intergenerational differences in the emphasis placed on education:

> When we would come home, parents and children would immediately think of work. It wasn't possible to go to school [beyond the mandatory years]. At that time it was considered natural that a child should work and school come second. My mother recently changed, now she thinks, as I do — that school is important.

While education and subsequent opportunities were recognized as important and desirable by parents, their children are more likely to take these things for granted and the unwillingness to study and work hard can be a source of disappointment to parents. Some of these feelings are embedded in the remarks made by a woman who came to Turin seventeen years ago from a neighboring rural area:

> Even now when we go to the country and we talk to our acquaintances, we see that they are not interested in studies. They know that their children will be 'contadini' [peasants]. It is very rare that they make their children study. I've always wished for my children something a little better. . . . But my son doesn't do well. Perhaps we haven't raised him well enough . . . but they don't let us talk. Even at the oratory they don't work hard enough; the priests let them play too much. At school he was given a book to read and he has had it for months now. I'm not satisfied with my son; he is not living up to his responsibilities.

Others, too, like this woman, entertain ambitions that exceed those of their children, want their children to strive much more than the children are willing, want their children to be motivated by opportunities that are not recognized as opportunities by children. These kinds of conflicts could be recognized by many American parents who have probably lived with them a generation longer than Italians. The Turinese are discovering that the very opportunities for which they have worked and hoped can become a source of conflict between them and their children.

A final issue concerning social change pertains to the expression of disenchantment with social institutions, especially educational and religious. There was some feeling among our respondents that these institutions are still functioning for a bygone era and have failed to assume new functions with changing conditions. The particular ways in which these institutions were thought to be failing in their missions vary considerably. For example, parents said schools are teaching things that "are no longer valid," they are not succeeding in conveying moral values, they are not paying sufficient attention to the real world, they are not motivating children, they are ignoring character development. Interestingly, there was also some sentiment that the schools should assume responsibility for sex education. Parents viewed this as a topic where factual information can best be taught by the schools and, in addition, school presentation would save parents from the embarrassment of discussing a tender subject with their children. Religion, too, received its share of criticism. It was seen both as too secular in its involvement in politics and not secular enough in its lack of attention to pressing social problems. Its opposition to divorce also attracted considerable comment.

The changes that are taking place, then, have found their way into the inner reaches of family life and have created a pervasive air of uncertainty and anxiety. Especially unsettling are changes that are seen as potentially dividing the old from the young, children from their parents. Such divisions are matters of utmost seriousness as far as parents are concerned and the observer comes away with the impression that much of the energy of parents is directed to warding off perceived threats to family cohesion.

PARENTAL CONTROL

A major means employed by Turinese parents to maintain the unity of the family in the midst of their changing world is to assume control and direction over the behavior of their children. Many American clinicians feel that granting independence and autonomy to children is necessary for healthy personality development, but most Turinese parents would view this theory as nonsensical. In their view independence is bad for children and reflects a callous lack of attention by parents to their own proper role. Parents are wiser than children and, therefore, know best what is good and bad for their children's welfare. To leave a child to his own judgment is the same as willfully exposing him to the harmful consequences of inexperience. In addition to making him more vulnerable to the dangers of the outside world, the child's independence encourages him to loosen his attachment to his family.

The feelings of parents regarding control and independence come across best in the respondents' own words. The wife of an industrial worker said:

> If in making a decision he always asked my advice and if he made me feel I had a lot of influence with him and if I agreed with what he wanted to do, then I would let him make his own decisions. My mother-in-law cries when her sons do not ask her advice. But it is her own fault. She brought them up independently. If she had been more severe, she wouldn't be unhappy now. I shall not let my son do as he likes.

The discouragement of signs and tendencies toward independence can extend to virtually every area of decision making and may be carried well into the adulthood of children. I quote again from the same mother:

> I shall decide about his education according to his abilities. If he is intelligent, then I shall give him a good education. . . . I shall decide about his free time. I shall decide when he can go to the cinema — with me — and when he must study and when he can play. I shall let him choose his own friends, but I should make sure that they are suitable for him.
>
> If he wanted to get married — after he is 25 — and if he wanted to marry a nice girl, then I would give my consent. I would have to know the girl well, though; by knowing the girl well, I mean that I would like my son to confide in me right from the start of the courtship. In this way I would know all about her and when he decided to marry her I would know whether she were suitable. If he wanted to marry a girl I did not consider suitable, then I would intervene.
>
> I feel that a mother is perfectly justified in interfering in her child's life if she feels he is making a wrong decision, even after he is 30.

These statements perhaps reflect a rather extreme position with regard to control, but it is one toward which many Turinese lean. Only two parents, both middle-class women, rejected outright any desire for their children to be dependent upon them. One explained that her own lack of independence left her completely unprepared for the demands of marriage, something she does not want her daughter to experience. The other is an artist, the wife of a physician, who travels extensively in connection with her art interests.

In the case of parents of daughters, and particularly those who have recently migrated from the South, independence is identified as a threat to "honor" and virginity and, consequently, is viewed with special horror by these people. The following are the words of a mother of two daughters, the wife of a policeman recently transferred from a city in Sicily to Turin:

> Here I see that girls are more free than in the South. If I send my daughters with girls who are loose, I would feel bad. I always say to my daughters, "my girl, you will find your bed as you make it." Because they are women, one knows, not because I don't trust them, but they are women. What should I do if they returned home pregnant?

Another mother, this one from the southern region of Calabria, voiced similar apprehensions about freedom for her daughters and also projected an image of Turin that would come as an outrageous surprise to the many natives who pride themselves on the tight reins they maintain over their children. She said:

> We keep our children closer to us than you [Turinese]. Above all, I hope they grow up well-behaved as I am and that they don't go with bad companions. I keep them very strictly and I don't want what happens to the people of Turin to happen to them. Rather than this, I pray to God that He takes them first.

From the perspective of parents, then, the major reason for keeping strict control over children is to protect them from such dangers as bad companions, unsuitable spouses and out-of-wedlock pregnancies. While these are manifest reasons, control also functions to enhance family solidarity. This is implicit in several remarks, such as those of the respondent who interpreted the fact that her husband no longer turned to his mother for advice as a sign of attenuation of attachment. Control by parents and acquiescence of children are the confirming signals of close family bonds. Solidarity based on these kinds of conditions might very well carry some unfavorable consequences. But from all indications it is a powerful solidarity nonetheless.

AFFECTION, SACRIFICE AND PARENTAL CONTROL. But how is control asserted? It is one thing for parents to *want* control and quite another to actually *achieve* it. The raw exercise of power and discipline is probably the least effective means for gaining control, for it cannot insure voluntary compliance on the part of children when they are outside the scope of direct supervision. More effective in this respect are at least two other mechanisms that can be identified through the interviews. These are affection and sacrifice, highly expressive elements that can have nonexpressive functions.

Consider first parental affection. Italians love their children without reservation, without condition and without "strings"; and nothing pleases them more than to have their children demonstrate affection for them. Yet, not infrequently our respondents suggested that more is involved than the intrinsic pleasure of affective relations; they also have a conscious interest in the uses and consequences of love and affection. They see affection, in other words, as instrumental for desired ends that are outside immediate parent-child expressive relations. The ends which may be served by affection are parental control and management. Though affection may be given for its own sake, this does not preclude an interest in how it can be used for the sake of other goals as well.

Here are the words of an upper-class woman who is quite explicit about the instrumental uses of affection. In comparing her two daughters, she said:

> Above all, I want my daughters to be affectionate. If they are affectionate and sensitive, they are easier to bring up. My oldest child is not at all affectionate and it has been twice as difficult to raise her. My second child is more affectionate and she appreciates all shades of my displeasures and is sensitive to my reproaches.

The mother links affectionate relations on the one hand to the management of her children on the other. That she has a warmer relationship to the younger daughter makes it easier to gain compliance from this child. Thus, control is clearly woven into the affection between the mother and her child. Another mother, a school teacher, also put the matter very pointedly when she stated: "I want to be, and at present am, my child's best friend. I feel that it is love that is at the basis of their obeying and respecting me."

Occasionally the relevance of affection to family solidarity was drawn directly by parents. One man, for example, thought about the time when his 11-year-old daughter would marry and what this would mean to her loyalty to her parents. Despite some obscurities in his speculations, it is apparent that he thought that the early creation of affectional bonds would insure her continued identification with her parents:

> I want my daughter to be affectionate to her parents, with deep-rooted ties to the family. If tomorrow she should marry a boy, this love for him should maintain ties with the family. That is, love for the boy would not exclude the family, but the boy would become incorporated into the family.

These words convey an intense desire that the child remain embedded in the family network; the most effective instrument to insure this enduring solidarity is affection.

Instrumental affection and conditional affection are not the same. Unlike the first, the latter involves the withdrawal — or threat of withdrawal — of love in order to gain compliance. While they are different, they can nevertheless appear together. This would be the case where affection would be withheld if it is not successful instrumentally. Such seems to be the implication in the following quotation, taken from the statement of a working-class mother:

> I think there should always be a great deal of friendship between a mother and child. My child should always make his decisions with me. If my son were not affectionate toward me, then . . . I think I might become indifferent toward him.

First, this mother saw her son's willingness to give her a part in his decisions as a sign of his affection for her. Should he not share his decisions, she would interpret this as evidence of a lack of affection. She, in turn, might then withdraw her affection for him. There are in this brief statement a number of interlocking elements. The use of love that is conditional upon the son's compliance to the mother's wishes is prominent among them.

We may say, somewhat digressively, that the instrumental uses of affection are not limited to parental control over children. At least one wife suggested that it is also a vital ingredient in the exercise of influence over husbands. She asserted that "affection is the most important thing, especially for [dealing with] a man. A man is always influenced by the woman he has by his side."

Italian parents, then, want love and affection between their children and themselves. But, while love might be enjoyed for its own sake, it is also employed as a means to manage and control the behavior of children. Parental control, in turn, serves to discourage independence and autonomy and to cement family solidarity. I shall discuss in Chapter VII some of the social factors underlying variations in expressed affection. But with these qualitative data it is possible to see what affection means to parents, how it is used and how it is associated by parents with the continuity of cohesive family relations.

Consider now feelings of sacrifice and self-denial in behalf of children that, when communicated to children, can serve the same control functions as instrumental affection. It is possible here to draw upon the survey to indicate just how prevalent such feelings are, for we asked mothers two questions that bear directly on this issue. One asked whether they thought they had given up part of their *enjoyment of life* for their children and the second if they thought they had given up part of their *happiness* for their children. As could be expected, expressions of sacrifice were inversely related to class. To the first question, 50 per cent of the middle-class and 67 per cent of the working-class mothers replied in the affirmative; the corresponding percentages for the second item are 12 and 33. The sense of sacrifice of enjoyment of life is fairly widespread, therefore, and, especially in the working class, the belief among mothers that they have forsaken happiness in behalf of their children is not uncommon.

The prevalence of sacrificial sentiments is less at point here, however, than the question of how sacrifice may be used in dealing with children. The themes of sacrifice that appeared in the interviews were sometimes coupled to suggestions that these sacrifices entailed an obligation or debt owed parents by children. In return for parental sacrifices, parents expected some reciprocal self-denial. And, typically, where such themes were found, parents wanted most that their children deny themselves their own autonomy and independence. Rebellion under these circumstances would be tantamount to the children belittling the things that their parents have denied themselves for their sake.

The interviews contained many allusions to sacrificial debts imposed on children, but one or two references will illustrate the process. The first points up how parental sacrifice as a lever of control over children is carried across generational lines. The respondent, a working-class woman stated:

> I think we owe our parents a great deal for the sacrifices they make for us. I gave up my chance for happiness for my parents and I feel that this was my duty. [She did not marry the man she loved because of parental disapproval.] Perhaps sometimes they demanded too much of me, but I will be just the same with my son. I believe a child should always remember the sacrifices that a mother has made for him. I demand of him ... that he try to give me what I have given him.

These words show how sacrifice was used as an awesome instrument to create in this mother a powerful sense of debt to her parents, and an instrument that she intended to employ in the same manner in dealing with her own son. By its very nature, sacrifice is an obligation than can never fully be satisfied, for there is no measure by which it can be agreed that the debt has been fully repaid. It is an obligation without end.

I have emphasized that parents want control over their children to insure the continuity of family solidarity. Solidarity, in turn, is important because it enables family members to withstand threats and uncertainties originating in the world outside the family. Among such uncertainties are those that are economic in nature. We could expect, therefore, that the sacrificial debt imposed on children would be applied to the time when parents may face economic difficulties. This was clearly put by a mechanic speaking of his son's occupational future:

> I would oppose my son very strongly if he wished to work away from home. In fact, after all the sacrifices I will have made over the years, it would be cruel abandon on his part. As soon as he is able to earn his living, he should help in the household.

Contained in this simple statement are the very direct connections between economic concerns, the desire to anchor children to the family and parental sacrifice. A *quid pro quo* is expected, not because the father is exploitative or selfish, but because of the conditions of life that make this sort of expected reciprocity meaningful and important. Where economic conditions are more certain and secure, this kind of statement would not be heard.

STATUS

Throughout this study class and status are major variables in the analyses of various family patterns. These matters also emerge in the interviews, and the final issue that I shall present is how Turinese themselves regard status and the meanings it has for them, particularly with respect to the family. Though we cannot estimate whether Turinese are more or less status conscious than others, the problem of status is important to them. They indicate a sensitivity to where they stand in relation to others — or where they would like to stand — and they are responsive to the esteem in which they are held by those about them. Status in Italy has the same symbolic and reward functions as in any stratified industrial system. But in a society where so much depends on who one is or who he appears to be, status and its accouterments may take on even greater importance in day-to-day affairs. It is also my impression that, to a greater degree in Turin than in American cities, status carries responsibilities that must be borne not by the parents alone, but by the entire family.

I doubt that there is a difference between the social classes in the degree to which people are conscious of status and prestige. There is a distinct difference between the higher and lower economic groups, however, in the ways that status consciousness is manifested. The middle and upper class are likely to express status concerns in desires for a distinctive style of life, one that signifies an economic position clearly set off from those below. This is not always easy to accomplish, for the style of life that provides symbolic and differentiating functions can push a family's resources to its limits. Here is a woman confronted with such a problem:

> My husband works in a bank. We are supposed to do what people of our condition do. We bought this apartment, but it has been a strain. It is necessary to do as I do [work hard] to keep this standard.

She is quite aware that they have overextended themselves but doesn't question its wisdom. Indeed, she does not even see it as a voluntaristic choice but as an obligation.

A style of life is essentially a device to establish and maintain status distance from those considered socially inferior. There are more direct devices to maintain status distance and one of these is limiting interaction across status lines. This is where children become significant, for they too have a part in the family's standing and are expected to be as selective in their social contacts as their parents. The following quotation from the wife of a white-collar worker illustrates this:

Children must see that good and bad exist. I explained to my children the social differences that exist and I made them understand the differences of origin, as otherwise they may have mixed with the mass, and this would not be nice.

This statement reflects the idea that the maintenance of status in Italy is the duty of children as well as parents. The status training this mother gives her child implies that each individual, regardless of age, is a representative of the family and its status. But at this point class differences appear. Middle-class parents may be interested in *who* the people are that the child interacts with, but working-class parents are more concerned about *how* the child behaves with others. Specifically, the working-class child should do nothing that contravenes the accepted standards and rules of "good" behavior. This is not an absolute class difference as much as one of emphasis. Its tone can be illustrated by a number of statements, such as one made by a working-class father while discussing his daughter's deportment:

At age 10, she must understand certain things; she must accept social rules. If we go to the house of an acquaintance and they present candy, she must not behave as though she had never seen it before.

Another parent, the mother of a son, spoke in a similar vein when she stated, "When he is in touch with people [adults], he should be able to speak with manners. We don't want people to have reason to criticize us."

Unlike those in the middle class, these parents are not stressing the selectivity of social contacts, or the importance of styles of life or status distance; instead they are concerned with the respect of the family. Like their middle-class counterparts, they, too, assign to children a role in upholding the family's status; however, the role prescription is different. In the middle class *the selectivity of social contacts* is emphasized, but in the working class it is *the avoidance of behavior* that would cast a shadow over the honor of the family and invite opprobrium. To prevent loss of respect, they insist that children conform to accepted social conventions. This may be one reason why working-class parents emphasize adherence to adult standards more than do middle-class parents (something about which we shall have more to say in the next chapter).

To some extent, then, working-class parents seek respect through the appearance they and their children can make in society. In fact, this was voiced very simply and pointedly by a woman who said, "With people it's how one behaves that counts. It's the exteriority that counts. Therefore, one should behave well." "Behaving well" involves the correct, acceptable presentation of self. Somewhat derisively we may call it "face work," but the Italians themselves have a more descriptive phrase — *far bella figura*. Literally it means to make an attractive figure, although its full meaning resists simple translation. It is exemplified in the following statement:

> We must show that we are decent. No one should have bad things to say about us. Even if I don't have much money, I would still want *far bella figura*. I give the best to others, even if I don't have money for it, and this makes me happy.

Whatever class similarities may exist in desires to establish and aggrandize status, the class differences in the ways of pursuing these interests are apparent. Working-class families are more likely to "give the best" and to rely on the presentation of self in seeking esteem. And if nothing can be done to enhance esteem, then nothing should be done to lose it; no one should have reason to criticize or say bad things about the family.

Each individual, then, is a representative of the family. Even children have the responsibility to maintain and advance the family's status or, at least, to refrain from behavior that would damage it. The prestige and honor of the entire family rises and falls with the actions of its individual members. This fact alone helps to understand some of the functions of parental control: it serves to discourage behavior that could bring shame to the family and result in a blow to its status.

DISCUSSION

The materials I have presented and my discussions of them have been intended to point to a number of interlaced elements in social and family life. A process can be abstracted from the interviews that may be outlined in these terms:

a. Parents' perceptions and experiences of their social world as potentially harmful and uncertain make the family the major setting offering psychological and material safety and security.

b. The vital importance of the family leads parents to be deeply concerned with its solidarity and viability, especially under conditions of massive social and economic change.

c. Parents see autonomy and independence of action among children as incompatible with solidarity and, consequently, want to exert control over their children's behavior.

d. This control appears not to rest so much on the exercise of direct authority as on more indirect techniques, such as the instrumental use of affection and self-sacrifice.

e. Finally, engagement in the status system involves the solidarity of family, and parental control may serve, in part, to enforce children's roles in these regards.

The essential point, and the one I have attempted to bring into focus, is that elements in the basic character of the family can be seen as adaptations to the constraints and imperatives imposed upon it by its social contexts. Much of what we observed in the family of Turin can be understood as processes that protect and enhance the solidarity of the family. But solidarity, in turn, is important because of what surrounding institutions fail to do for individuals and because of the threats — real or imagined — they pose for individuals.

A final point to mention concerns the effects on children of parental control and its mechanisms. Many authorities would probably view the denial of autonomy implied by extreme control inimical to healthy development. Yet, impressionistically, this does not seem to be the case; Turinese children do not appear any more neurotic in their behavior than their American age-mates. If this is a correct observation, I think it results partly from the unambiguity and certainty of parental actions. The concept of personality is not prevalent among Italians, particularly as a viable and developmental entity, shaped by parents and others. They recognize that children can be taught specific things by their parents, but they view the configuration of feelings and styles of behavior displayed by children as reflecting a biological thrust rather than environmental influences. Consequently, parents seem free of conflict or ambivalence concerning the way they raise their children. They appear to act more from a set of absolute values rather than from a range of options where each choice is presumed to have its own enduring impact. At the very least, children do not suffer the effects of uncertainty and ambiguity.

When I speak of absolute values, I do not mean that all Turinese parents possess the same values; far from it. Just as Americans, the characteristics they value in their children assume a diversity that corresponds to the circumstances they experience in their lives. This becomes clear in our examination of parental values.

IV

Parental Values

Most Turinese parents have a clear idea of the characteristics they would like to foster in their children. They are, in this respect, similar to parents of all nationalities. Every culture offers a wide array of characteristics that are equally acceptable, and from among these parents typically select some as particularly important for their children, others as less important. What they attempt to inculcate and what they choose to ignore largely depend on the order of importance they attach to various characteristics. In speaking of *parental values*, we refer to this hierarchical order of importance parents attribute to various characteristics. It is no accident that such an order is created in the minds of parents, for it helps them both to organize their socializing actions through time and to provide the benchmarks for evaluating their children's developmental progress. This chapter considers how parental value systems are formed by looking for the conditions underlying their variations.

Parents' own experiences as adults must ultimately be at the basis of the values they hold for their children. The nature of their experiences, in turn, is closely regulated by their locations within the social class system. By this reasoning alone we could expect parental values to vary with social class, and this is precisely what Kohn has found in the United States.[1] Values reflecting a stress on self-direction, he discovered, are more common to middle-class than to working-class Americans, who are more likely to prize conformity to external

This chapter is based in part on a revision of a previously published paper: Leonard I. Pearlin and Melvin L. Kohn, "Social Class, Occupation, and Parental Values: A Cross-national Study," *American Sociological Review*, 31 (1966), pp. 466 – 479.

[1]Melvin L. Kohn, "Social Class and Parental Values," *American Journal of Sociology*, 64 (1959), pp. 337 – 351.

proscription. *Self-control* is the particular value that exemplifies the middle-class emphasis; *obedience* best expresses the working-class emphasis.[2]

How does the relationship of class to values in Turin compare with that found to exist in the United States? The question of comparability of class effects, which occupies the first part of this chapter, actually probes an issue more fundamental to modern societies than might at first appear evident. Essentially, it asks if there are conditions so inherently common to social class structures that they lead to similar parental values in industrial societies that are dissimilar in history, culture, politics and material levels of life.

The comparability of findings from the two countries has been enhanced by adopting for use in Turin the same protocols previously used by Kohn to assess parental values in the United States. Respondents were handed a list of seventeen characteristics and were asked to indicate those that they thought were important to a child of their fifth-grader's age and sex. They were then instructed to designate from among those they considered important the single characteristic they viewed as foremost in importance, next, that which was second, and, last, the characteristic that was third most important. This technique serves to establish the rank order of the top three valued characteristics, to identify characteristics considered important but not among the first three and, finally, to determine which characteristics are thought to be of no importance. The items, of course, were translated and revised in Turin so as to keep the Italian version as close to the original as possible. To guard against the danger that the items would fail to tap or exhaust important values of Turinese parents, each respondent was asked if there were characteristics not on the list that he considered important. None suggested anything substantively different.

The first part of the analysis compares the relationship of class to values in the two countries, and the second part attempts to explain the relationship. The nature of social class tends to obscure a precise recognition of what may be responsible for its connections with parents' values. Social class is a global context, encompassing many conditions and experiences. The very richness and variety of social phenomena associated with class make it difficult to know which of them are influencing values. Parents' informal associations, the norms to which they are exposed and the roles and statuses they occupy

[2]Comparative data, albeit incomplete, indicate that working-class parents in several industrial societies place a high premium on obedience in their children. See Alex Inkeles, "Industrial Man: The Relation of Status to Experience, Perception, and Value," *American Journal of Sociology*, 66 (1960), pp. 20–21, and Table 9.

in various social institutions are among the important elements in a social life that are associated with class position. Undoubtedly several of these factors have some part in shaping parents' values for their children and in contributing to class differences in values. But rather than attempt to identify a range of class-related conditions that may underlie the different values we will focus our attention exclusively on certain features of occupational experience. For reasons that will be presented later, this is a theoretically meaningful analytic line to follow and also provides the most comprehensive opportunities for cross-national comparisons.

NATION, CLASS AND VALUES

Consider now the effects of class on parental values in the two countries. These are best assessed when first viewed against the more general background of similarities and differences between the two *cultures*. Table IV.1 presents separately the value choices of middle- and working-class fathers and mothers of each country. Comparing for the moment only by country, nationality has a profound effect on values. Some basic similarities exist between Italian and American parents; honesty, for example, is given the highest priority of all the seventeen characteristics in both Italy and the United States. But the rank-order of value choices is substantially different in the two countries. Regardless of social class, American parents are more likely than are Italian parents to value happiness, popularity and consideration; regardless of social class, Italian parents are more likely than are American parents to value good manners, obedience and seriousness. American parents' values are perhaps more child-centered, emphasizing the child's own development and gratifications, while Italian parental values seem more adult-centered, emphasizing the child's conformity to adult standards. Clearly, there are impressive cultural differences between the countries and they should not be obscured by the emphasis that we shall be giving to the similarity in the effects of class structure.

Despite the considerable differences between Italian and American parental values, almost all of the class relationships noted in the United States are also found in Italy.[3] Of the eight characteristics that have a statistically significant relationship to social class in the

[3]One other difference between the two countries is not shown in Table IV.1. In the United States, working-class parents are more likely to value certain characteristics for girls and others for boys. Italian parents make virtually no distinction between what is desirable for boys and girls. In fact, the sex of the child makes no difference for anything we shall discuss in this chapter. Thus, for simplicity of presentation, the data will not be presented separately for boys and for girls.

Table IV.1

Italian and American Parents' Selection of the Three Most Important
Characteristics for Children, by Social Class

| | ITALY | | | | UNITED STATES[a] | | | |
| | Fathers | | Mothers | | Fathers | | Mothers | |
Characteristic	Middle Class %	Working Class %	Middle Class %	Working Class %	Middle Class %	Working Class %	Middle Class %	Working Class %
1. That he is honest	54	54	55	55	52	58	44	53
2. That he has good manners	32*	44*	44	51	24	25	19	24
3. That he obeys his parents well	31*	45*	36*	48*	13*	39*	20*	33*
4. That he acts in a serious way	25	18	18	20	–	3	–	1
5. That he has self-control	23*	11*	16*	8*	20*	6*	22*	13*
6. That he is dependable	23*	13*	21*	10*	33*	8*	24	21
7. That he is able to defend himself	21	14	17*	8*	2*	17*	10	6
8. That he is ambitious	19	17	21	19	17	8	7	13
9. That he is happy	14*	7*	16	14	37	22	46*	36*
10. That he is considerate of others	11	9	10*	3*	35*	14*	39*	27*
11. That he is affectionate	10	12	13	12	2	8	5	4
12. That he is neat and clean	9	14	7*	14*	15	17	11*	20*
13. That he is popular with other children	9	7	6	4	15	25	15	18
14. That he is a good student	8*	24*	13*	24*	7	19	15	17
15. That he is liked by adults	4	9	5	9	–	8	5	4
16. That he is curious about things	3	1	2	1	13	8	18*	
17. That he is able to play by himself	1	2	–	1	2	6	1	6*
Numbers	(160)	(148)	(263)	(205)	(46)	(36)	(174)	(165)

United States, six are significantly related to social class in Italy, too [4] — obedience and neatness being more highly valued by the working than by the middle class in both countries, self-control, dependability, happiness and consideration being more highly valued by the middle than by the working class in both countries.[5] In both Italy and the United States, middle-class parents are more likely than working-class parents to value characteristics that bespeak the child's self-direction, and working-class parents are more likely than middle-class parents to value characteristics that bespeak his conformity to external prescription.

We should not exaggerate the *degree* to which social class is related to parental values in either the United States or Italy. The rank-order of middle-class parents' value choices does not differ greatly from that of working-class parents in either country; and the difference between the proportions of middle- and working-class parents who value any given characteristic is never very large. What is impressive is that the relationship of social class to parental values is so very nearly identical in the two countries — despite the considerable cultural difference between the two.

Self-control and obedience, in particular, embody most clearly the essential difference between the middle-class emphasis on self-direction and the working-class emphasis on conformity to external prescription. In fact, these two show a *completely* consistent relationship to

[4]Tests of significance are presented throughout this study for the reader's reference. These are not the only criteria generally used for judging the importance of relationships and for selecting lines of analyses and interpretation, however. The theoretical interests of relationships, their continuity within and between tables and their stability when using different indices are the criteria usually employed in deciding what merits analytic attention. Table IV.1 represents an exception, however; here the pattern of statistically significant results is so consistent with what is theoretically significant that it provides a definite aid to the analysis.

[5]The two instances where there is no cross-national correspondence are curiosity and ability to defend oneself. Middle-class American mothers, particularly upper-middle-class American mothers, value curiosity more highly than do working-class mothers. This is not so in Italy. A problem of language may be at issue, for we could find no Italian word equivalent for "curiosity" which was free of the connotation of voyeurism. In the United States, working-class fathers are more likely than middle-class fathers to value the child's ability to defend himself. In Italy, the middle class is more apt to value the ability to defend oneself. We suspect that in Italian context, to defend oneself has the connotation, "to be able to take care of oneself in a potentially hostile world." Two characteristics are not significantly related to social class in the United States but are in Italy — good manners and being a good student. Both are more highly valued by the working than the middle class.

social class: In both countries, middle-class mothers and fathers are more likely than working-class mothers and fathers to value self-control; and, although sex of the fifth-grade children is not shown in Table IV.1, we can report that this class difference holds for parents of sons and daughters alike. Also in both countries, working-class mothers and fathers are more likely than middle-class mothers and fathers to value obedience, both for sons and for daughters.

And so a rather striking answer to the first question has emerged: similar class structures do have similar effects in different cultures. Despite their very different traditions, the disparate levels of their economies, their distinctive religious climates and their diverse political systems, the similar social class orders of Turin and the United States give rise to similar parental conceptions of what is desirable and necessary for children. The valuation of self-control and obedience are particularly pivotal. In Turin, as in the United States, middle-class parents, regardless of their sex or the sex of their children, lean to the former and working-class parents to the latter. Because self-control and obedience so consistently distinguish the classes along theoretically important lines, we shall focus on them to see if the different occupational conditions of the classes help account for their different parental values.

THE RELATIONSHIP OF SELF-CONTROL
TO OBEDIENCE

To examine how occupational experiences enter into this picture first requires a re-examination of self-control and obedience and their inter-relationships. This is necessary because neither the magnitude nor the meaning of class differences can be fully appreciated by treating the valuation of self-control and obedience as though they were independent, as we do in Table IV.1. More incisive class differences are revealed by observing how individuals allocate their priorities between these two characteristics; that is, by seeing how their valuations of one are related to their valuations of the other.

Although proportionately more working- than middle-class parents rate obedience highly (selecting it as one of the three most important), there is very little difference between the classes when we add together those valuing obedience either highly or moderately (saying it is important, but not including it as one of the three most important). In other words, obedience is valued either moderately or highly by similar majorities of both classes: 60 per cent of the middle class, 65 per cent of the working class. The real difference between classes emerges only by comparing how those according some importance to obedience assess self-control. This reveals that middle-class parents are more likely than working-class parents to assert that self-control, along with obedience, is highly or moderately important. In contrast, working-class parents assigning some value to obedience are more likely than their middle-class counterparts to reject self-control altogether. These differences can be interpreted to mean that *external control is valued throughout the culture, but the middle class also emphasizes internal control.*

By sorting out the appropriate inter-relationships between the two values, it is possible to create a single index that will capture these important class differences. This index, shown in relation to the social class of Turinese fathers,[6] is presented in Table IV.2. It delineates those who value self-control highly or moderately, irrespective of their valuation of obedience (categories 1 and 2); those who consider neither characteristic important (category 3); and those who assign moderate or high importance to obedience but reject self-control as of no importance (categories 4 and 5). The first two categories include the many fathers who are not impervious to obedience, but who

Table IV.2

Turinese Fathers' Valuation of Self-control and Obedience, by Social Class

Valuation of Self-control and Obedience	Middle Class %	Working Class %
Self-control highly, regardless of their valuation of obedience	23	11
Self-control moderately, regardless of their valuation of obedience	29	24
Neither self-control nor obedience	26	25
Obedience moderately and self-control not at all	4	9
Obedience highly and self-control not at all	18	31
Numbers	(167)	(158)

Significance of χ^2
(linear regression) $p < .001$

[6]The picture is essentially the same for Italian mothers; we shall limit ourselves to the fathers because this is more relevant to the subsequent analyses of the effects of various dimensions of occupation on paternal values. Too few of the mothers have jobs to permit a systematic analysis of their occupational situations. Later we shall briefly consider the relevance of fathers' occupational circumstances to their wives' values.

nevertheless also single out self-control as desirable in their children. The last two categories include fathers valuing obedience but eschewing self-control completely.

Looking at the distribution of men of the two classes among these categories, this index of parental values would appear to get at the crux of class differences.[7] It clarifies class distinctions in value patterns by highlighting the fact that the middle class doesn't necessarily disavow obedience while subscribing to self-control, but that the working class is more likely to disavow self-control while subscribing to obedience. It is a meaningful and serviceable index of values and we will use it in the following analysis of occupation. For simplicity, however, we will reduce the five categories to three by combining category 1 with 2, 4 with 5.

THE STRUCTURAL SOURCES OF SELF-DIRECTION IN OCCUPATIONAL EXPERIENCES

Occupation is an area of life where many conditions and experiences converge. However, we are interested only in those that meet a limited set of conditions: (1) The conditions must be relatively constant aspects of occupation, durable over time, predictable, and patterned. In short, if they are to explain meaningfully class differences in values, they must be built into the structure of the occupation. (2) They must differ between middle- and working-class occupations; the only dimensions of occupational experience that can possibly enter into the relationship of class to parental values are those that are differentially distributed between middle-class and working-class occupations.[8] (3) They must have *a priori* relevance to the values under scrutiny.

What conditions of occupation are relevant to self-control and obedience? A central difference between middle- and working-class

[7]The test of significance used in Table IV.2 is Cochran's test for a linear regression of P, which is based on chi-square. This test will be used in all tables whose variables have a natural order, or to which ordinality is conceptually imputed. The technique partitions a relationship so that it is possible to test for that part which is linear. Since a regression line is based on one degree of freedom, the number of rows and columns in a table have no bearing on the number of degrees of freedom. See W. G. Cochran, "Some Methods of Strengthening the Common x^2 Tests," *Biometrics*, 10 (1954), pp. 417–451; A. E. Maxwell, *Analysing Qualitative Data* (London: Methuen and Company, 1961), pp. 63–72.

[8]This is easily understood as a requirement when we realize that before a third variable can account for the relationship between two other variables, it must be associated with each of them. For a discussion of the "arithmetic of controls," see Morris Rosenberg, *The Logic of Survey Analysis* (New York: Basic Books, 1968), pp. 259–271.

occupations that may eventually result in the difference between middle- and working-class values is that middle-class jobs require more self-direction; working-class occupations more typically demand that one follow explicit rules set down by someone in authority.[9] Our assumption is that the structural requirements of the job are easily transmuted into personal requirements for doing the job well, and that the characteristics needed in so major a segment of life as one's occupation come to be valued generally — for oneself, and for one's children as well. Middle-class jobs tend to allow — or demand — self-direction and this may underlie the high valuation in this class of self-control for children. Working-class jobs more often require following the directions established by someone in authority; indeed, they may penalize anything other than compliance to rules and directives handed down from above. From these enduring conditions of work, obedience comes to be valued and self-control ignored.

The task, then, is to specify and index those dimensions of occupation that reflect the above conditions and that define the overall occupational situation as conducive to self-direction or to conformity to external direction. There are three such dimensions: the closeness of supervision to which a person is subjected; whether the type of work he does principally involves dealing with things, people or ideas; and the degree to which the job requires self-reliance. These three dimensions of occupational self-direction are closely related empirically as well as conceptually. But since they are analytically distinct, we shall consider them *seriatim* and only then examine their combined effect on the relationship of class to values among Turinese fathers.

THE CLOSENESS OF SUPERVISION. A limiting condition for the exercise of self-direction is the closeness of supervision to which one is subjected. Under conditions of close supervision little leeway is possible. On the other hand, freedom from close supervision, while a condition for self-direction, does not necessarily signal autonomy. The absence of occupational surveillance might simply indicate a situation where work is so unvaryingly routine that it requires little or no overseeing. In general, however, an occupational situation of close supervision can be taken to mean a limitation on self-direction. We should expect closely supervised men to be more likely to value obedience for their children and less likely to value self-control than would less closely supervised men.

We measured closeness of supervision by three questions, which

[9]This distinction was originally formulated in Melvin L. Kohn, "Social Class and Parent-child Relationships: An Interpretation," *American Journal of Sociology*, 68 (1963), p. 476.

together form a reasonably satisfactory Guttman scale [10]: How much control does your direct supervisor exercise over your work? Do you feel that you are able to make decisions about the things that have true importance to your work? Do you have much influence on the way things go at your work? The scale pattern is such that men who report that their supervisors exert little or no control over them are likely also to claim decision-making power and considerable influence. Those who are unable to exert influence over their work claim little decision-making power and say they are subject to considerable control.

Only in the working class is any considerable proportion of men subjected to very close supervision. Nevertheless, the direction of the relationship between supervision and parental values is the same for both social classes, although the association is closer in the working class, as Table IV.3 demonstrates. The more a working-class man experiences his work as closely directed from above, the more likely he is to value obedience for his child exclusively. In the middle class, where the self-employed are shown separately, the relationship is less

Table IV.3

Closeness of Job Supervision and Turinese Fathers' Valuation
of Self-control and Obedience, by Social Class

Valuation of Self-control and Obedience	Middle Class				Working Class		
	Self-employed %	*Loose Super-vision* %	*Inter-mediate Super-vision* %	*Close Super-vision* %	*Loose Super-vision* %	*Inter-mediate Super-vision* %	*Close Super-vision* %
Value self-control	51	49	52	40	39	38	26
Value neither self-control nor obedience	26	30	24	10	31	25	19
Value obedience but not self-control	23	21	24	50	30	37	55
Numbers	(77)	(57)	(17)	(10)	(62)	(48)	(38)

Significance of χ^2 (linear regression)	$p < .30$	$p < .05$

[10]Reproducibility = 0.95, Scalability = 0.83.

linear, for only among the most closely supervised is there an increase in the valuation of obedience. In both classes, nevertheless, men whose work depends on adhering to the orders of others tend to value obedience for their children, and those who have greater freedom in their work situations are more likely to value self-control for their children.

THE PRINCIPAL COMPONENT OF WORK: THINGS, PEOPLE OR IDEAS. A second dimension of occupation intimately involved in the question of the degree to which one's actions are self-directed is the substance of work one does. Most working-class occupations deal with things, most middle-class occupations deal with interpersonal relationships or ideas. Work with things typically entails the least freedom for independent judgment, for it is most amenable to standardization and regulation by others. Work with ideas typically entails the most freedom, even necessity, for independent judgment, for it is intrinsically resistant to the intervention of others and necessarily under more direct control of the individual himself. Where the task involves ideas, there is a natural opportunity for autonomy of decision and action.

We asked fathers: "In almost all occupations it is necessary to work with ideas, people and things, but occupations differ in the extent to which they require these types of activities. Considering now a typical day's work, which of these three aspects of work is most important in your occupation?" As expected, the correspondence between social class and whether one works with things, people or ideas is close, but, fortunately for analytic purposes, not complete. Some middle-class men deal principally with things and some working-class men deal principally with ideas and people. The middle-class men who say that things are most important to their work are mostly small entrepreneur-craftsmen, dentists, engineers, highly trained technicians, managers and sales personnel whose work is very directly related to the manufacture or distribution of hard goods and a few clerks whose jobs are so routinized that they see themselves as working with things rather than data. The majority of working-class men who say that they work primarily with people are in service occupations; the remainder are foremen. Working-class men who say that ideas are most important to their work are concentrated in highly skilled jobs. What differentiates them from other skilled workers is that their jobs seem to require more independence of judgment or evaluation — as in the case of mechanics who specialize in diagnosis, or testers in the automobile factory.

Table IV.4 clearly shows that men of both classes who work mainly with things are the least disposed to value self-control, and that men

Table IV.4

The Major Component of Work and Turinese Fathers' Valuation
of Self-control and Obedience, by Social Class

	Middle Class			Working Class		
Valuation of Self-control and Obedience	*Things* %	*People* %	*Ideas* %	*Things* %	*People* %	*Ideas* %
Value self-control	27	51	64	23	45	62
Value neither self-control nor obedience	45	26	21	29	16	27
Value obedience but not self-control	28	23	15	48	39	11
Numbers	(22)	(73)	(58)	(96)	(31)	(26)
Significance of χ^2 (linear regression)		$p < .20$			$p < .20$	

who work mainly with ideas are the most disposed to value self-control. Obedience is most likely to be stressed by those men, whatever their social class, who work primarily with things. The relationships are strong and consistent independently of the class in which men are located.

THE REQUIREMENT OF SELF-RELIANCE IN WORK. The degree of supervision to which a man is subject and the type of work he does limit the degree of self-direction a job permits. Within these limits, some jobs in fact require that a man make independent judgments, take responsibility, invest himself in his work, while others, although they may permit it, do not actually require it. The last aspect of self-direction we indexed is the degree to which men see their jobs as requiring self-reliance.

In the interview, fathers were given a list of qualities and asked to indicate, on the basis of their own occupational experience, the rank order of the three that were most important to doing well at their work. For the remainder they were asked to distinguish between those that were important and unimportant. Four of these items form an index of "self-reliance." They are: to understand one's self; to be intelligent; to have trust in one's self; and to have a sense of responsibility. The index was formed by giving a weight of four when an item was ranked first in importance, three when it was ranked second, two when it was ranked third, and one where it was considered important even though unranked. These scores were then added for each respondent so that the higher a man's score, the more his work required self-reliance.[11] Understandably, a man's score on self-reliance is related to the closeness of the supervision he receives and even more closely to whether he works primarily with ideas, people, or things. The degree of self-reliance is also closely related to social class.

Looking now at the association between the degree to which a man thinks that his job requires self-reliance and his values for his children, a very substantial relationship is evident, as Table IV.5 shows. Regardless of their class, men who experience their jobs as requiring a large measure of self-reliance are overwhelmingly more likely to value self-control than are men who do not. Men who think their jobs require little or no self-reliance are overwhelmingly more likely to value obedience.

OCCUPATIONAL ELEMENTS
IN THE CLASS-VALUES RELATIONSHIP

Two remaining issues confront this analysis. One concerns the independence of the three dimensions of occupational self-direction. Closeness of supervision, components of work and the requirement for self-reliance are not only conceptually kindred but empirically intertwined as well. Indeed, as long as occupational roles have an internal integrity, the dimensions of occupation are bound to be interrelated. We cannot be certain, however, that they independently affect parental values, that they are not simply different ways of examining the same variance. It is necessary, therefore, that we consider whether each of the three dimensions has some effect on fathers' values independently of the other two. Then we can take up the second, and main, issue: the extent to which these conditions of occupation jointly explain the relationship between class and values.

We can assess the independent effects of the three occupational dimensions by observing separately the relationship of each of them to values while controlling the others. Does the need for self-reliance at work influence fathers' values, for example, regardless of whether the men work primarily with things, people or ideas? To answer this question we must include in our comparisons such

---

[11]We have some evidence for the unidimensionality of this index. The four items, taken three at a time and dichotomized on the basis of whether or not the attribute is considered important, form quite satisfactory Guttman scales. But the cutting points are such that we cannot use all four items in one scale, and the requirement that we score each item dichotomously (for independence) unduly restricts the power of the index. A simple additive scoring of the four items provides a less elegant but more useful index.

Table IV.5

The Degree of Self-reliance Required in Work and Turinese Fathers' Valuation of Self-control and Obedience, by Social Class

Valuation of Self-control and Obedience	Middle Class				Working Class			
	Least Self-reliance %	Next Least Self-reliance %	Next Greatest Self-reliance %	Greatest Self-reliance %	Least Self-reliance %	Next Least Self-reliance %	Next Greatest Self-reliance %	Greatest Self-reliance %
Value self-control	5	46	57	83	14	37	41	65
Value neither self-control nor obedience	58	26	24	—	33	28	21	21
Value Obedience, but not self-control	37	28	19	17	53	35	38	14
Numbers	(19)	(50)	(70)	(24)	(36)	(64)	(42)	(14)
Significance of χ^2 (linear regression)	p<.001				p<.01			

unlikely groups as men who work with things but with a high level of self-reliance, and those engaged with ideas but at jobs requiring little self-reliance. Despite the unevenness of the findings that results partly from the small numbers in these groups, the answer to our question, shown in Table IV.6, is essentially in the affirmative. In both social classes, regardless of whether men work with things, people or ideas, those whose jobs require high self-reliance are more likely to value self-control. We can read the same table in a different way to show that the effect on paternal values of working with things, people or ideas generally holds both for men whose jobs require a great deal of self-reliance and for men whose jobs do not.

The cumulative result is that men who both work primarily with things and on jobs that require little self-reliance are least likely to value self-control and most likely to value obedience alone; at the other extreme, men who work primarily with ideas on jobs that require much self-reliance are most likely to value self-control and least likely to value obedience alone. Comparable tables (not shown) using the other combinations of occupational dimensions produce similar independent and additive effects. Although there is a close correspondence between the three dimensions of occupational self-direction, therefore, each contributes separately to variations in parents' values.

It has been established that the occupational conditions supporting self-direction are predominantly found in middle-class occupations; the conditions reflecting compliance are concentrated in working-class occupations. Each of these conditions, furthermore, is independently related to fathers' values. Now we can consider the extent to which the three occupational conditions together explain the middle-class emphasis on self-control and the working-class stress on obedience. We cannot treat the three conditions simultaneously in their present form, because it would result in numbers impossibly small. Instead, we employed Rosenberg's technique of test factor standardization.[12] This technique allows us, in effect, to ask how much difference there would be between middle- and working-class fathers' values if their occupational experiences were the same in all three relevant respects.

Table IV.7 presents from Table IV.2 the original comparison of middle- with working-class fathers' values and the same comparison standardized on the three aspects of occupational experience. The original difference of 12 per cent in the proportion of men who value

12Morris Rosenberg, "Test Factor Standardization as a Method of Interpretation," Social Forces, 41 (1962), pp. 53 – 61.

Table IV.6

The Major Component of Work, the Degree of Self-reliance Required and Turinese Fathers' Valuation of Self-control and Obedience, by Social Class

MIDDLE CLASS

Valuation of Self-control and Obedience	Things		People		Ideas	
	Low Self-reliance %	*High Self-reliance[a]* %	*Low Self-reliance* %	*High Self-reliance* %	*Low Self-reliance* %	*High Self-reliance* %
Value self-control	13	—	46	56	41	75
Value neither self-control nor obedience	47	—	36	19	30	15
Value obedience, but not self-control	40	—	18	25	29	10
Numbers	(15)	(7)	(28)	(43)	(17)	(39)

[a]Percentages not given because of small number of cases,

WORKING CLASS

Valuation of Self-control and Obedience	Things		People		Ideas	
	Low Self-reliance %	*High Self-reliance* %	*Low Self-reliance* %	*High Self-reliance* %	*Low Self-reliance* %	*High Self-reliance* %
Value self-control	21	30	34	61	58	65
Value neither self-control nor obedience	31	26	22	8	34	21
Value obedience, but not self-control	48	44	44	31	8	14
Numbers	(67)	(27)	(18)	(13)	(12)	(14)

Table IV.7

Original and Standardized Percentages of Turinese Fathers' Valuation of Self-control and Obedience, by Social Class

Valuation of Self-control and Obedience	Original Comparison[a]		Standardized Comparison	
	Middle Class %	*Working Class* %	*Middle Class* %	*Working Class* %
Self-control highly, regardless of their valuation of obedience	23	11	18	14
Self-control moderately, regardless of their valuation of obedience	29	24	23	27
Neither self-control nor obedience	26	25	34	24
Obedience moderately and self-control not at all	4	9	6	15
Obedience highly and self-control not at all	18	31	19	20
Numbers	(144)	(141)	(144)	(141)
Significance of χ^2 (linear regression)	p < .001		n.s.	

[a]*The "original" comparison differs slightly from Table IV.2, for it excludes those fathers who could not be classified on all three dimensions of occupation.*

self-control highly is reduced to 4 per cent. Similarly, 52 per cent of the middle-class men and 35 per cent of the working-class men rated self-control either highly or moderately. In the standardized comparison there is no difference, for here 41 per cent of each class rates self-control at these two levels. Thus the original difference between 52 and 35 per cent is reduced to 0 when the prevailing conditions of occupational life in the two classes are taken into account. In short, the differential occupational experiences of middle- and working-class men largely account for their differential valuation of self-control.

At the other extreme, the original difference of 13 per cent in the proportion of men who value obedience highly is reduced to 1 per cent. Other aspects of social class continue to show some effect, however. The difference in proportions of men who value obedience either moderately or higher, originally 18 per cent, remains 10 per cent after standardization. Thus, the differential occupational experiences of middle- and working-class men largely account for the difference in the extreme valuation of obedience, but aspects of class not dealt with here still contribute substantially to the greater overall likelihood of working-class men valuing obedience.

Standardization further reveals that one effect of social class may be hidden by these three dimensions of occupation. In the original comparison, there is no difference between the proportion of middle- and working-class fathers who reject both values — who, presumably, do not value control, whether internal or external. The standardized comparison suggests that if not for these occupational experiences, middle-class men would be more likely to reject both values. For many middle-class fathers the alternatives are not self-control and obedience; were it not for their occupational experiences, they would value neither self-control nor obedience, but other characteristics altogether.

A CROSS-NATIONAL VIEW OF CLASS, OCCUPATION AND VALUES

There is reason to wonder if occupation plays the same part in accounting for class differences in fathers' values in other industrial areas as it does in Turin. Have we been recording the effects of cultural elements or of the enduring and structured experiences of men in their occupations? We pointed out in Chapter III that Italians are very sensitive to authority relations. It is important to their security that they be able to "size up" the power of others, to know when to comply and to know when they can exert what power they may possess. These skills can have an important bearing on one's fate in a particularistic society. Perhaps, then, the consequences of occupational self-direction and compliance enter into the family domain because these are pervasive concerns, reinforced by the nature of many encounters in the society.

Cultural differences notwithstanding, if occupational self-direction and compliance are intrinsic concomitants of class stratification, the same class-occupation-values relationship we find in Turin should also exist elsewhere. It is possible to make appropriate comparisons with data from a recently completed study by Kohn.[13] His investigation, which employed a national sample of all employed American males over twenty-one years of age, was partly concerned with the same question studied in Turin concerning the role of occupation in the

[13]Melvin L. Kohn, *Class and Conformity: A Study in Values* (Homewood, Ill.: Dorsey Press, 1969).

class-value relationship. Consequently, there is substantial overlap between the concerns of his study and those of this chapter.

The indices Kohn constructed for his study are different from, but still comparable to, those used in Turin. His three measures of occupational self-direction, while more elaborate, contain questions that tap the same dimensions as those conceptualized and indexed in Turin.[14] The two studies differ more in their indices of parental values than of occupational self-direction. In the American study Kohn factor analyzed several items to derive a factor of self-direction and conformity values for children.[15] However, included in his factor are the items used in Turin to assess the priorities accorded self-control and obedience. Because it includes these specific items, we assume that the self-direction and conformity factor, while broader than the index used here, nevertheless occupies the same continuum as that which is defined by self-control and obedience alone.

We could have presented separate tables with the American occupational data paralleling those from Turin. If we had, we would see that the factor scores favoring self-direction in children are disproportionately found among middle-class men (Hollingshead's classes 1 – 3) and scores favoring conformity are concentrated in the working class (classes 4 and 5). The three dimensions of occupational self-direction, furthermore, are each related to American fathers' valuation of self-direction and conformity in the same way they are associated with Turinese fathers' valuations of self-control and obedience.

But the cross-national correspondence can be seen most inclusively when we look at the United States data to see how the three conditions of occupation jointly account for the class-values relationship that appears in this study. The factor scores for the two American classes are expressed by means in Table IV.8; the lower the mean the greater the value placed on self-direction in children, the higher the mean the greater the value placed on conformity.

Looking first at the class differences without regard to occupation, we see that the mean score for middle-class fathers is —3.0, in contrast to 2.5 for working-class fathers. The product-moment correlation is .28. The table also compares the paternal values of both classes, this time controlling for the three occupational conditions by covariation. In effect, the standardized table shows the association

---

[14]Kohn's assessment of the principal components of work — whether with things, people or ideas — is virtually the same as used in Turin. He describes his indices of closeness of supervision and of self-reliance *ibid.*, pp. 139 – 140.

[15]The construction of the self-direction-conformity factor and the items that go into it are found *ibid.*, pp. 57 – 59.

Table IV.8

Mean Factor Scores of American Fathers' Valuation of Self-direction and Conformity, Before and After Controlling on Conditions of Occupational Self-direction, by Social Class[a]

	Original Comparison		Controlled Comparison	
	Middle Class	*Working Class*	*Middle Class*	*Working Class*
Mean self-direction- .conformity factor score	−3.0	2.5	−1.6	1.4
Numbers	(666)	(757)	(666)	(757)
Correlation coefficient	.28		.12	
Significance of χ^2 (linear regression)	p < .001		p < .001	

[a]*Provided by Melvin L. Kohn from unpublished data.*

of class and factor scores after the three occupational dimensions are removed from the relationship. The differences between the mean scores of the classes are now less, indicating that the original differences come about partly as a result of the distinctly different opportunities for occupational self-direction in the two classes. Just how much difference occupation makes can be most directly assessed by the change in the value of the correlation coefficient in the original and in the controlled comparison. It is a property of the product-moment correlation that its changes can be expressed in proportionate terms. Thus, the correlation between fathers' class and their values is reduced from .28 to .12, a change of 57 per cent. Well over half of the relationship of class to values, in other words, is accounted for by occupational self-direction. The importance of occupation to values is not unique to Turin, therefore in both countries the structured and patterned actions of men within the important sphere of occupation have direct consequences for parent-child relations.

DISCUSSION

This chapter has been concerned with: (1) whether the relationship ot social class to parental values found originally in the United States is also a concomitant of stratification in industrialized Turin; (2)

whether the differences in middle- and working-class parents' values are due to differences in their occupational conditions.

Although a cross-national comparison shows that Turinese parental values are more adult-centered and American more child-centered, the relationship of social class to parental values is much the same in both countries. In Italy as in the United States, middle-class parents put greater emphasis on the child's self-direction and working-class parents on the child's conformity to external prescription.

The strikingly similar effects of class in the two cultures strongly indicate that conditions intrinsic to stratification itself are responsible. Occupation stands out as one critical condition, especially aspects of work reflecting self-direction: closeness of supervision; work with things, people or data; and required self-reliance. These are structured elements of work resulting in imperatives and constraints that pierce cultural differences to affect values in very similar ways in Turin and the United States. Independently and cumulatively they account for a large part of the difference between middle- and working-class fathers' values.

The relationships that have been presented raise several important questions; some of them we can answer, at least partially, by available data; others we can only speculate about. One question concerns what is actually represented in the relationships of occupational self-direction and compliance to the paternal valuation of self-direction and obedience. An obvious possibility is that fathers, on the basis of their work experiences, prepare children for their occupational life to come. From the demands and requirements characteristic of their own occupations, they stress the development of characteristics that will best enable their children to meet similar demands when they enter into occupational life. It is likely that more than a specifically occupational preparation is involved. In a general and profound way, fathers come to value these characteristics as virtues in their own right and not simply as expedients to later occupational adaptation. One important piece of evidence buttresses this conclusion: exactly the same relationship exists between fathers' occupational experiences and values for daughters and for sons. Yet it is hardly likely that any large proportion of the fathers think their daughters will have occupational careers comparable to their own, particularly in Italy.

Another question generated by our analysis concerns women. Dealing, as we have, with fathers' experiences and fathers' values leads one to wonder how husbands' occupations may affect their wives' values. A later chapter considers the general issue of marital consensus and its antecedents. Looking only at the part played by occupation in maternal values, the Turin data indicate that husbands' occupational experiences are related to their wives' values just as to their own, albeit not quite so strongly in the working as in the middle class. Not surprisingly, therefore, a man's experiences affect his own values more strongly and those of his wife less, particularly in working-class marriages. What is notable is that wives are at all influenced by their husbands' occupational experiences, considering that these experiences unfold at places and at times so separated from the family domain.

Finally, our analysis presents the tough problem concerning the direction of relationships. The last chapter takes this up in detail, but some discussion of it here is also necessary. We have intentionally phrased our interpretations to point up the effects of class and occupation on values. But may not values affect class and occupation? It is doubtful if values shape the structural character of a class system or if they create conditions of work; these are better understood in terms of economic organization and industrial technology. Values do influence the fates of individuals within class and occupational systems, however, and in so doing may contribute to the acceptance and legitimation of the systems. Once they are inculcated with valued characteristics, individuals probably selectively seek out and best fit into the particular occupational situation requiring these very characteristics. Children from middle-class families eventually are drawn into occupations requiring self-direction; those of working-class origins may find such occupations psychologically uncongenial. The inequalities inherent in social stratification and in occupational settings are not supported by teaching children to submit reluctantly to the inevitable, therefore, but by acually training them to prize the behavior that will be expected of them.

These selective mechanisms are particularly evident in an examination of the future goals Turinese parents hold for their children. Relatively limited numbers of working-class parents want their children to achieve middle-class status; even fewer of them expect their children to achieve it. We consider the broad issue of parental aspirations in the next chapter.

V

Parental Aspirations—
And an Unanticipated Consequence

Aspirations refer to the social statuses parents want their children to achieve. Together with the characterological attributes valued by parents, aspirations are important elements in the preparation of the young for future roles. And, like parental values, the formation of aspirations is best understood when we recognize that aspirations are intermeshed with the social systems that touch upon the family. On the basis of their own statuses in education, occupation and economy, parents are made keenly aware of some opportunities and are blinded to others; they come to judge some goals as feasible, others as hopelessly remote. Thus achievement aspirations are inseparably bound to the larger society by the participation of parents in its institutions. Because of these connections, a study which seeks the effects of social structure on the family, as this study does, finds a rich harvest in parents' status aspirations for children.

The technological and industrial expansion of the kind that has been taking place in Turin seems to elevate profoundly parental aspirations. Yet, even with increased opportunities, parents differ considerably in the statuses to which they aspire. A major aim of this chapter is to learn why. The work of Herbert Hyman in the United States has already provided a partial, though most important, answer to this query.[1] He discovered that the appeal of high success goals, far from being universally held, declines markedly with economic resources. Those of limited economic means are, of course, in the least favorable position to compete for high status goals. Because they are

[1]Herbert Hyman, "The Value Systems of Different Classes: A Social Psychological Contribution to the Analysis of Stratification," in Reinhard Bendix and Seymour Martin Lipset (eds.), *Class, Status and Power* (Glencoe, Ill.: The Free Press, 1953), pp. 426 – 442.

73

the least likely to achieve these goals, they are also the least likely to want them in the first place. To take liberties with an old adage, Hyman's findings reflect a sentiment that it is better to have never wanted at all than to have wanted and failed. We shall see how the effects of economic resources on the aspirations of Turinese parents compare with the very powerful effects shown by Hyman in the United States.

Although the effects of social class are more potent than other circumstances, class is not the only condition that influences levels of parents' aspirations. Regardless of a family's economic standing, other circumstances may act as levers or depressors. Particularly relevant in this regard are husband and wife status relations. The relative status of the families from which spouses come continues to be important long after marriage, for certain status disparities in the structure of the marriage bear an interesting relationship to aspirations. Actual mobility experiences of parents are also significant in relation to hopes for children; this relationship, in turn, is part of a process that implicates subjective class identifications.

The second part of this chapter considers a single group of parents: *the disprivileged strivers*. They are disprivileged because of their very limited economic resources and they are strivers because they entertain the highest aspirations for their children. They form an interesting group, both because they represent a point at which somewhat divergent theoretical perspectives intersect and because of the rather special, though unintended, consequence of their aspirations for their children's behavior.

ASSESSMENT OF PARENTAL ASPIRATIONS

The interviews contained many questions bearing on parental aspirations. Those aspirations that are of concern here involve two institutional domains: education and occupation. Although formal education is more abbreviated in Italy than in the United States, it is no less important as a route to social and economic advancement there than it is here. The Italian educational system, uniform for the entire nation, is fairly complicated. It contains a number of points at which irreversible decisions must be made. These decisions are crucial, for each serves to funnel the student to particular courses of study while precluding others. Four principal levels existed at the time of this study and these can be identified in terms familiar to Americans: elementary, extending through the fifth grade; technical or vocational; secondary; and university. Fathers and mothers were asked which of these levels they would ideally like their children to achieve, and their answers are used to represent the levels of educational aspirations.

Parents also were asked to specify the occupations they would like their children to enter. These were classified as professional; managerial and entrepreneurial; technical and clerical; sales; foremen; and skilled, semi-skilled, or unskilled manual workers. Through a second question, which asked parents what they felt were the most important things their children should seek in an occupation, we could establish what parents considered desirable in this domain. Although these items serve well in revealing levels of aspiration, it is well to keep in mind that there are aspects of aspirations that they do not tap, such as the intensity with which they are desired or what they represent to their holders.[2] The information we do have is nevertheless suited to our present purposes.

CLASS AND PARENTAL ASPIRATIONS:
A COMPARATIVE VIEW

In Italy, as in any society where such options are meaningful, parents would like to see their children in educational and occupational echelons they consider to be rewarding and gratifying. Parents typically hope that their children will advance beyond their own occupational attainments. While only 8 per cent of the mothers and fathers in our sample attended a university, for example, 44 per cent of them desired a university education for their children. Virtually the same percentage of difference appears when comparing the occupational status fathers have attained with the occupational status they want for their children. Though Turinese parents live at a time and under conditions that have limited their own educational and occupational achievements, their aspirations in behalf of their children have nonetheless been stimulated by the industrial system in which they live and the changes that have been occurring in it. Indeed, as rapid as economic expansion has been in Turin in recent years, the expansion of aspirations may have been even greater.

This overview, however, tells only a general and partial story; aspirations cannot be understood fully until they are seen within the context of class. Since I shall compare the effects of class on aspirations in Turin with those analyzed by Hyman in the United States, I must adapt my indicators of class to his. The American studies from

[2]The intensity and meaning of aspirations for different classes are considered by Leonard Reissman, "Levels of Aspiration and Social Class," *American Sociological Review*, 18 (1953), pp. 233–242; and Ephraim Harold Mizruchi, *Success and Opportunity* (Glencoe, Ill.: The Free Press, 1964).

which Hyman drew much of his secondary data relied on interviewer ratings to judge the class of respondents. No such ratings were employed in the Turin study, so that strict equivalence is not possible. The underlying criterion in Hyman's interviewer ratings was economic, however, and for this reason we shall use reported income as the basis for our classification. This difference in the indicators of class in no way interferes with the opportunity to observe if economic divisions among people are similarly related to their aspirations in societies having very different cultures.

Table V.1 presents the importance attached to a college education by the different economic classes in Turin and the United States. The classificatory labels are adopted from Hyman, but the monthly income figures are for the Turinese. If we consider only differences between the two countries, we see that aspirations of Americans exceed those of the Turinese. This national difference is greatest among the poorer of the two populations, but at every economic level proportionately more Americans than Turinese value college education. Indeed, national differences become more impressive when we realize that the question asked in Turin inquired into preferences for one's own children, while that analyzed by Hyman inquired into adults' preferences for young people in general. Since the Turinese were talking about

Table V.I

Parents' Preference for a College Education for Children of Different Classes in Turin and the United States

Monthly Income Level	Per Cent Preferring College		
	Turin		*United States*[a]
	%	N	%
Prosperous (Over $480)	81	(64)	91
Upper middle ($240 to $480)	68	(172)	91
Lower middle ($160 to $240)	48	(219)	83
Lower (Below $160)	17	(336)	68

Significance of χ^2
(linear regression) $p < .001$

[a]*Adapted with permission of the Macmillan Company from Herbert Hyman, "The Value Systems of Different Classes: A Social Psychological Contribution to the Analysis of Stratification," from* Class, Status and Power, *2nd Edition, Edited by Reinhard Bendix and Seymour Martin Lipset. Copyright © 1966 by The Free Press, a Division of The Macmillan Company. The original material from which Hyman compiled these data reported no totals.*

their own offspring, their educational goals were probably maximal; since the Americans were talking about youth generally, their expressed aspirations were probably minimal. And, yet, Americans still outstripped the Turinese in their preferences for a university education.

These national differences, however impressive they may be, should not overshadow the cross-national similarities in the relationship of economic structure to parental aspirations. Quite obviously, in both countries the appeal of a university education diminishes with reduced economic means. In Turin this relationship is particularly marked, ranging from over 80 per cent of the prosperous group to 17 per cent of the poor group. The disparity between the low economic position of the latter group and its high aspirations characterizes the disprivileged strivers who will be the center of analysis later in the chapter.

Consider now how the two countries compare with regard to class differences in occupational aspirations. Hyman presented only the proportions of each class recommending two non-adjoining levels of the occupational scale: professional and skilled manual occupations. Since the question as it was asked in the United States concerned the future occupations of boys exclusively, only Turinese parents of sons who expressed a desire for professional or skilled manual levels are included in Table V.2. As with educational goals, the order of relationships is the same in each country: the highest economic group is more likely to favor professional occupations for its young males, the lowest group is more likely to recommend skilled manual occupations. Once again, the economic position of people can be seen as a condition for shaping conceptions of what is desirable. It is a condition sufficiently powerful to transcend cultural distinctions.

A final comparison concerns class differences in occupational desiderata in each country. Hyman dealt with a question that asked adults what they thought was the most important thing for a young man to consider in choosing an occupation. He then distinguished those answers that stressed either "congeniality to person" or "economic benefit." I have grouped in the same way the responses to a virtually identical item used in Turin. Parents giving first priority to "a chance to use his own interests or aptitudes," or "a chance to be original, use imagination" are classified as stressing elements of congeniality. Responses of an economic nature are those that single out either size of income or the stability and security of the occupation. These categories do not exhaust all answers, and, as in Table V.2, the column percentages in Table V.3 do not total 100 per cent for this reason. Between these two kinds of desiderata there are, in both countries, definite class predilections. Whether they be Turinese or American,

Table V.2

Occupational Levels Considered Most Desirable by Different Classes in Turin and the United States

Desired Occupational Level	Turin			United States[a]		
	Wealthy and Prosperous %	Middle Class %	Lower Class %	Wealthy and Prosperous %	Middle Class %	Lower Class %
Professional	76	63	22	50	38	32
Skilled manual	–	4	28	5	13	19
Numbers	(25)	(164)	(151)	(430)	(1303)	(721)
Significance of χ^2 (linear regression)	p < .001			p < .001		

[a]*Adapted with permission of The Macmillan Company from Herbert Hyman, "The Value Systems of Different Classes: A Social Psychological Contribution to the Analysis of Stratification," from Class, Status and Power, 2nd Edition, Edited by Reinhard Bendix and Seymour Martin Lipset. Copyright ©1966 by The Free Press, a Division of The Macmillan Company.*

Table V.3 shows that the well-to-do tend to be sensitive to the "fit" between the job and the individual; the poor are more likely concerned with material rewards and economic stability.

The patterns identified by Hyman for the United States, then, are certainly matched, if not exceeded, by those for Turin. In both countries the realities of class positions — the conditions of life they embody, and the opportunities they afford for social and personal advancement — tend to create concordant aspirations and goals. The countries are by no means identical in these respects. Judged by the cumulative evidence, there is a greater polarization of class-aspiration relationships in Italy than in the United States. The overall cross-national correspondence, however, provides ample support to conclude, with Hyman, that people are likely to want what they are most able to achieve. The unequal opportunities intrinsic to class systems also produce unequal motivations, thus perpetuating class positions across generations. Cultural differences, furthermore, are overridden by the powerful thrust of this phenomenon.

INTRA-FAMILIAL STATUS DIFFERENTIALS

As important as the economic resources of a family are to parental aspirations, other conditions influence parents' hopes for their children.

These conditions involve prestige and social status rather than the extent of the family's income. They enter into the family in various ways and with various effects on aspirations. In discussing the status antecedents of aspirations, I shall be examining relationships not found in published studies. Unfortunately, this precludes the possibility for direct cross-national comparisons. Unless comparisons are built into the design and content of a study, cross-national comparisons typically cannot be made beyond social class relationships. This is the case here and with most of the issues analyzed in subsequent chapters.

Status considerations can be drawn into the family by the social characteristics people have when they marry. It is an assumption of sociology that, regardless of the origins of spouses, all individual members of the nuclear family share a single status, usually determined by the occupational standing of the male breadwinner. This may be the case as far as judgments of a family's status by the society at large are concerned. But husbands and wives are apparently aware of status discrepancies that may exist between them; it is evident also that this awareness makes a difference, at least with regard to the aspirations parents adopt for their children.

The status background of spouses can be judged either by the occupational status of their respective fathers or by the extent of

Table V.3

Occupational Desiderata of Different Classes in Turin and the United States

	Turin			United States[a]		
Occupational Desiderata	Wealthy and Prosperous %	Middle Class %	Lower Class %	Wealthy and Prosperous %	Middle Class %	Lower Class %
Congeniality	48	43	33	64	51	34
Economic	19	29	41	16	21	31
Numbers	(31)	(189)	(162)	(428)	(1303)	(721)

Significance of χ^2 (linear regression)	p < .01	p < .001

[a]*Adapted with permission of The Macmillan Company from Herbert Hyman, "The Value Systems of Different Classes: A Social Psychological Contribution to the Analysis of Stratification," from* Class, Status and Power, *2nd Edition, Edited by Reinhard Bendix and Seymour Martin Lipset. Copyright © 1966 by The Free Press, a Division of The Macmillan Company.*

husbands' and wives' formal educations. In each case we can determine if they brought to the marriage the same status, or if the status of one of them is higher. We can then see whether intra-familial status differentials have any bearing on levels of parental aspiration.

Table V.4 contains the results of this comparison. In order to obtain a better distribution of respondents I included in the highest income group all those whose family income was over $240 per month. Also, I used the occupational standing of spouses' fathers to assess spouses' status equality or inequality. I classified as unequal any difference in the status background of husband and wife, regardless of its magnitude. For the aspirational data, I used parents' hopes for children's occupational status. (Using educational background and educational aspirations produces very similar results.) Finally, since the comparisons entail the relative status of husbands and wives, I excluded all those cases where only one of the spouses was interviewed, thus, reducing the total number.

In none of the partials of Table V.4 are the aspirational differences between parents whose spouses are of equal or unequal status background very great. What we can emphasize, however, is the complete consistency with which relationships occurred. In each income group, both husbands and wives are likely to have the highest occupational aspirations when they are part of a marriage where the spouses come from different status backgrounds. But, for these differences to be made meaningful, and in order that they be seen in their true magnitude, we must know which spouse is higher in status, the husband or wife.

Table V.5 clearly indicates that the particular condition relevant to aspirations is the higher status of wives. *The aspirations of both mothers and fathers are likely to be elevated when the wife is of higher status,* except in the highest income group where it makes no difference which spouse is higher.

These results form a coherent pattern when certain things are kept in mind. First, if the husband comes from a status higher than his wife, the inequality is handled simply by the wife's adoption of her husband's higher status; this, of course, is entirely consistent with the way society accords status. Now consider families where the wife has the higher status, the condition most closely associated with high aspirations. While the wife is still free to accommodate to her husband's lower status, chances are that she will not want to. Indeed, she is likely to feel a sense of loss to the extent that she must identify with her husband's status. The lower status husband, even if he wanted to, would be unable to assume his wife's higher status, for society will not accord him this status. Both the wife and the

Table V.4
Turinese Husband-Wife Status Relations and Occupational Aspirations for Their Children, by Monthly Family Income

	A. MOTHERS					
	Less than $160		$160 to $240		More than $240	
Occupational Aspirations	Equal Status %	Unequal Status %	Equal Status %	Unequal Status %	Equal Status %	Unequal Status %
Professional, managerial	18	23	42	57	71	82
Technical, clerical, sales	61	56	55	36	25	16
Manual	21	21	3	7	4	2
Numbers	(71)	(39)	(33)	(28)	(28)	(43)

Significance of χ^2
(linear regression)
On equality of status only: $p < .02$

	B. FATHERS					
	Less than $160		$160 to $240		More than $240	
Occupational Aspirations	Equal Status %	Unequal Status %	Equal Status %	Unequal Status %	Equal Status %	Unequal Status %
Professional, managerial	20	31	38	52	70	81
Technical, clerical, sales	61	51	49	42	30	19
Manual	19	18	13	6	–	–
Numbers	(66)	(43)	(37)	(33)	(23)	(41)

Significance of χ^2
(linear regression)
On equality of status only: $p < .01$

husband in these families are limited in their ability to resolve this disequilibrium — the wife because she does not want to yield her higher status, and the husband because he is socially unable to escape his lower status. This same differential poses no problem for those in

Table V.5

Relative Status of Turinese Husbands and Wives and Occupational Aspirations for Their Children, by Monthly Family Income

A. MOTHERS

Occupational Aspirations	Less than $160			$160 to $240			More than $240		
	Equal Status %	*Husband Higher* %	*Wife Higher* %	*Equal Status* %	*Husband Higher* %	*Wife Higher* %	*Equal Status* %	*Husband Higher* %	*Wife Higher* %
Professional, managerial	18	12	32	42	42	89	71	81	82
Technical, clerical, sales	61	59	55	55	48	11	25	15	18
Manual	21	29	13	3	10	–	4	4	–
Numbers	(71)	(17)	(22)	(33)	(19)	(9)	(28)	(26)	(17)

Significance of χ²
(linear regression) By relative status only: p < .01

B. FATHERS

Occupational Aspirations	Less than $160			$160 to $240			More than $240		
	Equal Status %	*Husband Higher* %	*Wife Higher* %	*Equal Status* %	*Husband Higher* %	*Wife Higher* %	*Equal Status* %	*Husband Higher* %	*Wife Higher* %
Professional, managerial	20	25	39	38	40	69	70	80	81
Technical, clerical, sales	61	58	44	49	55	23	30	20	19
Manual	20	17	17	13	5	8	–	–	–
Numbers	(66)	(24)	(18)	(37)	(20)	(13)	(23)	(25)	(16)

Significance of χ²

the highest income bracket. Here, whatever disequilibrium was created by the wife's originally higher status is eased by the relatively substantial earnings of her husband. Because of their economic position, the wife is not threatened by loss nor the husband by deprivation. It is in families where earnings are more limited that the originally higher status of the wife retains a presence. The future success of children born into these families constitutes a way to resolve eventually the intra-familial status disequilibrium. This condition of status inequality exerts leverage even on the aspirations of the most economically disprivileged.

MOBILITY AND IDENTIFICATION

Status influences parental aspirations in yet another way, through the achievement of status by parents themselves. Probably nothing more encourages hope for success than success itself. Parents who live in a state of immobility are not likely to attach much reality to advancement for their children because it is so removed from their own experience. Some mobility by parents, however, brings mobility for children into the realm of a meaningful possibility. In fact, it may stimulate aspirations on behalf of children to levels that are well beyond the actual accomplishments of the parents themselves. One reason for this is that the class identifications of mobile parents elevate at a more rapid rate than parents' objective movement and these identifications, in turn, are a source of new standards of achievement for children.[3] Even for the poor, modest advancement shifts identifications which then result in expanded hopes for children.

The evidence for these statements includes, first, the relationship of actual mobility to aspirations. I assessed mobility between generations by comparing the husband's occupational status with that of his father or, in the case of the wife, with that of her father. Any change, regardless of its magnitude, represented inter-generational mobility. This is necessary in order to distinguish at the lower income levels those who have experienced some upward change, however small. Respondents whose fathers were farmers presented a special problem, for there was no way to determine the scope of the farming in which they were engaged. Somewhat arbitrarily — though meaningfully in terms of probabilities — any respondent who currently worked at skilled labor or higher and whose father was a farmer I considered

[3] There is evidence that the increased aspirations of mobile parents are also absorbed by their children. See Richard L. Simpson, "Parental Influence, Anticipatory Socialization, and Social Mobility," *American Sociological Review*, 27 (1962), pp. 517 – 522.

mobile, while I classified unskilled and semi-skilled workers whose fathers were engaged in farming as stationary. Finally, I employed education to evaluate levels of parental aspirations, though occupation would have yielded essentially similar results.

Table V.6 shows that in the two lower income groups, mobility elevated levels of educational aspiration. Those parents earning less than $160 per month who have experienced no upward movement were less likely than any other in this income category to want a university education for their children. In the next higher income category the immobile still had the lower aspirations, though the downwardly mobile exceeded the upward group in the proportion wanting a university education. Finally, the income of the highest income group diminished the contribution that mobility made to aspirations in the other groups; regardless of their mobility history, the university was a normative expectation for a substantial majority of this group. Of course, the sheer amount of resources available to a family is still the most potent determinant of aspirations. But even within the severely limiting conditions imposed by low income, *a little direct experience with advancement can stimulate considerable aspirations in behalf of children.*

I suggested earlier that class identification is involved with actual mobility in the stimulation of aspirations. Apparently when a family experiences some objective upward mobility there is a corresponding rise in subjective class identification. The elevation of class identification results in a commensurate elevation of aspirations. For this hypothesized process to be confirmed, we would have to find, first, that the class identifications of the mobile are higher than of the stationary, even when their income is the same; and we would have to find that aspirations are likely to be highest among those with the highest class identifications, even while holding actual mobility constant.

Both of these conditions do prevail. We have determined this by including in Table V.7 income, mobility, identification and aspirations. For simplicity it omits the downwardly mobile and combines the few individuals whose self-designation was "lower class" with those who identified themselves with the working class. The impact of mobility on identification is best assessed by a simple examination of the marginal numbers across the bottom row of the table. Consider the lowest income group, for example. Among the mobile 21 out of 76 people (28 per cent) have middle-class identifications, but only 20 (12 per cent) of the 169 stationaries so identify themselves. Parallel differences exist in the next higher income group, although among the most prosperous identifications are so overwhelmingly middle class that the influence of mobility cannot be seen. Despite this, it is

Table V.6

Intergenerational Mobility and Educational Aspirations in Turin, by Family Income

Educational Aspirations	Less than $160			$160 to $240			More than $240		
	Upwardly Mobile %	Down-wardly Mobile %	Stationary %	Upwardly Mobile %	Down-wardly Mobile %	Stationary %	Upwardly Mobile %	Down-wardly Mobile %	Stationary %
University	29	16	12	53	64	34	74	63	70
Secondary	49	53	62	37	33	53	23	33	29
Elementary, vocational	22	31	26	10	3	13	3	4	1
Numbers	(86)	(36)	(186)	(112)	(30)	(68)	(137)	(27)	(69)

Significance of χ^2
(linear regression) By mobility only: p < .001

Table V.7
Intergenerational Mobility, Class Identification and Educational
Aspirations in Turin, by Family Income

Educational Aspirations	LESS THAN $160						$160 TO $240						MORE THAN $240					
	Upwardly Mobile			Stationary			Upwardly Mobile			Stationary			Upwardly Mobile			Stationary		
	UMC %	LMC %	WC %	UMC %	LMC %	WC %	UMC %	LMC %	WC %	UMC %	LMC %	WC %	UMC %	LMC %	WC %	UMC %	LMC %	WC %
University	–	38	27	–	31	9	(1)	59	46	(1)	48	19	85	75	43	79	76	17
Secondary	–	48	47	(1)	59	62	–	35	38	–	45	62	15	22	57	21	24	83
Elementary, vocational	–	14	26	–	10	29	–	6	16	–	7	19	–	3	–	–	–	–
Numbers	(–)	(21)	(55)	(1)	(19)	(149)	(1)	(69)	(26)	(1)	(27)	(32)	(13)	(103)	(7)	(14)	(42)	(6)

Significance of χ^2
(linear regression) Comparing for Class Identification only: p < .001

UMC – Upper-middle-class identification
LMC – Lower-middle-class identification
WC – Working-class identification

clear that actual mobility is accompanied by higher identifications. It is even more clear that those with the higher identifications are also more likely to have the higher aspirations. Whether they have a history of mobility or immobility, and regardless of the size of their incomes, it is evident in Table V.7 that parents who see themselves as belonging to higher classes are apt also to entertain the higher ambitions for their children.

Very likely, then, actual mobility heightens aspirations through the intervening arousal of class identifications. Consequently, aspirations are not as keenly affected when mobility and elevated identifications occur by themselves as when they are jointly part of parents' experience. Parents who have experienced some degree of advancement beyond their own parents' attainments are prompted to raise their class identifications. These new identifications embrace new standards and norms of success that, in turn, are expressed in increased aspirational levels for children.

BEHAVIORAL CONSEQUENCES OF DISPRIVILEGED STRIVING[4]

Both Hyman's study and the comparative data from Turin clearly indicate that high aspirations are forsaken because of limited opportunities. Yet, in his classic analysis of the structural sources of anomie, Merton centers on those who strive after success despite blocked access to legitimate means.[5] While these perspectives are distinct in their emphases, they are by no means incompatible. There is unmistakable evidence that aspirations for one's self and one's children are in fact depressed by limited economic resources. Still, each of the preceding tables shows the presence of a sizeable minority of disprivileged strivers, people at the lowest economic levels who entertain the highest aspirations. And, as Merton himself suggests in discussing the implication of Hyman's work for anomie, this minority should not be ignored simply because it is a minority.[6] Quite possibly its importance exceeds its proportions in a population, for the disprivileged strivers are likely to be the "innovators" who challenge

[4]This section is a revised and abridged version of Leonard I. Pearlin, Marian Radke Yarrow and Harry A. Scarr, "Unintended Effects of Parental Aspirations: The Case of Children's Cheating," *American Journal of Sociology*, 73 (1967), pp. 73 – 83. Copyright 1967 by The University of Chicago.

[5]Robert K. Merton, "Social Structure and Anomie," in Robert K. Merton, *Social Theory and Social Structure*, 2nd ed. (Glencoe, Ill.: The Free Press, 1957), pp. 131 – 160.

[6]Robert K. Merton, "Social Structure and Anomie: Continuities," *ibid.*, pp. 161 – 194.

traditional means of advancement and exert leverage for the creation of new legitimate means to success.

The aspirations of the disprivileged strivers are in a direction clearly counter to the normative grain of others in the same economic circumstances. Because they are so unlike their economic peers, because their goals for their children are so disparately out of line with their resources, one wonders whether their high aspirations are not simply the fruits of fantasy, not to be taken too seriously. There is ample reason to believe that this is not the case, that disprivileged strivers are characterized by a powerful motivational thrust. The evidence for this belief is that in achievement situations such parents act upon their children in ways distinctly different from others of their economic condition. Their actions, furthermore, are sufficiently consistent to bring about in their children behavior distinctly different from that of other children with parents in the same economic position. The behavior is cheating.

Cheating is an excellent example of behavior that, although probably disdained and held in contempt, can inadvertently result from the socialization practices of parents. There can be, and frequently is, little apparent connection between the behavior parents would like to develop in their children and the actual behavior that children display. In the course of striving for one effect, parents unwittingly contribute to others. Thus, disprivileged strivers, through a process I shall describe, in effect, but without recognition what they are doing, induce their children to cheat.

Cheating has been the subject of considerable research. Its most prominent origin is the work of Hartshorne and May.[7] Their studies were designed to discover whether dishonesty is a specific response to specific situational arousal or a characteristic mode of behavior cutting across situational contexts.[8] Since then interest in cheating has shifted to a search for its social antecedents. One type of study has sought to find relationships between moral development in young children and maternal styles of childrearing.[9] More recent are studies of

---

[7]Hugh Hartshorne and Mark A. May, *Studies in Deceit* (New York: The Macmillan Co., 1928).

[8]See Roger V. Burton, "Generality of Honesty Reconsidered," *Psychological Review*, 70 (1963), pp. 481 – 499. Burton provides an excellent current statement of the issue of generality vs. specificity of cheating, and through a re-analysis of the Hartshorne and May data shows more generality than might be granted to this class of behavior from their original interpretations. He points out that Hartshorne and May themselves actually did not take the extreme position of specificity often attributed to them.

[9]For examples of maternal attitudes, modes of discipline and rearing practices that have been studied in relation to cheating, see Roger V. Burton, Eleanor E.

academic dishonesty that view cheating practices of campus groups as a function of variations in institutional constraints and supports and suggest that academic cheating reflects the acquisition of existing social norms.[10] Regardless of the many ways in which it can differ, contemporary research converges at a common view of cheating as a result of the learning which takes place through interpersonal interaction and social experience.

This analysis differs from previous studies in several respects. Unlike some of the campus studies, for example, it did not consider the prevalence of cheating in collectivities. Indeed, this study experimentally maximized cheating, giving a compressed picture of how it might occur under natural conditions. Furthermore, in seeking the ways cheating might be inadvertently learned, it went beyond immediate contexts to consider the broader social system.[11] Finally, it conceived of cheating as representing a more inclusive type of socialized behavior: that which is acquired less from immediate circumstances than from enduring social conditions.

PARENT-CHILD OBSERVATIONS. Direct observations of parent-child interaction were made in a sub-sample of 79 homes in which both parents had previously been interviewed. This sub-sample was selected to achieve approximately an equal number of working- and middle-class families and an equal number of male and female fifth-graders. An interval of from three to eight months occurred between survey interviews with the parents and the parent-child observations. The present data deal only with the sub-sample.

Measures of the child's cheating and of parent-child interactions were derived from the subjects' behavior in coping with six problem-solving tasks, three of them with the child and his mother and three

Maccoby and Wesley Allinsmith, "Antecedents to Resistance to Temptation in Four-year-old Children," *Child Development*, 32 (1961), pp. 689–710.

[10]Rose K. Goldsen, Morris Rosenberg, Robin M. Williams and Edward A. Suchman, *What College Students Think* (Princeton: D. Van Nostrand Co., 1960), pp. 74–80; and William J. Bowers, *Student Dishonesty and Its Control in College* (New York: Bureau of Applied Social Research, 1964).

[11]In this connection, two studies merit particular attention, one by Harp and Taietz and the other by Tallman. Although both employed college student subjects, they were less concerned with the prevalence of academic cheating than understanding it within the framework of Merton's established theory of deviant behavior. Such an understanding helps to bring into focus implications of social structural conditions for cheating. John Harp and Philip Taietz, "Academic Integrity and Social Structure: A Study of Cheating Among College Students," *Social Problems*, 13 (1966), pp. 365–373; and Irving Tallman, "Adaptation to Blocked Opportunity: An Experimental Study," *Sociometry*, 29 (1966), pp. 121–134.

with the child and his father. The tasks were allocated to insure that an equal number of the four parent-child sex combinations would be observed at each task. In presenting the tasks the observers emphasized the importance of doing well by telling parent and child that their scores would be compared to those of American children and to other Italian children; they also told the parent and child a fictitiously high score that children "usually" made on the particular task, and in other ways they encouraged the parent and child to extend themselves. The sessions were thus clearly structured in terms of achievement, a factor crucial to the relationships which we present later.

Parents were forbidden to perform the tasks for their children, but they were free to assume their own roles within this broad limit. After the initiation of each task, the observer withdrew to a corner of the room and quietly recorded a detailed, running account of the actions and interactions of parent and child. The transcriptions of the behavioral records were then coded on such dimensions as the attention and interest of parents, their praise and criticism, and their positive and negative affective expressions in interacting with their children.[12]

Only two of the six problem-solving tasks presented figure into the assessment of cheating, and both were adapted from tests used by Hartshorne and May.[13] Each test is constructed in such a way that neither skill nor effort can appreciably contribute to success. One consists of a series of printed concentric squares with a common center. The space between the successively larger squares is less than one inch. The child is asked to pencil a line, with his eyes closed, around the perimeter of each square without touching either the sides or corners of the printed squares. The second task consists of a ring of ten circles of declining sizes; here the child is required to place an "X" within each circle while keeping his eyes closed. Both tests, while captivating, are very difficult, and it is most unlikely that anyone can have a high score without opening his eyes. Adherence to the rules results in poor performance; success depends on cheating. The nature of the tests, therefore, lent itself to our design to maximize the probability of cheating by those so disposed.

The raw scores on both "peeping" tests were simply based on the

[12]Observers were trained to observe in terms of the pre-established categories in which their observations would be coded. Practice sessions were staged to pre-test the categories and the codes. Correlation coefficients based on agreement of assignment of recorded acts to specific categories ranged from .72 to .91, with a median .81.

[13]Hartshorne and May, *Studies in Deceit*, pp. 61 – 65.

proportion of successes to attempts. The scores were then standardized by using the same standard deviations from the mean for both tests, thus permitting us to ignore the particular test as a variable. It was possible to score all but one of the children. Those classified as not having cheated cleared fewer than 45 per cent of the corners on the squares test or were successful in no more than 31 per cent of their attempts to place an "X" within a circle. Those classified as "possible" cheaters cleared up to 70 per cent of the square corners or were successful in 55 per cent of their attempts at the circles test. The unambiguous cheaters were those whose successes exceeded these levels. It is most improbable that they could have achieved such high successes without either peeping by the child or the collusive intervention of the parent.

A final issue of method pertains to the unit that was taken for analysis. We observed 79 families. This resulted, of course, in unequal numbers of parents and children: there were 158 parents, each engaged alone with his child in an observational session, while there were only 79 children. To have grouped mothers or fathers into single parental units or to have grouped the separate performances of children with their mothers and fathers into single scores would have resulted in a loss of independence of observations. Although the same child was engaged in two sessions, his behavior with regard to cheating was tabulated with mothers and fathers separately.

PARENTAL PRESSURE FOR SUCCESS. The conditions most immediate to the cheating observed during the course of the experimental sessions inhere in parental actions toward their children that signal pressure for successful performance. Because success at the experimental tasks could be gained only by violating the rules, we anticipated that cheating would be a prominent response to parental pressure for success.

Among the behaviors recorded, three in particular enabled us to assess the degree of pressure for success imposed by mothers and fathers on their children. The first was the frequency of highly specific "do this, now do that" directives parents gave their children. Such directions bordered on violating the instructions, which emphasized that the child himself was to go through the manipulations required by the tasks. A second aspect of behavior reflecting pressure was the number of strategic suggestions parents made concerning general approaches to the tasks that they wanted their children to adopt in order to maximize their performance. A final reflection of pressure was the extent to which parents maintained a restrained, unintrusive interest while their children were at work at the achievement tasks. This was not the same as withdrawal of interest, which we coded separately. It reflected sustained attentiveness to what the child was doing without beratement, encouragement or intrusiveness of any kind.

These three items of behavior form a Guttman scale. The pattern of greatest pressure occurred when a parent gave many specific directions (nine or more), was also relatively active in making strategic suggestions (four or more) and was quietly attentive to the child's independent efforts for fewer than eight intervals of sufficient duration to be recorded. We gave parents fitting this pattern the maximum score of three. Parents who did not give as many specific directions but who were still active in making general suggestions and lacked restrained attention received a score of two. Parents who were neither active in making suggestions nor in giving directions but who gave little attention received a score of one. Parents who gave few or no directions and who made few or no suggestions and who were quietly attentive received a score of zero.[14]

Despite its shortness, this scale was useful in ordering parents by the extent to which they exerted on their children a focused pressure for successful performance. Indeed, at the high end of this scale are parents so eager for their children to do well and so involved in the execution of the tasks that we cannot distinguish children who might have cheated in actual collusion with their parents from those who cheated by themselves. We can show, however, that children who are pushed the hardest are the most likely to cheat.

Table V.8 presents the pressure exerted by mothers and fathers and the cheating behavior of their children. Regardless of the sex of the parent with whom a child is working, the likelihood of his cheating was greatest when the parental pressure he experienced was extreme. The magnitude of these relationships leaves no doubt of the importance of this facet of parent-child interaction as a direct lever for cheating. Parents who pressure their children might only be eager for them to achieve, but they are also contributing, probably unwittingly, to the learning of other behavior that is undesired.

DISADVANTAGED STRIVING AND PARENTAL PRESSURE. The levels of the aspirations that parents entertain for their children seem to be among the most pertinent conditions behind parental pressure. The stress placed on achievement in the experimental situation was not likely to have a particularly unsettling effect on parents with limited aspirations; they could remain unintrusive, even while witnessing their children perform poorly at the tasks. Those with higher hopes and achievement aspirations could not be indifferent to failure, however,

---

[14]The coefficient of reproducibility for this scale is .93; the coefficient of scalability by item is .76.

Table V.8

Pressure by Turinese Parents for Success, and Cheating by Their Children

	Pressure by Fathers				Pressure by Mothers			
	High			Low	High			Low
Cheating	3	2	1	0	3	2	1	0
Behavior	%	%	%	%	%	%	%	%
Cheated	60	27	16	11	81	25	22	20
Possibly cheated	20	32	25	11	6	25	19	7
Did not cheat	20	41	59	78	13	50	59	73
Numbers	(15)	(22)	(32)	(9)	(16)	(20)	(27)	(15)

Significance of χ^2
(linear regression) $p < .001$ $p < .001$

and were more inclined to ply their children with directives and urgings.

Generally we found that mothers and fathers with the highest aspirations imposed the greatest pressure. This association was surprisingly small and somewhat uneven, however, indicating that the levels of aspirations alone do not adequately explain parental pressure. Even more significant is the level of aspirations in relation to the income of parents. The same goals might appear to one person as easily attainable and unproblematic and to another, with fewer resources and more limited life chances, as remote, elusive, fraught with difficulties. Among parents with high hopes and low resources, the very fact that the actual achievement of their aspirations is so very problematic seems to create a greater urgency for success and more intense pressure on children. Consequently, the disparity between aspiration and material status is more important to parental actions than either aspiration or income separately. The combination of high hope and low structural baseline is the critical condition.

Table V.9 illustrates this by presenting desired levels of education (though we could have used occupational aspirations with similar results) together with income in relation to the pressure parents exerted on their children in the experimental situation. (There is some loss of cases in this table because of the lack of income information.) The important variations are found among those hoping for a university education. Thus, 53 per cent of the parents in families earning less than $160 per month imposed extreme pressure, in contrast to

8 per cent of the parents having the same goal but earning over $240. Obviously, the parents with the highest goals and most limited resources were most likely to urge their children on to successful performance. Parents holding the same high goals but with a better income were considerably less disposed to use pressure, and the same was true of parents who aspirations are lower, regardless of their resources. It appears that the uncertainties of disadvantaged strivers in realizing success goals propel them to active intervention in the achievement efforts of their children. The success motivations of such parents are probably even more intense than for others; if this were not so, they would abandon their hopes in the face of the improbability of attainment, just as most people in the same economic circumstances have done. Through their actions, these parents convey to children the urgent importance of success — perhaps by any means.

DISADVANTAGED STRIVING AND CHEATING. Cheating, then, appears to be an unintended consequence of a process that has important roots in culturally cherished aspirations. Blocked or limited access to these goals — conditions for anomie — results in extreme parental demands on children for evidence of achievement. Children, either to avoid disappointing their parents in an area of obvious importance to them or because they share with their parents a cynical view of accepted means, respond to this pressure by cheating. In this fashion, cheating

Table V.9

Educational Aspirations for Turinese Children in Relation to Income and Parental Pressure

	UNIVERSITY ASPIRATIONS Family Income:			ASPIRATIONS BELOW UNIVERSITY Family Income:		
Parental Pressure	*Less than $160* %	*$160 to $240* %	*More than $240* %	*Less than $160* %	*$160 to $240* %	*More than $240* %
High 3	53	21	8	19	17	—
2	20	16	19	27	50	33
1	20	42	50	42	21	47
Low 0	7	21	23	12	12	20
Numbers	(15)	(19)	(26)	(52)	(24)	(15)

Significance of χ^2
(linear regression) $p < .01$ $p < .30$

can become an inadvertent companion of desired achievement behavior.

Since parental pressures are related to cheating and goal-resources disparities contribute to pressures, we can expect an association between disparities and cheating. Cheating, in fact, did occur disproportionately among children whose parents have both limited financial resources and high hopes for education and occupation. The relationships, however, were less close than we might have anticipated. The reason for this is that disparities, while vitally important to the process, constitute more of a precondition for parental pressure than a direct force for cheating. Stated another way, disadvantaged striving results in cheating through the intervention of parental pressure.

The nature of the contributions to cheating made by the means-aspirations disparity and parental pressure can be shown more exactly by examining them simultaneously. We classified as "disparate" those parents aspiring to the highest level of occupation but having a family income that is less than $240 per month. We classified as "consonant" those parents having either more modest aspirations, regardless of income, or more substantial means, regardless of aspirations. We classified as "high pressure" those parents scoring three or two and we classified as "low" the remainder.

Despite the few children involved, we can now see the circumstances under which cheating is most concentrated. A majority of parents holding goals disparate with their resources imposed extreme pressure for achievement and the children of these parents were most likely to be cheaters. Disparity without the intervention of parental pressure was substantially less associated with cheating, as was pressure without disparity. Thus, there was a marked cumulative effect on cheating when these circumstances were coupled. Cheating, therefore, is an unintended product of a process made up of a number of interconnected conditions involving parental aspirations, location within the context of economic class, and the expression of these conditions in parent-child relations.

Paradoxically, then, disprivileged parents who adopt the widely valued hope that their children will surpass their own stations in life tend to implement these aspirations in ways inducing their children to behave in violation of other values of the society.

DISCUSSION

All industrialized societies require populations highly motivated to advancement. When economic expansion is underway, as in Turin, aspirations for status aggrandizement probably also are expanded.

Table V.10

Disparity Between Occupational Aspirations and Income
in Relation to Parental Pressure and Cheating by Turinese Children

	FATHERS				MOTHERS			
	Aspirations Disparate		Aspirations Consonant		Aspirations Disparate		Aspirations Consonant	
Cheating Behavior	*High Pressure* %	*Low Pressure* %	*High Pressure* %	*Low Pressure* %	*High Pressure* %	*Low Pressure* %	*High Pressure* %	*Low Pressure* %
Cheated	63	—	35	16	80	14	43	18
Possibly cheated	25	33	26	19	—	14	21	15
Did not cheat	12	67	39	65	20	72	36	67
Numbers	(8)	(6)	(23)	(32)	(10)	(7)	(14)	(33)
Significance of χ² (linear regression)	p < .02		p < .05		p < .02		p < .05	

These aspirations are generated and sustained by the differential distribution of rewards, both material and honorific. The desire for advancement is not confined to one's self but extends across generations to children and is, as a result, reflected in socialization practices.

Yet, it is a mistake to ascribe to all segments of society the same desire for the same levels of success. Hyman has brought together convincing evidence that the goals that people strive for are molded to the realities of their chances for achieving them. Overall, people are likely to want most those very ends that are most within their reach. Thus, economic class structure has a most powerful effect on the levels to which parents aspire in behalf of their children. The occurrence of this effect in both Turin and the United States should dispel any notion that the relationship of class to aspirations is a cultural by-product.

Economic position is not, however, the only condition underlying parental aspirations. A disparity in the status backgrounds of parents, represented particularly in the higher status of the wife, also acts as a lever on parents' aspirations. So, too, does a family's direct experience with social mobility. Regardless of how small the upward movement may be, it serves to raise class identifications, which in turn provide higher standards for aspirations. Although we cannot look at the full range of contributing factors, we can say that apparently aspirations to a large extent arise out of enduring and structured social conditions and experiences.

Even the aspirations of those who are economically most disadvantaged are stimulated by these conditions. A minority of parents, consequently, run against the grain of the general accommodation of ends to means. They are exposed to circumstances that serve to elevate their hopes but can do nothing to alter the disprivileged material conditions of their lives. Rather than forsaking their hopes in the face of the improbabilities of realizing them, they are even more strongly motivated to see their children achieve than parents in more privileged positions. This very motivation leads them to be importune and inadvertently to bring about behavior in their children that they probably disdain.

When we look at the entire process by which disadvantaged striving leads to cheating, we are struck by its correspondence to Merton's conceptualization of the structural sources of innovated means to cherished ends. Here we could see also that structural conditions of anomie that Merton specified affect not only those directly exposed to them — parents — but children also through the interventions their parents employ. In this manner, the behavior of those who have not yet assumed for themselves problematic cultural goals is nevertheless affected by such goals. The consequences of high hopes and low economic standing spill over generational lines through the socializing actions of parents.

Children do not cheat, of course, because they — or their parents — prefer it above all other means of achieving success. It is an adaptation to conflict arising from hindered access to desired goals and, as such, has an obvious and direct implication for any social action program designed to elevate the disprivileged by elevating their motivation for achievement. Unless this effort is also coupled with material changes in the opportunity structure, such a program could only add to a reservoir of frustrated aspirations that, among other consequences, could eventually lead to the circumvention of normative standards of behavior.

The point that deserves most emphasis is that much of what we call socialization is a result of conditions that are subtle and unrecognized, but nonetheless very real in prompting and structuring behavior. Culminating in the cheating by children was a host of antecedents involving the interlacing of culturally prized goals, economic structure, parents' own status relations and mobility experiences and the joint influence of these factors on how parents deal with their children in an achievement situation. The complexity of the inter-relationships understandably means that much important social behavior that is learned is neither taught nor intended.

It is also quite understandable that the conditions influencing a parent's vision of his child's future status is prominently social in origin. Future status has meaning only insofar as it is located within the institutional organization of society. Parents' own locations in social institutions serve to bring into focus some goals and rewards and to block others from view; some goals will appear within easy reach, others will be so distant that they can have no concrete reality. Apparently, then, the social circumstances of parents should be related to the aspirations they hold for their children, and these relationships should be similar in different cultures. The connections between social conditions and some other aspects of parent-child relations — for example, parental discipline — may be less readily apparent, however.

VI

Parental Discipline

We have seen that values and aspirations are social products, acquired on the basis of parents' roles and statuses in society. Since these values and goals in substantial measure emerge out of the structured social experiences of adults, they hardly have crystallized in the minds and actions of young children. More often, the characteristics and statuses parents consider important to their children's futures are beyond the concern or ken of the children themselves. For this reason, much socialization is directed toward preparing the young for distant goals to which they are not yet particularly oriented or motivated.

Thus, parents, whether Turinese, American or another nationality, must oversee the behavior of the young and continually judge it. When children's behavior deviates from a course consonant with ends parents consider desirable or necessary, they may apply sanctions. The socialization of children, therefore, entails a stream of actions serving to direct, redirect and reinforce patterns of behavior in a direction consistent with social ideals.

Parents can take many measures to channel and maintain desired behavior. Some might be unique to a given culture or subculture, or even family; others might be used at one age and discarded at another. Embodied in the very different techniques used by parents to control the behavior of their children, however, are two universal elements: discipline and affection. The first reflects a direct control of children and includes correcting or discouraging transgressions from the acceptable; the second is more indirect and, in effect, rewards "voluntary" compliance to the acceptable. This chapter considers only discipline but these elements are not mutually exclusive; discipline and affection are each likely to be used by the same parent to mold and pattern his child's behavior.

Parents differ considerably in their disciplinary practices, both with

99

regard to the type of discipline they employ and the frequency with which they exercise it. These differences are systematic and are unexplained by the random disciplinary reactions which normally erupt from ephemeral provocations in parent-child encounters. Nor can personality characteristics, as important as they may be, fully explain why some parents are more disciplinarian or punitive than others. Much of the variation in disciplinary practices among parents corresponds to differences in the social conditions of their lives.

No single condition has a preponderant role in influencing parental disciplinary practices. Several conditions are important to discipline, but primarily as they converge on the family together and not as they exist apart from one another. As I suggested at the outset, the values and aspirations parents have for children and their assessment of children's behavior in terms of these ideals are crucial elements in discipline. However, the relationship of parental ideals to parental punishment is not direct or unconditional. Whether or not punishment results from a set of values and aspirations depends on parents' social class, their sex and the sex of their children. The following analysis briefly considers class and sex roles and then proceeds to examine the confluence of these conditions with aspirations and values in affecting disciplinary actions. Then it examines the modes of authority to which fathers are exposed in their occupations in relation to their use of discipline in the home.

PHYSICAL PUNISHMENT AND ITS CORRELATES

Parental discipline was measured by a question which simply asked each parent how often in the past six months he had physically punished his child. There is an understandable uncertainty over the reliability of a single-item indicator, particularly one which requires recall, as this does. Physical punishment, furthermore, is an extreme action, omitting more moderate disciplinary measures. To buttress confidence in the retrospective reports of parents and to determine how physical punishment is related to a broader spectrum of constraint, we related this information to other data relevant to discipline.

Included in the interviews with Turinese parents were questions about five situations which commonly arouse parental reactions: wild play, fighting with sibs, fighting with other children, loss of temper, and refusal to obey. We asked parents if their fifth-grade child ever engaged in the particular behavior. In each of the five instances many parents stated that the situation did not arise in their experience. In cases where the answer to the first question was affirmative, however, we instructed parents to describe the behavior. We then asked them how they dealt with the behavior. Answers to the last question revealed a variety of constraints and sanctions used by parents to cope with these behaviors. At one extreme are parents who used the direct physical means of discipline. Others used techniques involving restrictions (e.g., isolation) and the loss of privileges. Less extreme are parents who verbally scolded or shouted. Then are parents who relied on reasoning or on attempts to alter the conditions of the situation precipitating the undesired behavior. Finally, at the other extreme are parents who asserted that, although they were aware of the behavior, they purposely ignored it. The responses thus include direct actions against the child, actions aimed at changing the immediate aspects of the situation precipitating or supporting the misbehavior, and ignoring the misbehavior.[1] For the reported frequency of punishment in a six-month period to serve as a useful indicator of parental discipline, it should be meaningfully related to parents' reactions to children's transgressions in the five concrete situations. Taking "wild play" as the example, although the other situations would serve as well, such a relationship is quite apparent, as Table VI.1 shows. Only 8 per cent of the middle-class parents reporting no physical punishment in the past six months used physical means to control their children's wild play; the corresponding percentages for the occasional group (from one to four times) and those using force frequently (more than four times) are 24 and 30. In contrast, those reporting no physical discipline are much more likely to appeal to the child, attempt to alter the situation, or ignore the behavior altogether. In the working class the order of relationships is similar.

The frequency of employment of the extreme action of physical punishment over a six-month period, therefore, mirrors a characteristic way of responding to provocative actions of children that are likely to arise in everyday situations. Parents who physically punish frequently are generally disposed to move punitively *against the child*; parents using physical means only occasionally or less are more likely to deal with transgressions by *altering the circumstances* evoking misbehavior or by ignoring it. These associations mean that frequency of punishment encompasses more than a simple distinction between parents who do or do not use physical means. It is, I believe, a reliable indicator of constraint, subsuming a general readiness to impose direct measures against the child.

[1] I originally intended to use these situational items, taken from Kohn's Washington study, to index the range of parental constraints. I had to abandon them for this purpose, however, because of the many parents who reported that their children did not engage in the behaviors included in each of the five situations.

Table VI.1

Frequency of Physical Punishment by Turinese Parents in Past Six Months and Their Reactions to Wild Play, by Social Class

Reactions to Wild Play	Middle-Class Parents Who Punished:			Working-Class Parents Who Punished:		
	Never %	*Occasionally* %	*Frequently* %	*Never* %	*Occasionally* %	*Frequently* %
Physical punishment	8	24	30	6	30	30
Deprivation	4	3	13	8	2	2
Scolding	40	31	30	31	36	47
Altering situation	10	8	4	8	7	2
Ignoring	38	34	23	47	25	19
Numbers	(100)	(62)	(46)	(52)	(56)	(47)

Significance of χ^2 (linear regression)   p < .001   p < .001

CLASS AND SEX

By itself, class bears only a modest relationship to physical punishment: Only 8 per cent more middle- than working-class parents reported that they had not resorted to any physical punishment in the past six months.[2] As unprepossessing as this variation is, class is not unimportant to discipline. Its relevance, however, is best assessed in conjunction with parents' sex.

The actual relationship of parental sex to corporal punishment is contrary to theories that view the father as the main agent of discipline.[3] It is contrary, also, to an image of the Italian family in which the father is a stern patriarch. The evidence, shown in Table VI.2, indicates that the mother is more disposed to administer corporal punishment than the father. This is true, furthermore, in the middle as well as the working class, although working-class mothers are even more likely than their middle-class counterparts to punish frequently. And, finally, the pattern of relationships of class and sex to discipline is not peculiar to the culture of Turin, for it appears in corresponding form in the Washington data as well.[4]

[2]There is some lack of consistency in the findings of American studies regarding class differences in the use of physical punishment. The particular studies reviewed by Bronfenbrenner show general agreement that physical discipline is more commonly used by working-class parents. Kohn, however, finds no appreciable differences among Washingtonians and even less than is found among the Turinese. Urie Bronfenbrenner, "Socialization and Social Class Through Time and Space," in Eleanor E. Maccoby, Theodore M. Newcomb, and Eugene L. Hartley (eds.), *Readings in Social Psychology* (New York: Henry Holt and Company, 1958), pp. 400 – 425. Melvin L. Kohn, "Social Class and Parental Authority," *American Sociological Review*, 24 (1959), pp. 352 – 366.

[3]Parsons sees the father as the main disciplinarian. This would be consistent with paternal responsibilities for the sustenance and safety of the family. He sees the mother as responsible for the stability of the family. She fulfills this functional requirement by providing children with emotional gratification through expressive relations. Children, in the course of their socialization, identify with and internalize these roles. Talcott Parsons and Robert F. Bales, *Family, Socialization and Interaction Process* (Glencoe, Ill.: The Free Press, 1955), pp. 45 – 54. In the same volume is a chapter dealing with the allocation of expressive and instrumental roles within fifty-six societies for which adequate ethnographic reports are available. See Morris Zelditch, "Role Differentiation in the Nuclear Family: A Comparative Study," *ibid.*, pp. 307 – 352.

[4]Other studies also reveal that mothers are the dominant disciplinary figures both in the United States and Italy. A study of American families longitudinally covering eighteen years, found that not only are mothers of the present generation more authoritative than fathers, but that these differences go back to their parents' generation, where the same differences existed. Wanda C. Bronson, Edith S. Katten and Norman Livson, "Patterns of Authority and Affection in Two Generations," *The Journal of Abnormal and Social Psychology*, 58 (1959), pp.

Fathers may be less punitive because they are removed from the household for substantial blocs of time and are less often witness to their children's misbehavior. Mothers are not necessarily tougher disciplinarians, perhaps, but simply find themselves more often in situations demanding severe discipline. If the differential exposure to children accounts for mother-father differences, then the frequency of discipline by mothers employed outside the home should be no more than that of men and less than that of unemployed mothers. However, *employed mothers of both classes are found to be punitive more frequently than the housewives.* Sheer exposure to children cannot explain mother-father differences; more likely these differences result from definitions of their respective sex roles.

We can examine sex role variations in fuller detail by considering the sex of the child. There is no doubt that girls are less frequently the object of spankings than boys. While this is the case in both the middle and working classes, working-class sons are particularly likely to be spanked. And, although the data are not shown, these findings are again consistent with the patterns among Washingtonians.

When parents' sex is added to an overall class comparison, we see that women are the primary sources of physical discipline, particularly in the working class. When we also consider children's sex, we see that mothers of *boys* are most likely to employ physical constraint, again particularly in the working class. Some of these class and sex variations will be more understandable if we examine the ideals that parents hold for their children and the rather special relevance of these ideals to the discipline of sons.

LEVELS AND PROBLEMS
OF ASPIRATIONS

Earlier I emphasized that the characteristics parents value in their children and the status aspirations they have for them serve as criteria for judging the acceptability of behavior. Parents impose constraints on children when their actions are inconsistent with the ideals parents hold for them. In effect, disciplinary practices are influenced by desiderata anchored in the distant future. This influence of parental

---

143 – 152. However, Italian mothers, at least those from Sicily, may be more disciplinarian than American mothers. A cross-national factor-analytic comparison of Sicilian and American parents found that the former were appreciably more controlling, primarily with respect to sexual and aggressive behavior. This study did not distinguish by class, but a comparison by parental sex shows Sicilian mothers to be the group most active in control. Donald R. Peterson and Giuseppe Migliorino, "Pancultural Factors of Parental Behavior in Sicily and the United States," *Child Development*, 38 (1967), pp. 967 – 991.

Table VI.2

Sex of Parents and Frequency of Physical Punishment in Turin and Washington, by Social Class

Frequency of Physical Punishment	TURIN				WASHINGTON[a]			
	Middle Class		Working Class		Middle Class		Working Class	
	Mothers %	*Fathers* %	*Mothers* %	*Fathers* %	*Mothers* %	*Fathers* %	*Mothers* %	*Fathers* %
Never	47	65	35	60	46	57	41	58
Occasionally	33	26	37	27	42	37	43	39
Frequently	20	9	28	13	12	6	16	3
Numbers	(266)	(164)	(215)	(156)	(153)	(46)	(159)	(35)
Significance of χ^2 (linear regression)	p < .001		p < .001		p < .20		p < .05	

[a]*From unpublished data provided by Melvin L. Kohn.*

Table VI.3

Sex of Turinese Parents, Sex of Their Children, and Frequency of Physical Punishment, by Social Class

	MIDDLE CLASS				WORKING CLASS			
	Mothers		Fathers		Mothers		Fathers	
Frequency of Physical Punishment	Sons %	Daughters %	Sons %	Daughters %	Sons %	Daughters %	Sons %	Daughters %
Never	40	56	65	65	26	45	47	76
Occasionally	34	30	22	29	39	35	36	16
Frequently	25	15	13	6	35	20	17	8
Numbers	(144)	(122)	(83)	(81)	(116)	(100)	(83)	(73)
Significance of χ^2 (linear regression)	$p < .01$		n.s.		$p < .01$		$p < .01$	

ideals on discipline is neither simple nor direct, however, because the same goals call forth different reactions from parents of different class position and the same goals also are differently related to the disciplining of sons and daughters. *The relationships of aspirations and values to physical discipline are thus conditioned by social class and the sex of children.*

Table VI.4 demonstrates these relationships by examining educational aspirations. This table can only distinguish two levels of aspiration among middle-class parents since so few of them indicated that they wanted anything less than a secondary education for their children. The table also does not recognize the sex of parents since relationships among mothers and fathers, while not identical, are similar. In both classes and for both sons and daughters the frequency of discipline differs with the levels of parents' aspirations. However, levels of aspiration make more difference in the punishment of boys than of girls in both classes. This finding is entirely consistent with the fact that the future statuses of boys depend on their own achievements, while those of girls depend more on the statuses of their future husbands. Thus there may be an element of urgency in parents' aspirations for boys that is absent in those for girls.

But the most intriguing finding in Table VI.4 is the distinctive direction of the relationship of aspirations to punishment among middle-class parents of sons. Except for this group, physical discipline is least often used by those with the highest aspirations. Most parents eschew severe discipline as a means of generating and maintaining motivation toward distant ends, relying, perhaps, on other sanctions and supports. The middle-class parents of boys, however, are less likely to resort to physical discipline when their sights are set lower rather than higher — exactly the reverse of the condition found in each of the other class and sex groups.

This is an important and revealing exception, for middle-class boys are in the best position to actually achieve a university education. Yet, although as a group they are most likely to satisfy rather than fail their parents' high aspirations, they are punished more than other children whose parents hold the same high aspirations. Several reasons probably account for this. The meaning and consequences of aspirations depend somewhat on standards that vary with the class and sex. A university education for the middle-class son, for example, represents the continuation of the family's status; the same education for a working-class boy is more of a windfall, for it means that he will exceed his family's status. Perhaps there is a more intense normative imperative behind the former circumstance.

Evidence suggests that middle-class parents of sons associate long-

Table VI.4

Sex of Turinese Children, Parents' Educational Aspirations, and Frequency of Physical Punishment, by Social Class

| | MIDDLE-CLASS PARENTS OF: | | | | WORKING-CLASS PARENTS OF: | | | | | |
| | Sons | | Daughters | | Sons | | | Daughters | | |
Frequency of Physical Punishment	Univer-sity %	Less %	Univer-sity %	Less %	Univer-sity %	Second-ary %	Less %	Univer-sity %	Second-ary %	Less %
Never	43	68	64	54	50	36	18	74	56	54
Occasionally	35	18	31	28	36	39	39	22	27	28
Frequently	22	14	5	18	14	25	43	4	17	18
Numbers	(162)	(50)	(103)	(95)	(44)	(106)	(44)	(23)	(93)	(50)
Significance of χ² (linear regression)	p < .02		p < .02		p < .001			p < .20		

range goals with self-denial and delay of gratification. Self-denial may be a characteristic that parents expect in their children as well as something they impose on themselves. There is an element of this expectation in one of the parental values listed in Table IV.1 — "That he is ambitious." Table VI.5 distinguishes, by class and sex of children, parents who rated this as an important or unimportant characteristic for their children to possess. This long-range success value makes a difference, once again, only to disciplining middle-class sons. Middle-class parents, I submit, think achievement depends upon self-restriction and denial, and they see in misbehavior their sons' failure to recognize that these qualities are necessary for achievement. In these circumstances, middle-class parents assume the responsibility for enforcing behavior they consider consistent with their success goals and values. The severity of the measures they use is commensurate with the importance they place on future achievement.

This interpretation is speculative, of course. We can state with far greater certainty, however, that the middle and working classes take different approaches to socializing their children for distant goals. Where long-range achievement in areas important to the future of children is involved, middle-class boys are not left to their own constraints. Perhaps when they reach adolescence their parents will have more confidence in their internal controls, but when they are in the fifth grade their high-aspiring parents are not reluctant to impose corporal punishment. Achievement is serious business to middle-class parents of sons and they employ serious measures.

One circumstance associated with aspirations unconditionally leads mothers and fathers in both classes to resort more frequently to physical punishment in dealing with sons and daughters: *the anticipation that the child will fail to realize parental aspirations.* This is true at each level of aspiration, whether in the educational or occupational realm. We judged failure, in the case of education, by parents' answers to a question that asked how far they expected their children to go in school. Expectations below aspirations indicated anticipated failure; aspirations matched by expectations represented anticipated success. Since the effects of anticipatory success and failure were in the same direction for parents and children of either sex, these distinctions are omitted from Table VI.6. Clearly, parents who feared their children would not measure up to their hopes were more disposed to the use of corporal punishment than those more confident of ultimate success. At least two different explanations of this relationship may be applicable. Perhaps discipline comes about as an expression of the disappointment that parents feel in reaction to an outcome they already accept as a *fait accompli.* Or perhaps they are hoping they can stave

Table VI.5

Sex of Turinese Children, the Importance Parents Accord Ambition, and Frequency of Physical Punishment, by Social Class

| | MIDDLE-CLASS PARENTS OF: | | | | WORKING-CLASS PARENTS OF: | | | |
| | Sons | | Daughters | | Sons | | Daughters | |
Frequency of Physical Punishment	Ambition Important %	Ambition Unimportant %	Ambition Important %	Ambition Unimportant %	Ambition Important %	Ambition Unimportant %	Ambition Important %	Ambition Unimportant %
Never	38	60	54	64	33	37	52	63
Occasionally	36	25	34	26	36	38	34	23
Frequently	26	15	12	10	31	25	14	14
Numbers	(110)	(115)	(93)	(109)	(87)	(105)	(73)	(97)
Significance of χ^2 (linear regression)	p < .01		p < .30		n.s.		n.s.	

Table VI.6

Educational Aspirations of Turinese Parents, the Anticipation of Success or Failure, and Frequency of Physical Punishment, by Social Class

| | MIDDLE-CLASS PARENTS | | | | WORKING-CLASS PARENTS | | | | | |
| | Want University | | Want Less | | Want University | | Want Secondary | | Want Less | |
Frequency of Physical Punishment	*Antici-pate Success* %	*Antici-pate Failure* %	*Antici-pate Success* %	*Antici-pate Failure* %	*Antici-pate Success* %	*Antici-pate Failure* %	*Antici-pate Success* %	*Antici-pate Failure* %	*Antici-pate Success* %	*Antici-pate Failure* %
Never	55	37	61	48	68	39	48	36	42	8
Occasionally	30	47	25	26	25	44	33	34	28	61
Frequently	15	16	14	26	7	17	19	30	30	31
Numbers	(203)	(62)	(126)	(19)	(44)	(23)	(149)	(50)	(81)	(13)

Significance of χ^2 (linear regression)   p < .02   p < .02

Success vs. failure only.

off a likely failure by invoking severe physical discipline. Whichever it is, discipline of children is intimately linked to the statuses parents expect their children will actually achieve relative to the statuses they ideally would like them to achieve. No group of parents regards its aspirations for children as trivial; in the face of the possibility that their children will fail them, all parents, regardless of class or sex conditions, are likely to resort to more frequent physical punishment.

More generally, we can conceptualize parental discipline as one type of control used to maintain children's behavior on a course consistent with what parents feel are desirable ends. When these ends demand a high level of achievement, middle-class sons are likely to find that their parents reinforce effort and motivation by relatively frequent use of physical punishment. We saw that middle-class parents of sons, in particular, regard stern discipline and strict control as necessary for long-range achievement. Thus the same ideals do not call forth the same disciplinary practices from different parents, for the meaning of these ideals varies with social class and sex of children. The frequency of physical discipline results from the confluence of all three conditions: class, sex, and ideals. It results from other conditions as well, however, and important among these is the occupational experience of fathers.

OCCUPATIONAL EXPERIENCE AND
PATERNAL PUNISHMENT

The constraints and inhibitions that fathers must exercise to carry out their jobs, the successes and failures they experience as they pursue occupational goals, their place in the hierarchy of power relations and several structural properties of the authority system are all relevant to their use of physical punishment as a constraining technique. The father's day-after-day encounters with various features of his occupation influence the roles he takes within the family domain and the relationships he establishes with other family members. They influence, also, what he comes to view as necessary and proper to control and gain acquiescence from his children. Perhaps in no other area are the connections between work and parenthood more multiple — though not always clear — than in the area of discipline.

THE DEFERMENT OF OCCUPATIONAL GRATIFICATIONS. Earlier I emphasized that levels of educational aspiration embody the deferment of gratification, a concomitant of most long-range goals. For children to realize their parents' ambitions requires discipline, and, however much parents may want behavior controlled from within, they are not reluctant to impose extreme external control, especially middle-class parents of sons. The deferment of gratification as a salient characteristic of fathers' own occupational experiences is also related to paternal discipline. We can expect such a relationship to the extent that structured experiences in the occupational realm shape fathers' conceptions of what is necessary for children.

We gave fathers a list of characteristics, discussed in Chapter IV, and asked them to indicate the importance of each as requirements for doing well at their work. Several items are indicative of occupational goal deferment, but one in particular states the issue very directly: "Being able to sacrifice today for tomorrow's results." The responses to this item, which we also asked the self-employed, are classified in Table VI.7 by whether fathers considered this an important or unimportant requirement of their work. Evidently, perceived deferment of rewards at work is associated with physical punishment, especially for middle-class fathers and most strikingly for middle-class fathers whose fifth-graders are sons. Repeatedly, then, middle-class sons stand out as being subject to physical punishment under certain conditions. If middle-class fathers see the delay of rewards as necessary to their work, then most likely they will consider severe discipline necessary in dealing with their sons, at least as an auxiliary control.

Much the same results appear when we examine related requirements of fathers' work, such as "perseverance" and "ambition to succeed." Together with sacrifice for future rewards, they form a picture of patient self-denial, dedication to the task, hard work. Indeed, even though most Turinese are Catholics, these attitudes reflect elements of the Protestant Ethic. Patterns of delay and denial do not have the same impact on disciplinary practices in the different classes, however. Members of the middle class are most likely to associate striving after future rewards with restriction and denial, and they also seem to rely most heavily on physical punishment as a major means to train children — most notably sons — to follow the same deferment patterns. Consistent with earlier observations that high aspiring middle-class parents of sons are more disposed to physical means of punishment, we find once more that this very group is most likely to transmute the father's occupational self-sacrifice into physical constraint. The forbearance and self-denial that their occupations may require apparently contribute to a generally restrictive orientation of middle-class fathers toward male children, expressed in the relatively frequent employment of corporal punishment.

Yet, the deferment of goals is not the same as the frustration of goals, nor is its consequences for punishment the same. Those fathers who judge their opportunities for financial or occupational advancement as limited are no more disposed to use physical means than

Table VI.7

Sex of Turinese Children, the Importance to Fathers of "Sacrificing Today for Tomorrow's Results," and the Use of Physical Punishment, by Social Class

Frequency of Physical Punishment	MIDDLE-CLASS FATHERS OF:				WORKING-CLASS FATHERS OF:			
	Sons		Daughters		Sons		Daughters	
	Sacrifice Important %	*Sacrifice Unimportant* %	*Sacrifice Important* %	*Sacrifice Unimportant* %	*Sacrifice Important* %	*Sacrifice Unimportant* %	*Sacrifice Important* %	*Sacrifice Unimportant* %
Never	37	81	52	76	41	49	71	77
Occasionally	37	15	45	18	35	39	21	15
Frequently	26	4	3	6	24	12	8	8
Numbers	(30)	(52)	(29)	(50)	(29)	(51)	(24)	(47)
Significance of χ^2 (linear regression)	$p < .001$		$p < .20$		$p < .30$		n.s.	

those who see them optimistically, although the former are presumably experiencing more occupational frustration. Corporal punishment, therefore, is not an expression of blocked goals; it is more a training practice consistent with the constraints that fathers experience as they go about their work.

POWER OBJECTS AND POWER WIELDERS. Occupational constraints derive from aspects of work other than the deferment of rewards. Of the many facets of occupational constraint that might be pertinent to punishment, none is more directly implicated than the formal controls that impinge on fathers at their jobs. One way to assess these controls is through fathers' subordinate-superordinate roles in the authority systems regulating their work. We could argue that the more subject a man is to the power of others and the less he possesses, the more likely he is to employ punishment in dealing with his children. Being mainly an *object* of direct control and constraint in one institution would dispose him to exploit whatever opportunities he has to exercise power and control in other institutional settings. Such assumptions are consistent with the general view that parental actions inside the family may serve as compensatory mechanisms for the deprivation of power and autonomy outside.[5]

Several questions in our interview schedule were designed to describe the hierarchy in which fathers work. One of them asked how much control was exercised over their work by their most relevant superordinate. (We did not ask the self-employed these questions.) The answers are given in Table VI.8 in relation to physical punishment. This table further distinguishes fathers by the sex of their fifth-grade child since, in the working class, this made a difference.

The results indicate that physical punishment is most likely to be used by those subjected to the stricter controls — that is, those who said they were controlled almost completely or closely. Fathers reporting little or no control were much more likely to say that they never used physical punishment. The one exception is working-class fathers of daughters, where occupational control makes no difference. It would appear, tentatively, that those fathers who themselves experience stringent constraints are disposed "to take it out" on their children.

This explanation is incomplete, however. Discipline increases not only as one is subject to the authority of others but also as his scope of authority over others increases. We determined if fathers possessed power through a question that asked them if they had supervisory responsibility for others and, if so, how many others. Thus, we could

[5]For example, see Donald Gilbert McKinley, *Social Class and Family Life* (New York: The Free Press of Glencoe, 1964), pp. 118 – 151.

Table VI.8

Sex of Turinese Children, Subjection of Fathers to Occupational Control, and Physical Punishment, by Social Class

| | MIDDLE-CLASS FATHERS OF: | | | | WORKING-CLASS FATHERS OF: | | | |
| | Sons | | Daughters | | Sons | | Daughters | |
Frequency of Physical Punishment	*Strict Control* %	*Little Control* %	*Strict Control* %	*Little Control* %	*Strict Control* %	*Little Control* %	*Strict Control* %	*Little Control* %
Never	52	88	67	81	41	57	75	77
Occasionally	32	12	21	14	36	36	17	15
Frequently	16	–	12	5	23	7	8	8
Numbers	(25)	(14)	(24)	(22)	(53)	(28)	(59)	(13)
Significance of χ^2 (linear regression)	p < .05		p < .30		p < .10		n.s.	

identify those who were power wielders and judge something of the range of their power. In presenting the answers to this question in relation to physical punishment, fathers of sons and of daughters are combined in order to compensate for the small numbers in the working class who have any supervisory responsibilities.

Table VI.9 indicates that in the middle class, the possession of power makes a substantial difference for physical punishment but in the working class it makes almost none. What is interesting here is that occupational superordination in the middle class does not militate against punitiveness at home. To the contrary, it is a condition remarkably conducive to physical punishment. That is, as the scope of power increases so does the proportion of men employing at least "occasional" physical punishment. Among middle-class men, at least, discipline cannot be explained simply as a reaction to the deprivation of occupational authority, for wielders of power, as well as objects of power, are more frequently punitive. Any account of the absence of difference in the working class must be highly speculative. Quite possibly, however, it reflects a somewhat less intense and complete power than possessed by middle-class power wielders.

Obviously, the relationships that do appear challenge any supposition that corporal punishment of children is solely a result of being at the bottom of the pecking order, for in the middle class those without superordinate powers are not the most punitive; they are the least. A tenable interpretation must accommodate both the fact that punishment increases as one is increasingly an object of power, and that, in the middle class, it also increases with the power one wields. Most relevant to the frequency of punishment is the active participation of a man in the hierarchical distribution of power and constraint. The extremes of power, whether they be at the bottom or top, are built into a man's daily occupational experiences and come to serve as a model for establishing relations outside the work setting — even with his own children. It is not simply that the frustration of autonomy leads to punitiveness. Rather, when one's actions and interactions in the work setting closely depend on power and authority, either as a subordinate or superordinate, one tends to structure relations with others on the same axis. In this way the disciplinary roles of fathers are shaped by their interpersonal experiences in the occupational setting.

BUREAUCRATIC VS. PERSONAL AUTHORITY. Structural features of authority other than the subordination to and possession of power have a bearing on the use of physical punishment. The relatively limited number of fathers in our sample prohibits us from seeing how these features may fit together in relation to punishment practices. But the

Table VI.9

Turinese Fathers' Possession of Supervisory Responsibilities and Frequency of Physical Punishment, by Social Class

Frequency of Physical Punishment	Middle-Class Fathers			Working-Class Fathers		
	No Supervisory Responsibility %	*Supervises 1 to 10 men* %	*Supervises over 10 men* %	*No Supervisory Responsibility* %	*Supervises 1 to 10 men* %	*Supervises over 10 men* %
Never	79	65	48	59	65	67
Occasionally	12	26	39	28	26	22
Frequently	9	9	13	13	9	11
Numbers	(34)	(34)	(23)	(121)	(23)	(9)
Significance of χ^2 (linear regression)		p <.05			n.s.	

evidence that can be pieced together suggests that, even for those who are primarily objects of power, the bureaucratization, diffusion and impersonalization of authority in fathers' occupation settings are conditions that inhibit the use of physical means of punishment.

One indication of this is drawn simply from the number of people making up the functional work groups in which fathers are employed. Information on the size of the work unit came from a question asking how many people were in the fathers' immediate section. The relationship between the size of the work section and predisposition to use physical punishment is particularly clear in comparing fathers employed in sections of forty or fewer with those in work groups of more than forty. We can describe briefly the results of this comparison without presenting the data. Whether a man was in a middle- or working-class occupation, he was more likely to have punished his child in the last six months if he were a member of a small unit. I emphasize this finding precisely because size embodies many organizational and experiential conditions. It is difficult to be certain which of them is influencing this relationship; but it is reasonable to assume that the larger functional work units are characterized by greater formalization and bureaucratization, by an authority system that operates more impersonally and by a more diffused allocation of authority. The net effect is that authority is likely to be exercised in a prescribed fashion involving several echelons. These characteristics stand in contrast to the act of physical punishment, which is very direct, typically a personal action and dictated by spontaneous feeling rather than rule or plan.

The set of questions permitting an assessment of the diffusion and indirectness of authority in the work setting asked, first, for a listing, in hierarchical order, of all people in the work group in positions superordinate to the respondent. Next, respondents were asked to indicate with which of these superordinates they had systematic daily contact. From this question we determined the total number of authorities with whom fathers were in contact on a regular face-to-face basis.

We find in Table VI.10 that the number of superordinates to whom a father is responsible in his daily work is related to his disciplinary actions. This occupational condition influences fathers' punishment of sons only, however; thus the table does not include fathers of fifth-grade daughters. It is apparent that boys, at least, have a substantially greater chance of being physically punished if their fathers work under the direct authority of only one superordinate. Where authority over a father is multiple and, consequently, involves a larger and more diffused segment of a formal hierarchical order, he uses physical means of punishment less often.

Table VI.10

Number of Superordinates With Whom Turinese Fathers Have Daily Contact and Frequency of Physical Punishment of Sons, by Social Class

	Middle-Class Fathers		Working-Class Fathers	
Frequency of Physical Punishment	Contact With One Super- ordinate %	Contact With Two or More Super- ordinates %	Contact With One Super- ordinate %	Contact With Two or More Super- ordinates %
Never	53	75	36	55
Occasionally	32	20	44	31
Frequently	16	5	20	14
Numbers	(19)	(20)	(39)	(42)
Significance of χ^2 (linear regression)	p < .20		p < .20	

We can now fit together some of the elements in the portrait of the occupational underdog that are relevant to discipline: he has little or no determination over his own work; the completeness of his supervision is aided by his being part of a relatively small work group; and responsibility for the supervision of his work resides exclusively in the hands of a single superordinate. This man is likely to spank his child frequently, particularly if the child is a male. The underdog is not completely alone in this respect, for men who wield considerable authority, especially in the middle-class, are also relatively disposed to use corporal punishment. While this picture is incomplete, it suggests an isomorphism between the structural properties of the authority system in which fathers are located and the properties inherent in physical discipline. A father's location at the extremes of the authority system relates to the extremes of power involved in the physical punishment by a father of his child; and, similarly, the father's direct exposure to the authority of a single superordinate parallels the direct and face-to-face confrontation that goes with physical discipline.

More generally, we can state that the intensity and quality of the controls and sanctions fathers experience at work influence the ways they apply sanctions and controls in dealing with their children. Embodied in the occupational sphere is a host of demands and many arrangements for enforcing these demands. These represent to fathers the conditions of the real world. What they learn about these conditions and what they accept and reject of them come to constitute the terms they employ for judging and dealing with their children's behavior.

DISCUSSION

Parental discipline is much more than a vehicle for giving vent to feelings that exist at the moment. It is not exercised for its own sake, but is an important and patterned aspect of parent-child relations, instrumental to the socialization process.

Discipline may be conceptualized as a systematic reaction to the behavior of children that parents judge to be either a direct threat to parental values and aspirations or an insufficient effort by children to attain these distant ideals. The values and goals parents hold for children are not dormant fancies. They represent the ends toward which much striving and effort is directed. When these ends appear to be jeopardized by the actions of children, parents may react with severe measures. Discipline, of course, is not the only mechanism in the parental armamentarium: Behavior may also be controlled by exhortation, by example, or by emotional supportiveness. The severity of the controls, however, is likely to depend on the gravity of the perceived threat to important goals and the extent to which children are seen to lack sustained motivation to achieve the goals.

While this is a useful conceptual framework from which to approach disciplinary practices, it cannot completely explain some of the actual variations that occur in the use of physical punishment. The reason for this is that the effects of the same values and aspirations are regulated by the social structural factors of class and sex. Thus, different disciplinary practices are used by middle-and working-class parents and by mothers and fathers dealing with sons and daughters. Generally, parents who have goals for their children that are remote in time and difficult to achieve employ physical discipline *less* frequently than parents having more immediate and less problematic goals. Middle-class parents of sons are a major exception; here there is *more* frequent punishment by those with the highest goals. Both their class position and the sex of their children lead these parents to rely heavily on constraint and denial in maintaining the behavior of their sons on a course consistent with success goals.

Quite aside from parents' values and aspirations, from their own experiences they come to acquire conceptions of the proper and efficacious modes of dealing with children's transgressions. We have already seen how occupation is a sphere of experience relevant to the formation of parental values. Now we see it is important to discipline, also. More is involved here than a displacement of occupational frustrations, however. The location of men in the authority system at work and their exposure to power that is both direct and resides in a single superordinate are factors disposing men to employ physical discipline. The structure of constraints regulating the behavior of men at work serves as a basis of what men come to think as *necessary* to manage the misbehavior of their children. By employing with children a style of constraint consistent with that they experience, perhaps fathers are unknowingly training their children for the same kinds of occupational contexts in which they are located.

We could not make cross-national comparisons throughout the range of this analysis. Fortunately, what comparisons were possible involved the basic social characteristics of class and sex roles. To the extent that judgments can be made from these fundamental conditions, it would appear that similar social structural factors have similar effects on parental discipline in Turin and the United States. Although these cross-national comparisons are limited, they indicate that the requirements of industrialized societies create a correspondence in socialization practices that transcends formidable cultural differences.

Several conditions flow into the family and eventuate in disciplinary practices. Some of these we could observe directly, others we inferred from empirical evidence that is available and still others undoubtedly we have omitted from consideration altogether. Nor have we discussed the possible consequences of physical discipline for personality development and socialization. In this area contention is more abundant than knowledge; we know enough, however, to caution us against too ready assumptions about the deleterious effects of physical punishment.[6] Obviously, considerable work needs to be done to extend our knowledge of the social antecedents and consequences of disciplinary practices and to buttress the data and interpretations presented in this chapter. Nevertheless, the evidence brought together here permits this unequivocal assertion: Disciplinary practices result from durable social conditions and are not solely reactions to ephemeral provocative events or expressions of particular personality characteristics. It will be possible to make the same statement with regard to parental affection, the issue to which I turn now.

[6]The consequences of physical punishment would depend on other elements in parent-child relations, such as affection. It would also depend, I believe, on the particular aspect of personality under consideration. In this regard, Coopersmith shows that the children of parents favoring strictness tend to have high self-esteem, but those of parents using corporal punishment as a mode of control have lower self-esteem. Stanley Coopersmith, *The Antecedents of Self-esteem* (San Francisco: W. N. Freeman and Company, 1967), pp. 181 – 198.

VII

Parental Affection

The elements of parent-child relations that we have studied thus far function either to set socialization goals or to enforce such goals. Parental values and aspirations serve to establish important ends around which much of child training becomes organized and toward which parents want their children to progress. Discipline, on the other hand, is clearly different. Whereas values and aspirations help to select and formulate the ends of socialization, parents invoke discipline to insure that children's behavior does not deviate from a direction consistent with these ends. How does parental affection fit into this scheme? Like discipline, one of its functions is to support and enforce parents' goals for children. In this regard it is less direct a mechanism than discipline, but probably no less effective. And, despite its intimate character, parental affection appears to be no less influenced by social conditions than discipline.

Affection is an inclusive concept, embracing behaviors of considerable scope and richness. Most of these are necessarily left out of consideration in the present analysis. It is not possible, for example, to deal with the many fine shades of affection that exist between parents and children; nor can we examine the specialized languages and gestures used in a family to convey feelings. Even the negative feelings of parents, which may be intertwined with positive affect, are not easily captured. Because negative feelings toward one's own children run counter to powerful cultural dictates, they are difficult to uncover. The difficulty is not that parents refuse to talk about such feelings, but rather that they are not likely to recognize or accept them in themselves. We would have gained little, therefore, by asking survey questions aimed at finding if parents feel negatively toward their children. Such questions would only have discovered, I am sure, that virtually no Turinese dislike their children and, further-

123

more, that very few are consciously aware that this is even a meaningful possibility.

The aspect of parental affection that is treated here is one that has been the focus of a number of studies: the mode of affectionate expressiveness. We asked parents how they react when their fifth-grade children do something that pleases them. We graded their answers according to the level of responsiveness that they indicated. Parents at the most *active* level said they expressed their pleasure physically, typically by a hug or kiss. Parents at a less active level said they expressed their pleasure *verbally* in some statement of praise, encouragement or expression of thanks. Finally, *passive* parents said that they took their children's actions as a matter of course and did nothing to express their pleasure or, in a few instances, said that their children never did anything that pleased them.

There are several advantages to the use of this question and the data it yields. First, the question is meaningful and is anchored to everyday experience. It does not arouse any apparent threat, and, consequently, it is a query to which parents can readily respond without unusual difficulty. The question, furthermore, is directed to an important aspect of parent-child relations. The manner in which parents characteristically present their feelings to their children must be considered a vital element in their transactions, one that has far-reaching consequences. Finally, since affectionate expressiveness has been scrutinized by other studies, it permits us to make a general cross-national comparison with the findings from Turin. In fact, it is possible to make very direct comparisons, for the question used in Turin is identical to that used originally by Kohn in his Washington study and to that employed by him again in his recent national study.[1] This makes available two bodies of data with which comparisons can be made, although for reasons noted below the Washington data are not suited to systematic comparison.

Somewhat surprisingly virtually no relationship exists between the demonstration of affection and the frequency of physical punishment. Children may be showered with affection and still be frequently subjected to corporal punishment, or their parents may be affectionately indifferent but never employ harsh discipline in dealing with them. Despite the absence of a direct association between punishment and affection, some of the social circumstances relevant to discipline are also relevant to parental differences in expressiveness, particularly

[1]This same study provided the comparative data regarding parental values in Chapter IV. Melvin L. Kohn, *Class and Conformity: A Study in Values* (Homewood, Ill.: Dorsey Press, 1969).

class and sex roles. But class and sex, while important to affection in their own right, are also important because they set the stage for other conditions.

CLASS AND SEX ROLES

Various studies have identified the expression of affection as parental nurturance or warmth.[2] Regardless of the label they employ, however, these studies are commonly interested in observing the variations that occur with social-class membership and with parents' and children's sex. Considering that the relation of class and sex to affection have been examined empirically by a fair number of studies, one would expect a well-established body of knowledge to exist in this area, providing many opportunities for cross-national comparison. This is not the case, however. A review of the literature indicates substantial uncertainty and ambiguity concerning parent-child affective relations and their social correlates. Partly, this results from different research workers using different indicators of the same concepts or, in other instances, from using similar indicators of essentially dissimilar concepts.[3] The ages of the children involved in various studies also cover a wide range, making the generality of conclusions problematic. These kinds of issues have militated against the comparability of studies and the cumulative development of reliable knowledge.

Such difficulties notwithstanding, we can derive one important conclusion: middle-class parents are more actively affectionate toward their children than working-class parents. The reliability of this finding is supported by a substantial degree of consistency in the results of studies conducted over a considerable period of time.[4] Are there class

[2]Two review articles discuss many of the studies relating class to parental affection or kindred concepts. One is by Urie Bronfenbrenner, "Socialization and Social Class Through Time and Space," in Eleanor E. Maccoby, Theodore M. Newcomb and Eugene L. Hartley (eds.), *Readings in Social Psychology*, 3rd ed. (New York: Henry Holt and Company, 1958), pp. 400–425. More recent is the review by John A. Clausen and Judith R. Williams, "Sociological Correlates of Child Behavior," in Harold W. Stevenson, *Child Psychology: The Sixty-second Yearbook of The National Society for the Study of Education*, Part I (Chicago: National Society for the Study of Education, 1963), pp. 62–107.

[3]Bronfenbrenner, "Socialization and Social Class."

[4]These studies typically use small samples, raising some question about the credibility of their findings. The greater affectionate demonstrativeness of middle-class parents, however, has been a consistent finding of studies in this area, giving the relationship an unusual reliability. For examples see Nancy Bayley and Earl S. Schaeffer, "Relationships Between Socioeconomic Variables and the Behavior of Mothers Toward Young Children," *The Journal of Genetic Psychology*, 96 (1960), pp. 61–77; Martha Sturm White, "Social Class, Child Rearing

differences in Turin in regard to affection? How do they correspond to those that exist in the United States? If we compare all middle- to all working-class Turinese parents, we find the former more phys- ically demonstrative, less limited to verbal expressions of affection, and less passive than the latter, as shown in Table VII.1.

Since the item used to assess the levels of expressiveness in Turin was first used in Washington, it would be particularly relevant to compare the parents from these two cities. The responses of the Washingtonians are much more highly concentrated at the verbal level; fewer parents are actively affectionate and even fewer are passive. This concentration is sufficiently great to preclude a systematic comparison between the parents of the two cities. The class differences that exist in Washington, however, are in a direction entirely consist- ent with those found in other American studies and with those in Turin. Piecing together all the evidence, we can say the relationship of social class to the expression of affection is similar for the Turinese and Americans.

Consider now the sex of parents. It may seem hardly worthwhile to compare the affectionateness of mothers and fathers, for it is "common knowledge" that mothers are more expressive than fathers. This difference is sufficiently universal, apparently, to support a theory placing functional responsibility for the emotional gratification of

Table VII.1

Social Class and Expression of Affection in Turin

Expression of Affection	Middle-Class Parents %	Working-Class Parents %
Active	35	24
Verbal	37	44
Passive	28	32
Numbers	(439)	(380)

Significance of χ^2
(linear regression) $p < .01$

Practices and Child Behavior," *American Sociological Review*, 22 (1957), pp. 704 – 712; and Robert R. Sears, Eleanor E. Maccoby and Harry Levin, *Patterns of Child Rearing* (Evanston, Ill.: Row Peterson and Company, 1957), pp. 423 – 433. Urie Bronfenbrenner discusses the greater expressiveness of middle- class parents in "The Changing American Child. A Speculative Analysis," *The Journal of Social Issues*, 17 (1961), pp. 6 – 18.

children with the mother.[5] But this does not mean that mothers are uniformly warm and actively loving people. Their social class and the sex of the child with whom they are interacting have a good deal to do with their expressive behavior.

Looking first at parental sex within the context of the two classes, we see in Table VII.2 that middle-class mothers exceed all other parents in the proportion that is actively affectionate. Indeed, because of middle-class mothers' disposition toward physical demonstrativeness, there is a larger difference between mothers and fathers in the middle than in the working class. Clearly, the overall class difference that appears in Table VII.1 results primarily from the behavior of middle-class mothers toward their children.

It will be useful to subsequent analysis to define further these variations by looking at the sex of children as well as of their parents. Table VII.3 divides parents first by the sex of their fifth-graders, then by their own sex.[6] This table contains a number of interesting relationships but I wish to call particular attention to the fact that we find the largest proportion of actively expressive parents among middle-class mothers responding to sons. As a consequence, the mother-father

Table VII.2

Sex of Turinese Parent and the Expression of Affection, by Social Class

Expression of Affection	Middle Class		Working Class	
	Mothers %	Fathers %	Mothers %	Fathers %
Active	42	24	29	18
Verbal	34	41	40	49
Passive	24	35	31	33
Numbers	(274)	(165)	(221)	(159)

Significance of χ^2
(linear regression) p < .001   p < .20

[5]Talcott Parsons and Robert F. Bales, *Family, Socialization and Interaction Process* (Glencoe, Ill.: The Free Press, 1955), pp. 45 – 54.

[6]It is interesting to note as a methodological sidelight that although much has been written about social class, parents' and children's sex, these variables rarely appear in the same analysis. Their simultaneous examination helps considerably in clarifying the role of each. This problem is also referred to in Bayley and Schaeffer, "Socioeconomic Variables and Behavior of Mothers," p. 75.

difference is greatest in this class among parents of sons. We said earlier that mothers are the main contributors to the greater affectionateness in the middle class; now we note that middle-class mothers of sons have a somewhat greater part in these class differences than middle-class mothers of daughters.

Social class and parents' and children's sex roles are each conditions under which the effects of the others will vary. Social class and sex, it should be emphasized, are fundamental elements in social organization. They are social statuses that structure behavior and define relations among people throughout society. What is remarkable is that they are also related to affectionateness, that their effects extend to the most intimate of transactions within the inner reaches of the family. Of course, to know that basic features of social organization are related to the expression of affection is not the same as understanding how these relationships come about. Why, specifically, are middle-class mothers, particularly in responding to sons, so outstandingly expressive? Their class and their sex define the relationship, but they do not account for it. For this, we must bring into the analysis other considerations.

PARENTAL CONTROL

Affection is not necessarily aroused by any particular event or transaction between parent and child; normally it is a spontaneous expression of a prevailing state. Remember, however, that the question used in this analysis asked parents what they did when they were pleased by their child. Thus, the query was intended to discover specific parental responses to specific acts. Implicit in such an intent is the assumption that the demonstration of affection is, at least to some extent, anchored to approved behavior. In this framework, affection is a rewarding reaction to the behavior of children that parents wish to encourage. Affection, perhaps more powerfully and effectively than discipline, is in this way a potential instrument to channel and reinforce desired behavioral patterns in children. While it may be expressed for the sheer gratification it yields, affection also is capable of serving as a mechanism to regulate and control children's behavior.[7]

For many parents, of course, the expression of affection has no relevance whatever to control. In part, this is because control itself is of little or no importance. To explore the possible connections

[7]Other writers have linked affection and control as elements intrinsic to socialization. Winch, for example, sees "nurturance" and control as joint variables in producing identification and, consequently, role learning. Robert F. Winch, *Identification and Its Familial Determinants* (New York: Bobbs-Merrill Company, Inc., 1962), pp. 56 – 92.

Table VII.3

Sex of Turinese Children, Sex of Their Parents, and the Expression of Affection, by Social Class

Expression of Affection	MIDDLE CLASS				WORKING CLASS			
	Sons		Daughters		Sons		Daughters	
	Mothers %	*Fathers* %	*Mothers* %	*Fathers* %	*Mothers* %	*Fathers* %	*Mothers* %	*Fathers* %
Active	44	22	40	26	28	18	31	18
Verbal	36	45	32	37	44	47	36	50
Passive	20	33	28	37	28	35	33	32
Numbers	(152)	(84)	(122)	(81)	(119)	(81)	(102)	(78)
Significance of χ^2 (linear regression)	p < .001		p < .05		p < .20		p < .30	

between affectionateness and control, therefore, we must first distinguish parents according to their concern with control. This is done by modifying the index of parental values developed in Chapter IV. This index was intended originally to identify three major groups: those valuing self-control, those stressing obedience, and those subscribing to neither self-control nor obedience. Here it is necessary only to differentiate parents who accord some degree of importance either to self-control or obedience from those attaching importance to neither. In effect, this treats control from within and control from without as interchangeable, since both emphasize parental valuation of control. The locus of control is not pertinent to the present problem; the only critical issue is whether or not parents are oriented to control.

Does expressiveness vary with a concern for control? Table VII.4 answers this question affirmatively, but the relationship is quite different for different groups. Specifically, middle-class mothers emerge once again as distinct from all other groups. They alone are likely to be actively expressive when they feel that control is important. The story is just the reverse for working-class mothers and fathers. When these parents regard control as important they are not more, but less, disposed to demonstrate affection actively. The two classes, then, are quite different. Whereas the affectionate behavior of middle-class mothers appears to be aroused by an orientation to control, the same orientation appears to inhibit the affectionate expressiveness of working-class parents. While the former are particularly apt to be demonstrative when they are concerned with control, the latter are more freely demonstrative when they are free of this concern. Parents of both classes and sexes are approximately equal in the proportions viewing control as important. What distinguishes them is the marked tendency of middle-class mothers to place affectionateness in the company of their orientation to control. It would appear, in other words, that these mothers employ the demonstration of affection in support of control.

Consistent with the earlier finding that middle-class sons are somewhat more likely than daughters to be objects of their mothers' affectionate display, we could expect the relationship of control to expressiveness to be particularly close where the child in question is a boy. This is precisely what emerges. The sex of the child, that is, makes a greater difference to the reactions of middle-class mothers than to any other parent; the net result is that control oriented middle-class mothers in interaction with sons are by far the most demonstrative. Rather than presenting the many associations generated by the simultaneous examination of class, sex of parent, sex of child and

Table VII.4

Sex of Turinese Parents, Importance Accorded Control, and the Expression of Affection, by Social Class

| | MIDDLE CLASS | | | | WORKING CLASS | | | |
| | Mothers Who Think Control: | | Fathers Who Think Control: | | Mothers Who Think Control: | | Fathers Who Think Control: | |
Expression of Affection	*Important* %	*Unimportant* %	*Important* %	*Unimportant* %	*Important* %	*Unimportant* %	*Important* %	*Unimportant* %
Active	46	29	24	24	25	39	15	27
Verbal	29	50	38	50	43	33	52	41
Passive	25	21	38	26	32	28	33	32
Numbers	(202)	(68)	(123)	(42)	(158)	(57)	(112)	(44)
Significance of χ^2 (linear regression)	$p < .30$		n.s.		$p < .20$		$p < .30$	

the concern with control, Table VII.5 is simplified and presents only the results for middle-class mothers, the focal group. The mothers of this class who regard control of their sons to be important are by a large margin the most actively expressive. When mothers of the same class view control of their sons as of no consequence, they are considerably more disposed to verbal expressions or to passiveness. With regard to daughters, on the other hand, middle-class mothers' orientation to control makes a difference only between passiveness and verbal expressions of affection. Also, the direction of this difference is not the same for girls as for boys, for control oriented mothers tend to be less, rather than more, responsive toward daughters.

Now we can understand why middle-class mothers are so actively responsive to their sons. They, more than others, rely on affection to reward and, thereby, reinforce behavior of which they approve. Affection serves as a lever for the positive control of behavior. This need not be, and in most cases probably is not, an insidious or blatant manipulation of feelings for the purpose of winning compliance. More likely, it develops because the middle-class mother and her child each find the expression of affection an emotionally gratifying element in their exchanges and not only because they recognize affection to be an effective regulatory mechanism. Once the expression of affection is established as a mutually gratifying element in the mother-child relation, however, it may function to maintain behavior in a desired direction.

If we juxtapose what we learned earlier of the discipline of middle-class boys with the active affection they receive, it might appear that

Table VII.5

Sex of Child, Importance Accorded Control, and the Expression of Affection by Middle-Class Turinese Mothers

	Mothers of Sons Who Think Control:		Mothers of Daughters Who Think Control:	
Expression of Affection	*Important* %	*Unimportant* %	*Important* %	*Unimportant* %
Active	50	15	41	39
Verbal	31	63	26	41
Passive	19	22	33	20
Numbers	(121)	(27)	(81)	(41)

Significance of χ^2
(linear regression)   p < .02   n.s.

contradictory patterns exist. Chapter VI stated that boys are subject to relatively frequent physical punishment by middle-class parents who entertain high aspirations for them. Yet, we learn now that underlying their strict discipline is also a good deal of active affection, used by mothers to support their concern with control. Many middle-class Turinese boys, therefore, are recipients of both strict constraint and actively expressed love. Bronfenbrenner has also noted the confluence of these patterns in the United States.[8] Such "desirable" characteristics as responsibility, achievement motivations, leadership and competitiveness, he observed, are best developed in boys where there is a balance between affection and discipline. If his observation is correct, then middle-class boys are socialized to acquire a number of attributes that enhance their competitive opportunities for later achievement. The joint use of affection and discipline probably changes as the child matures; but the combination may contribute to the acquisition of personality attributes functional for the attainment of distant goals.

OCCUPATIONAL DISAFFECTION
AND PATERNAL AFFECTION

We have said little of the expressiveness of fathers, except in comparison to mothers. We should not ignore them, however. Despite their being less active than mothers, they nevertheless participate importantly in the family's affective relations and contribute to its overall emotional climate. Underlying the style and quality of their affective behavior are certain occupational experiences. We already know that occupation influences fathers' values, the goals toward which they want their children to strive and the disciplinary practices they adopt to enforce their values and aspirations. It is not at all surprising, then, that experiences in the occupational realm would also influence the feelings that fathers express for their children.

Indeed, previous studies have attempted to establish the links between work and affective elements in father-child interaction. McKinley's study is particularly useful in this regard, for his approach provides a clear point of departure in the present analysis. He has shown that hostility of fathers toward sons increases as work autonomy and occupational satisfaction decrease.[9] Understandably, he inter-

[8]Urie Bronfenbrenner, "Some Familial Antecedents of Responsibility and Leadership in Adolescents," in Luigi Petrullo and Bernard M. Bass (eds.), *Leadership and Interpersonal Behavior* (New York: Holt, Rinehart and Winston, Inc., 1961), pp. 239 – 271; and "The Changing American Child: A Speculative Analysis," *The Journal of Social Issues*, 17 (1961), pp. 6 – 18.

[9]Donald Gilbert McKinley, *Social Class and Family Life* (New York: The Free Press, 1964).

preted these relationships within a frustration-aggression framework. The present findings, however, suggest that reactions to occupational frustration do not indiscriminately spill over into the family to sour fathers' relations with others. To the extent that the effects of frustrations are displaced into the family at all, they influence fathers' relations with boys and girls in quite different and highly selective ways. The influence of the same frustrating circumstances, we shall see, varies according to fathers' socialization functions for sons and daughters.

Consider first fathers' overall satisfaction or dissatisfaction with their jobs as one indicator of occupational frustration. When fathers who say they are "very satisfied" with their present jobs are compared with those reporting less satisfaction, the former are found to be somewhat more actively expressive than the latter, although the difference is greater in the working than in the middle class. If the analysis were not carried beyond this point, one could conclude that the frustrations attendant upon unsatisfying work result in a lower level of expressiveness toward children. However, a closer look reveals that the case is not this simple, for the expressive consequences of fathers' occupational disaffection are opposite for sons and daughters.

This is evident in Table VII.6 where the degree of job satisfaction is held constant in order to emphasize how its relationships to expressiveness vary with the sex of the child. (Self-employed fathers were not asked about job satisfaction, thus accounting for the smaller numbers in the middle class.) Although children's sex makes almost no difference at the most active level, fathers very satisfied with their work are far more likely to be verbally responsive and less apt to be passive in relation to sons than to daughters. That is, a high level of occupational satisfaction results in affective responsiveness to sons — albeit mostly verbal — and more passive detachment from daughters. In the middle class, only 22 per cent of the occupationally satisfied are passive toward sons compared to 45 per cent toward daughters; in the working class the respective percentages are 29 and 44. But among fathers who voice less occupational satisfaction the story is quite different. In the middle class, fathers' expressiveness toward sons and daughters is now similar and in the working class there is actually a reversal. That is, the occupationally disaffected are more responsive to daughters than to sons.

By any criterion, we cannot consider as great the differential effects of occupational dissatisfaction by sex of child shown in Table VII.6. Confidence in the relationships is somewhat enhanced by their general similarity in the two classes, and it can be further bolstered by seeing if relationships are reproduced with different indicators of

Table VII.6
Turinese Fathers' Job Satisfaction, Sex of Child, and the Expression
of Affection, by Social Class

| | MIDDLE CLASS | | | | WORKING CLASS | | | |
| | Occupationally Satisfied Fathers of: | | Occupationally Dissatisfied Fathers of: | | Occupationally Satisfied Fathers of: | | Occupationally Dissatisfied Fathers of: | |
Expression of Affection	Sons %	Daughters %	Sons %	Daughters %	Sons %	Daughters %	Sons %	Daughters %
Active	26	22	25	21	23	26	13	14
Verbal	52	33	40	45	48	30	47	60
Passive	22	45	35	34	29	44	40	26
Numbers	(23)	(18)	(20)	(29)	(35)	(27)	(45)	(50)
Significance of χ^2 (linear regression)	p < .30		n.s.		n.s.		p < .30	

occupational satisfaction-dissatisfaction. When more specific job rewards and deprivations are used in place of general satisfaction, similar patterns of relationships do occur. The amount of earnings one can look forward to is a case in point. Fathers, except the self-employed, were asked to assess their chances for an increase in salary. The overall class comparison in Table VII.7 is again rather inconclusive, and the most interesting results emerge only after the influence of the same occupational condition is observed separately for fathers' responsiveness to sons and to daughters. As in the case of overall job satisfaction, fathers who think their prospects for increased earnings are "very good" or "good" will be comparatively less passive in responding to sons but more passive in interaction with daughters. Among fathers who see their chances for earning more money as "little" or "none," however, these relationships are once again turned around. Where there is disenchantment with opportunities for economic improvement, there is also relatively greater responsiveness to daughters than to sons.

It is possible to accumulate more evidence in support of these relationships. Results closely paralleling the above occur, for example, when we look either at fathers' evaluations of their chances for occupational advancement or at the closeness with which they are supervised at work, indicating the frustration of a desire for autonomy. Also, there is a tendency for fathers who are occupationally disaffected, who anticipate the deprivation of rewards and who are most closely supervised to report themselves as frequently irritated with their children, particularly with their sons.

Does occupational fulfillment among American fathers also reduce emotional distance from their sons and increase it from daughters as among Turinese fathers? And does the frustration of occupational rewards also make fathers here less responsive to their sons and more to their daughters? These are complex connections that depend on the fusion of a number of conditions and, consequently, that make cross-national similarities problematic. Possible cultural differences in sex role definitions alone could prevent such similarities. If, for example, there has been in this country a confluence of socialization practices for boys and girls, the consequences of occupational experiences may not be dramatically different for fathers' relations with sons and daughters. There is an opportunity to pursue these questions empirically, for data similar to those I have presented were also gathered by Kohn in his national study of employed American men. The item regarding affectionate behavior, in fact, is identical in the two studies.

Since his nationwide sample was representative, it included men who are the heads of various sized households and who are fathers

Table VII.7

Turinese Fathers' Chances of Earning More Money, Sex of Child, and the Expression of Affection, by Social Class

	MIDDLE CLASS				WORKING CLASS			
	Chances Very Good-Good		Chances Little-None		Chances Very Good-Good		Chances Little-None	
	Fathers of:		Fathers of:		Fathers of:		Fathers of:	
Expression of Affection	Sons %	Daughters %	Sons %	Daughters %	Sons %	Daughters %	Sons %	Daughters %
Active	32	21	10	38	15	16	22	21
Verbal	40	38	50	33	53	42	43	54
Passive	28	41	40	29	32	42	35	25
Numbers	(47)	(53)	(30)	(24)	(34)	(31)	(46)	(46)
Significance of χ^2 (linear regression)	n.s.		$p < .10$		n.s.		n.s.	

of children of all ages. His interviewers listed all children in the family, recording their ages and sex. They then presented their questions about child-training values and practices with reference to a single designated child. The child selected as the focus of these questions was chosen by a prescribed procedure designed to insure that children of all ages and both sexes would have an equal chance to be the objects of the questions. Like the respondents in the earlier Washington study, the large majority of American fathers confine themselves to verbal expressions of affection, and especially so when children are over twelve years. Toward children beyond the age of twelve years, American fathers rarely demonstrate their affection actively by a hug or kiss. A sufficiently large number of fathers whose "focused-on" child was twelve or younger and who were actively expressive, however, permitted us to observe the relationship of occupation disaffection to affectionate behavior toward sons and daughters in the United States.

Several items in Kohn's study can be used to assess fathers' occupational fulfillment or disaffection. None are precisely the same as those employed in Turin, but they are nevertheless amenable to comparison. One question, for example, asked the American fathers how satisfied they were with their opportunities for occupational advancement. Their answers, along with the sex of their child about whom questions concerning expressiveness were directed, are presented in Table VII.8. The passive are combined with the verbally expressive because very few fathers — 28 in all — could be classified as passive.

Although there are some differences between the two countries, in essential respects there is a remarkable similarity. American fathers are not more likely to turn actively to sons than to daughters when they are satisfied. But when they are occupationally dissatisfied, two things happen: First, the proportion actively affectionate toward sons declines and, second, the proportion actively affectionate toward daughters markedly increases. American and Turinese fathers of both classes are similar, therefore, in that occupational frustration lessens expressiveness toward sons, but supports an active affectionate relation between fathers and daughters. While Americans and Turinese are not identical, it is most obvious that expressions of feelings for children are not blind reactions to satisfactions or frustrations.

If the relationship of occupational disaffection to expressiveness were the same for sons and daughters, then a frustration-aggression explanation would be the most parsimonious. The necessity to account for the differential impact of adverse occupational experiences by sex of child, however, imposes too great a burden on this explanation.

A more meaningful interpretation lies, I believe, in the different

Table VII.8

American Fathers' Satisfaction with Opportunities for Occupational Advancement and the Expression of Affection, by Sex of Child and Social Class[a]

	MIDDLE CLASS						WORKING CLASS					
	Very Satisfied Fathers of:		Moderately Satisfied Fathers of:		Dissatisfied Fathers of:		Very Satisfied Fathers of:		Moderately Satisfied Fathers of:		Dissatisfied Fathers of:	
Expression of Affection	*Sons* %	*Daughters* %	*Sons* %	*Daughters* %	*Sons* %	*Daughters* %	*Sons* %	*Daughters* %	*Sons* %	*Daughters* %	*Sons* %	*Daughters* %
Active Verbal or	20	23	21	27	15	45	20	24	19	31	9	37
passive	80	77	79	73	85	55	80	76	81	69	91	63
Numbers	(101)	(126)	(134)	(126)	(13)	(11)	(83)	(74)	(178)	(137)	(23)	(27)
Significance of χ^2 (linear Regression)	n.s.		p < .30		p < .20		n.s.		p < .02		p < .02	

[a]*Provided by Melvin L. Kohn from unpublished data.*

socialization functions of fathers for sons and for daughters. We can reasonably assume that it falls primarily to the father to serve as a model for the anticipatory occupational preparation of his son. He is best able to be a model when his own occupational experiences are gratifying and rewarding. In order that the occupationally fulfilled father be accepted by his son as a meaningful and motivating example, he must establish a positive affective relation with him. In the case of fathers of daughters, the same gratifying occupational experiences do not have the same consequences, simply because they do not have the same relevance to future roles of females. Where, however, the father fails to achieve rewards and gratifications from his work, he is inclined to forfeit his instrumental role vis-à-vis his son along with its expressive foundations. If his child is a female, he turns to her for a more expressive relationship, perhaps to compensate for what he lacks at work. Occupational frustration does not result in a generalized aggressiveness, but rather selective emotional detachments from and attachments to children. The patterns of selectivity that exist are apparently similar among industrialized nations.

DISCUSSION

Parents' feelings are not pure and simple. They encompass many dimensions, some of which may be in conflict; and they may be supported by a variety of conditions and have a variety of functions. From the flow and swirl of emotional transactions that course through the relations of parents and children, this chapter has chosen to examine affectionate expressiveness. While any choice from such a rich body of transactions is perforce limited, the one exercised here is, I believe, strategic. Expressiveness is anchored to specific behaviors that can easily be reported by parents without an inventory of feelings that requires a self-searching analysis. The characteristic manner of expressing feelings, furthermore, is not part of the unshared inner life of an individual; it is an experience that shapes the parent-child relationship and influences personality development. Finally, and very important from the perspective of this study, expressive behaviors help reveal some of the connections between the communication and exchange of emotions within the family setting and social circumstances.

What are these social circumstances and what is the nature of their relationships to parental expressiveness? Generally, parents' feelings and their expressions are intertwined with enduring patterns of socialization; these patterns, in turn, are shaped from parents' values and their experiences outside the family.

This process is illustrated by such facts as the expressiveness of middle-class mothers in interacting with sons. That expressiveness should vary with such social statuses as class and sex is by itself interesting. However, in asking why this should be so, the analysis leads to a set of relationships even more intriguing. These relationships suggest, essentially, that middle-class mothers are most actively responsive to sons because they are most likely to place their affection in the service of controlling their sons. They are not more oriented to control than other parents; but, when they are so oriented, they are also more likely to be highly affectionate. The major point to be underscored is that affection may be used as a rewarding response; as such it sustains behavior that parents wish their children to internalize during the socialization period. The expression of affection certainly does not function as a reinforcing mechanism for all parents. But those who do employ it in this way must find it not only emotionally gratifying, but a potent controlling mechanism as well.

Although fathers are secondary to mothers as sources of affection, their expressive behavior provides another illustration of the complex ways in which social conditions find their way into family relations. Specifically, there is an interaction between their occupational experiences and the sex of their children in influencing their expressiveness. Occupational fulfillment reduces emotional distance and irritability between fathers and sons; occupational frustration, on the other hand, makes fathers more responsive to daughters, but less responsive and more frequently irritable with sons. These relationships exist in both classes and they appear when different indicators of occupational disaffection are used. Their consistency supports the observation that the affectionate behavior of fathers is patterned by their socializing functions regarding sons and daughters. Fathers serve more directly as socializing models for sons than for daughters. How well they are able to do this, though, depends on how well they have mastered the conditions of their own occupations. For this reason the consequences of occupational frustration for expressiveness vary with the sex of the child.

Other studies conducted in the United States provide a basis for cross-national comparisons. There is at least one apparent cultural difference that has appeared: Americans are neither as passive nor as actively responsive as Turinese, but are much more likely to be verbally expressive. Nevertheless, in Washington and across the nation the relationships of the basic conditions of social class and parental sex to expressiveness are the same as in Turin. The cross-national correspondence was observed between the data from Kohn's study of American men and our study of Turinese fathers. These two investigations use the same question concerning expressiveness and quite comparable questions to determine occupational satisfaction. In most crucial respects, the very elaborate relationships between the occupational experiences of fathers, the sex of the children to whom they are reacting and the level of their demonstrativeness are similar. Such similarity across such dissimilar nations again points up the constraints and imperatives of social structural conditions on family relations.

This chapter completes our examination of parent-child relations in the Turinese family. We have looked at parents' values, their aspirations, the discipline they use and the affection they demonstrate. But the last four chapters have aimed at much more than these specific issues. They have attempted to provide a glimpse of the wondrous network of interrelationships that exists both between family members and between the family and society. Although these interrelationships have involved diverse issues, there is, I believe, a coherence among them. It is derived from the pervasive effects of social structure and the requirements of socialization on the internal processes of the family. And, judging by the basic cross-national correspondence that exists, the consequences of these conditions for parent-child relations are similar in nations of different cultural heritage.

It should be forcefully emphasized that these relations are very much more than blind and mechanical adaptations to impersonal forces. They are much more, also, than effective arrangements for accomplishing the job of child training. Parents, American or Turinese, have a tremendous emotional investment in their children and in the family. No institution surpasses it in its importance to individuals, or the extent to which it preempts their thoughts, feelings and actions. Family relations, although they change with time and maturity, are generally relations that people want to see perpetuated indefinitely. Some of the elements in parent-child relations function not to impart specific skills or behavioral patterns, but to create an attachment to the family that will preserve its solidarity long after the period of childhood is over.

The issue of family solidarity will be more clearly and explicitly involved in the following chapters. The first of these chapters deals with relations between husbands and wives. Of course, the spouses in this study are also the mothers and fathers of the fifth-graders, but there is more to marriage than the bonds resulting from spouses being parents of the same child. We will consider next some of the factors that nurture — and challenge — the solidarity of the marriage partnership.

VIII

Husbands and Wives

What conditions divide and unify spouses? In one form or another, this is the question most frequently asked by observers of modern marriage, and it is the question that guides the present chapter as well. Interest in what holds couples together and what pulls them apart seems to have accompanied the recognition that, as changes occur in society, the foundations of marriage must also change.[1] Not everything about marriage changes, of course. Even in the face of sweeping social alterations, certain basic elements of marriage are constant through time. The many requirements and obligations that must be satisfied to sustain the family are still divided between husbands and wives, as they were in earlier generations. Although the nature and content of marital roles undergo changes, spouses still depend upon each other for the performance of required tasks.[2] This interdependence of roles is itself an important and enduring source of marital unity.

[1]Most current treatments of marriage and family relations are cast in the framework of social change. As examples, see: Ernest W. Burgess, Harvey J. Locke and Mary Margaret Thomas, *The Family*, 3rd ed. (New York: The American Book Company, 1963); William J. Goode, *World Revolution and Family Patterns* (New York: The Free Press, 1963).

[2]The interdependence of roles and role allocations have been major themes in research into marriage in the United States. It is interesting that American students find the effect of wives' employment on the balance of dominance, power and authority particularly fascinating. Examples are: David M. Heer, "Dominance and the Working Wife," *Social Forces*, 36 (1958), pp. 341–347; Robert O. Blood and Robert L. Hamblin, "The Effect of Wife's Employment on the Family Power Structure," *Social Forces*, 36 (1958), pp. 347–352; Donald M. Wolfe, "Power and Authority in the Family," in Darwin Cartwright (ed.), *Studies in Social Power* (Ann Arbor: University of Michigan Press, 1959), pp. 99–117.

But the solidarity of modern marriage rests on other supports as well. Increasingly marriage bonds depend on what spouses share and less on how they functionally divide their roles. The kitchen, the children and the family economy continue to require the organization and allocation of effort. But traditional divisions are no longer as sharply drawn as they once were, nor do they define marital relations as completely as they once did. Increased leisure time, smaller families and the gainful employment of women have created new arrangements between husbands and wives. The essential qualities of these arrangements are reflected in *consensus* and *companionship*. Each emphasizes marital bonds based not on a division of labor, but on sharing and joint participation. Most of this chapter focuses on these two aspects of marriage.

We can understand consensus and companionship best by considering them against the background of changes that are affecting marital relations in Turin. There is no question that an alteration and reintegration of role relations are occurring in the family. By itself, change does not make Turinese families different from those in other societies. What is distinctive, however, and what makes Turin a particularly advantageous site in which to examine consensus and companionship, is that the alterations in roles are abrasively contrary to traditional social norms and legal codes, especially those placing the status of women below that of their husbands. Consequently, the emergence of new elements in marital relations that bespeak reciprocity and sharing may lead to tension and discord. As these elements become institutionalized and absorbed by husbands and wives, they leave a wake of conflict between older norms and current conceptions. I do not want to paint a picture of marriage in Turin as fragile and vulnerable to disaffection; but neither do I want to imply that it is permeated throughout by harmony, consensus and companionship. Indeed, the same marriage typically embraces a number of diverse and contradictory elements that reflect both distance and closeness. For most Turinese spouses change is something that has not run its course but is still very much in progress.

THE CHANGING NORMATIVE CONTEXT OF MARRIAGE

In many — perhaps most — Turinese marriages double standards of rights, privileges and penalties exist. These differences are built into the day-to-day relations between husbands and wives and are supported by pervasive cultural norms, by the legal codes of Italy that favor the husband and by religious mores. Not surprisingly, in numerous partnerships each spouse still accepts as unquestioningly proper the superordinate-subordinate arrangement of roles. Such marriages are free of tensions that arise from clashing role definitions. These tensions are also absent in marriages that no longer bear any vestige of hierarchical husband-wife relations. But most Turinese are neither blind in their allegiance to traditional norms nor completely free of them. Typically, couples are in the process of discarding such norms, in some instances with ease, in other instances only because of considerable opposition to the norms from women. Much of the following materials are primarily relevant to the latter group.

We can gain some sense of the prevailing normative context of marriage from the answers to an open-ended question that asked wives what they thought were the main differences between men and women in present-day Italy. Since we addressed this question only to women we cannot know the corresponding views of their husbands. Almost all the women acknowledging important differences pointed to husband-wife inequalities. Most comments identified the various areas of inequality: the greater freedom and rights enjoyed by husbands, a double standard of morality, the greater burden and responsibility of women. Some comments also revealed what women considered the sources of inequality. Some placed the blame directly on the legal codes, others ascribed it generally to tradition and some to the peculiarities of their own husbands.

The comments of the women aptly illustrated what they considered unjust. "According to the law," one said, "men are the bosses and I don't feel that this is right. There should be equal rights for both." A few wives directed their ire at specific legal codes: "They (women) do not have equal rights in marriage; for instance, it is humiliating that a child's legal guardian is not its mother if the father dies." And, of course, they expressed bitterness concerning the differential penalties meted out to men and women for the same transgressions. "Because of the law there are ridiculous differences. Women are subject to imprisonment if they leave their husbands or are unfaithful to them, even if they are separated." Regardless of whether or not these are accurate interpretations of the law, many Turinese women regard it as both a cause of and a mechanism for enforcing their inferior status, and the law is thus deeply resented. The resentment, perhaps, has played some part in the current review by the national parliament of Italian laws bearing on the rights and status of women.

By and large, however, the law is quite remote from daily experience, and Italian women, like people everywhere, are mainly concerned with the things that are visible and with which they must grapple directly. Consequently, most remarks concerned the everyday conditions they experience as wives and as those responsible for running the household. These roles demand a lot of work and attention, and some women think they bear the burden exclusively and unfairly. One complained, "Women are tied to their house and children and must work like dogs." Another said, "Women's 'independence' consists of working twice as much. Husbands still demand as much from a wife as they once did, and on top of this the wife works outside the house."

Women are irritated not because they do too much, but because husbands acknowledge too little. They do not want to be recognized only as useful helpmates; more important to them, they want appreciation and esteem as worthy *persons*. One woman expressed some of this sentiment when she said, "Men have all the advantages, women have the burden of the home and family. Life is always worse for the woman; it is an annulment of personality." Another agreed, "How lucky to be born a man! If a woman talks, she is stupid; if a man talks, he is right." A third woman stated, "Men feel too important. They feel that because they are the head of the family they have the right to do what they like. They never ask the woman's advice, though she may have clear ideas. She is never held in consideration." Finally, one complained, "A woman in Italy is half-slave to her husband."

Their husbands may view them as worthless, as hand maidens, as inferior, but women do not see themselves in this way. In fact, they can convert the injustices of their lot to serve as signs of moral superiority over men. One wife, after saying that Italian women had less freedom than those of other nations, stated that maybe this was beneficial since it enabled women to set a good example for their children. Thus, although they are in a subordinate position, women possess the important virtues. "In marriage the man has the authority which has to be respected and it is the woman who acts with diplomacy and kindness." Furthermore, the authority of men, rather than reflecting strength, may betray weakness. "My husband always wants to feel himself the boss," a woman said, "because he cares too much what people say. We care less." Their subjugation and suffering, then, signify to some women their own nobility. It is one mechanism that perhaps enables them to salvage self-esteem where their husbands' esteem for them is lacking. Other examples indicate that the ascendancy of males mirrors such characterological deficiencies as "egotism" or "superficiality." In contrast, women described themselves in such terms as "sensitive" and having good "common sense." In this way they prevent subordination of *role* from becoming the inferiority of *person*, and they make the oppressor morally and characterologically inferior to the oppressed. Nevertheless, it is not enough for a woman to think well of herself; she would like her husband to acknowledge her virtues, too.

By no means do all Turinese women think inequalities are bad. Several indicated that traditional husband-wife relations embody proper and natural distinctions between sex roles and, indeed, preserve the essential and important feminine-masculine differences. Some considered the United States the land of lost sex identity: "The Italian man wants to be boss. However, I prefer it this way. I wouldn't like to have a husband who lets himself be bossed as they do in America." In a similar vein, another wife stated, "A woman must always feel protected by the man and must always ask his advice. I don't like it in America where the women are the bosses and they feel superior to men because they work too. I prefer to be protected by a man." The issue of sex identification was firmly anchored to the kitchen for another housewife who said, "If my husband were to wash the plates for me, I wouldn't feel that he were a man any longer." In the eyes of a few women relations between the sexes have already changed too much. One succinct statement expressed this sentiment: "Today women are superordinate to men. Instead men should be men and women should be women." A clear note of alarm was sounded in another view of the changes taking place: "Women nowadays have too much emancipation. They have the same rights as men — they even smoke in the streets. It's exaggerated! They are losing their femininity."

The changes in motion, then, are to many women a source of discontent. Some see themselves unwillingly trapped in traditional roles, subordinate to their husbands and unable to enjoy the same rights, opportunities, privileges or protection by the law. The thrust of the changes is in a direction counter to older role definitions, resulting in dissatisfaction and impatience. Even the traditionalists are alarmed by change, though for very different reasons. Their femininity is threatened as established sex-role differentiation breaks down. Being a housewife in Turin is no easy job, but it appears to provide for some women a domain that they can feel is their own. They do not welcome change as an opportunity, but regard it as a challenge to a role they are able to claim exclusively as theirs. For these women, change is a threat to the correct, proper and natural expression of male-female relations.

Whether Turinese women actively resent their subordination, accept it as the natural order of things or are indifferent to it, we should not underestimate their power and their ability to influence their husbands. Even though they accept the male head of the family as the "boss," many wives regard them as rather dependent fellows who need a woman's clear head and steady hand. This conclusion results from answers to an openended question asking, "Do you find that men need the guidance and protection of a strong woman?" A majority either denied this outright or accepted it only under limited conditions. A sizeable minority, however, indicated that their experience led to an affirmative answer.

Some women also regarded men in general and their own husbands in particular as childlike. One woman reported that she told her husband, "You men are always children who have to be cared for, first by your mothers and then by your wives." And another said, "They are like big children — I have to do everything for him." Wives were not always so willing to humor their husbands, for sometimes they became impatient and angry. "If the woman is weak, the marriage is reduced to failure. It is the woman who must do almost everything and who shouts at her husband as well as her sons." This lady made no distinction between the management of her husband and of her children.

Several wives were convinced that to withhold active guidance and control is to invite dire consequences. One, apparently doubtful of the willingness or ability of men to maintain fidelity, said that without her watchfulness her husband would take "a bad address." Others were particularly concerned about their husband's susceptibility to squandering money. Clearly, these wives regarded men as more vulnerable to temptations than women. The matter was put explicitly by a wife who said, "Men are weak and only after marriage we understand this."

Faced with the necessity to guide and protect their men, not all women said they resorted to shouting and cajoling. In fact, many thought that the most effective guidance is that which is not recognized. Thus, one lady stated, "They need it [guidance] but we must not tell them. My husband himself says to me 'Without you, I feel I am lost.'" Another put it even more plainly: "In front of a husband it is best not to seem a strong woman; but I try to have influence over him without letting him notice it." Women are not altogether without power in families that show a traditional subordination of wives to husbands.

These statements help to point up the presence of normative inequality in marriage, the various reactions of women to a status socially defined as inferior to their husbands' and some of the mechanisms they employ in dealing with a subordination many of them find noxious. By intention we have emphasized the irritations, disaffections and conflicts between spouses. They deserve emphasis because they are indicative of pressures and counterpressures on changing role relations. But conflict and division do not characterize and cannot fully describe husband-wife relations in Turin. Even when feelings of injustice and abuse exist in a marriage, the couple may stand as one in many respects. For example, they probably hold the same values for their children and strive after the same goals. When an important issue arises requiring that a decision be made, it is likely to be made jointly.[3] And, as we shall now see, many couples possess the same perceptions and sentiments and look to each other for support and shared experiences.

CONSENSUS

It matters little whether or not one sees eye-to-eye on important issues with the grocery clerk, a neighbor or an employer, but it does matter to spouses. Their relations are continuous, they are invested with deep emotions, they span countless problems and they confront a parade of questions that must be dealt with. Given the nature of the interaction it entails, marriage cannot be impervious to disaccord, at least that which exists in important areas. Consensus, however, should not be confused with happiness nor disagreement with marital discontent, for shared values and practices may arise out of conditions that have no relevance to harmony or disharmony. Perhaps the absence of consensus makes marital solidarity difficult to achieve; but its presence is no sure sign that solidarity exists. Nevertheless, consensus is probably both a consequence of and a condition for husband-wife communication and is thus critically relevant to the kinds of adaptations couples can make to the circumstances of their lives.[4]

Eventually the analysis of consensus must ask what the consensus is about. The practices and precepts potentially entering the interactions of spouses define a wide spectrum. A plethora of situations and problems intersect at marriage and family, and each encounter with these situations and problems could conceivably make agreement and disagreement a critical matter for spouses. But consensus is not equally relevant to all situations nor to all issues, for certain priorities reduce some disagreements to trivialities while elevating others to considerable importance. Indeed, examining the correspond-

[3]Husbands and wives were independently asked which of them was responsible for major decisions. An overwhelming majority of spouses agreed that important decisions were made jointly.

[4]In his attempts to establish ways to study marital consensus, Morgan treats consensus and communication as intimately linked. James N. Morgan, "Some Pilot Studies of Communication and Consensus in the Family," *Public Opinion Quarterly*, 32 (1968), pp. 113 – 121.

ence between spouses in the priorities they assign to various matters is itself a fruitful way to look at consensus.

Here we cannot even sample the many issues to which consensus is of consequence. Those we can examine are confined to the family domain and, more specifically, to children. Remember that the husbands and wives in our sample are all parents of fifth-grade children and that many of them have older children as well. They are deeply launched into marriage, with the days of mate selection, courtship and marriage without children well behind them. Our inquiry entered their lives during a time when their energies and concerns were directed toward raising and socializing children. Against the disadvantage of looking only at child-related issues is the advantage that parents are deeply involved in these issues and consensus on them is thus a matter of some consequence to husbands and wives alike. Nevertheless, the question of the generality of consensus and disaccord between partners will be unanswered; we shall not know, that is, whether agreement or disagreement concerning children is related to consensus and divergence on other issues.

The available data permit a useful distinction between *role consensus* and *value consensus*. We evaluated role consensus by a battery of questions directed independently to husband and wives asking them to designate the spouse primarily responsible for different child-rearing tasks. For example, we asked which parent was more strict with the fifth-grader. By comparing their answers to such an item, we could determine whether they agreed or disagreed. We could also pinpoint the nature of the consensus to discover whether the mother, father or neither parent was dominant. Similarly, we could distinguish disagreement according to whether either parent claimed for himself a more active role than was accorded to him by his partner or if either parent claimed more for his partner than for himself. Variations in the internal patterns of consensus and disagreement merit a rather extensive analysis of their own, but here I will be concerned only with the extent of agreement and disagreement in response to selected questions that yield a measure of consensual perception of role allocation between the spouses.

The questions used to determine role consensus covered several issues, but they mainly concentrated on the restraint of children. We developed a composite index of consensus within this area from four items asking: which parent was more strict, which was more inclined to limit the child, which was more inclined to act with absolute firmness and which was more inclined to impose his wishes. We scored husband-wife pairs on a scale from four, indicating that they agreed on all items, to zero, indicating that they agreed on none.

The determination of value consensus required a different approach. Value consensus hinges on agreement about the characteristics and priorities parents think desirable for the child. We used the parental values analyzed in Chapter IV to assess the degree of value consensus. Consensus on values was determined by comparing the characteristics wives considered first in importance among the list of seventeen with the priority accorded to the same characteristic by their husbands. Thus, if the value rated as first in importance by a wife was also given first or second priority by her husband, we concluded that this represented close consensus. If he ranked her first choice as his third, or indicated that he considered it important but not among the top three, we regarded consensus as moderate. Finally, if he regarded his wife's top choice as altogether unimportant, we concluded that there was a lack of consensus. Built into this procedure, therefore, is a gradation of consensus and disagreement. We can reverse the procedure, of course, to observe wives' priorities of husbands' first-ranked characteristics. This yields a slightly different distribution, but one still sensitive to the underlying conditions associated with consensus. We turn now to these conditions and their relationship to role and value consensus.

SOCIAL DIFFERENTIATION. One obvious yet important condition would seem to exert considerable force toward achieving consensus in most marriages: the same socio-economic background of husbands and wives. This alone produces perceptual and value convergence between spouses. Yet, in highly differentiated societies spouses not uncommonly bring to marriage different background characteristics and attitudes that interfere with the formation of shared perspectives.

One respect in which husbands and wives may differ is their status origins. We showed earlier that the levels of parental aspirations are highest when the occupational statuses of wives' fathers are higher than those of their husbands. In regard to consensus only the equality or inequality of status backgrounds is relevant, not which spouse's father was higher or lower in occupational standing. Does status differentiation influence consensus in marriage? Table VIII.1 indicates that it does. The tabulated units are married pairs rather than individuals and the status characteristics and consensus scores are attributes of the marriage and not of husbands and wives separate from each other. In marriages where the spouses come from unequal status backgrounds there is less likely to be agreement as to responsibility for the child's restraint. These differences are not great, particularly in the working class. But any effect of this global background characteristic is most remarkable, for we must remember that its influence on consensus remains after the accumulation of all the

Table VIII.1

Relative Occupational Status of Turinese Spouses' Fathers and Role Consensus, by Social Class

Number of Restrictive Items Agreed Upon	Middle-Class Spouses		Working-Class Spouses	
	Status Equal %	*Status Unequal* %	*Status Equal* %	*Status Unequal* %
3-4 (high consensus)	57	42	40	31
2	24	31	36	45
0-1 (low consensus)	19	27	24	24
Numbers	(59)	(78)	(98)	(29)

Significance of χ^2
(linear regression) $p < .10$ n.s.

shared experiences accrued during a minimum of eleven years of marriage. Thus, status characteristics ascribed long before marriage continue to influence the structure of marital relations and the formation of consensus.

These status discrepancies affect value consensus in the same way they influence role consensus. Table VIII.2 demonstrates that within each class closest agreement again exists between partners of equal status backgrounds and least agreement between partners of unequal status backgrounds. In the middle class, for example, 45 per cent of the husbands in equal-status marriages considered the value to which their wives gave first priority as their own first or second choice in comparison to 31 per cent of the husbands whose status backgrounds were different from their wives'. The latter group were commensurately more likely to assess their wives' first choices as wholly unimportant. The directions of these relationships are the same among working-class partners. Differential status, which divides people in so many important respects in the larger society, apparently has a divisive consequence in marriage also.[5]

---

[5]Goode notes that families opposed to inter-class marriages — usually those of the ascendant class — base their opposition on predicted husband-wife conflict and on the confusion it creates in the socialization of children. Although a function of such opposition is to maintain class homogony, the justifications for resisting inter-class marriage would appear from this evidence to have some basis in fact. William J. Goode, *The Family* (Englewood Cliffs, N.J.: Prentice-Hall, 1964), pp. 82 – 83.

Religiousness is another factor affecting role and value consensus. The effects of religiousness on the two areas of consensus under examination are certainly not profound, but they provide an additional bit of evidence indicating that differentiating elements brought into marriage militate against consensus. The Protestants and Jews in Turin are too few to have merited a question about religious affiliation. We asked all respondents, though, whether they were believers. In the majority of cases both husbands and wives stated that they were. In a very few instances, husbands and their wives jointly disclaimed religious beliefs or expressed some strong reservations about religious institutionalization or clergy. And, particularly pertinent to our present interest, in several cases one of the spouses, almost always the husband, reported either disbelief or negative feelings while the other expressed unreserved belief. Let us compare the consensus of couples who have the same religious posture with that of those who differ in their religiousness.

Looking first at consensus regarding restrictive roles, we find that in marriages where spouses differed on religion, a smaller proportion agreed on the items than where both were unequivocably religious or where both held reservations about religious beliefs. This tendency was the same in each class, though the differences in the working class are quite small.

In the case of value consensus, there is a clear likelihood that

Table VIII.2

Relative Occupational Status of Turinese Spouses' Fathers
and Value Consensus, by Social Class

Husbands' Ranking of Wives' First- Ranked Parental Value	Middle-Class Spouses		Working-Class Spouses	
	Status Equal %	*Status Unequal* %	*Status Equal* %	*Status Unequal* %
First or second (high consensus)	45	31	39	29
Third or important	24	31	30	26
Unimportant (low consensus)	31	38	31	45
Numbers	(65)	(83)	(104)	(31)

Significance of χ^2
(linear regression)   p < .20   p < .20

Table VIII.3

Religious Differentiation of Turinese Spouses and Role Consensus, by Social Class

Number of Restrictive Items Agreed Upon	Middle-Class Spouses		Working-Class Spouses	
	Similar Religiousness %	Different Religiousness %	Similar Religiousness %	Different Religiousness %
3-4 (high consensus)	43	32	38	36
2	35	40	41	21
0-1 (low consensus)	22	28	21	43
Numbers	(112)	(25)	(121)	(14)

Significance of χ^2
(linear regression)   n.s. $p < .30$

husbands whose religious feelings are similar to those of their wives will be more disposed to give first or second place to the value their wives rank first; this will occur less frequently among partners whose religious views are at variance. And, conversely, in both classes husbands whose religiousness does not correspond to their wives' are also most likely to regard the very value that is of utmost importance to their wives as being entirely without importance. Table VIII.4 demonstrates this relationship.

Table VIII.4

Religious Differentiation of Turinese Spouses and Value Consensus, by Social Class

Husbands' Ranking of Wives' First-Ranked Parental Value	Middle-Class Spouses		Working-Class Spouses	
	Similar Religiousness %	Different Religiousness %	Similar Religiousness %	Different Religiousness %
First or second	39	31	39	25
Third or important	32	29	27	35
Unimportant	29	40	34	40
Numbers	(112)	(35)	(122)	(20)

Significance of χ^2
(linear regression) $p < .30$ n.s.

The importance of the associations between status and religious differentiation and role and value consensus does not lie with their magnitude, however. What is impressive is that there are any consistent relationships at all. We could assume that social differentiations would matter less and less under the daily flow of interaction and that they would no longer constitute conditions for disaccord after so many years of marriage. They continue, however, to exert some influence.

One differentiating characteristic of spouses has a greater impact on consensus than either status or religious divisions: the relative age of the couple. I do not refer to the absolute ages of individual husbands and wives but to the age disparity between them. Unlike status inequality, this structural feature of marriage is not something rooted only to the past. It has a constancy, a presence, which can pervade daily interactions, influence communications and, consequently, very directly implicate consensus. Tables VIII.5 and VIII.6 categorize marriages by the magnitude of age differences between husbands and wives. In relationship to agreement about responsibility for restraint of the child, consensus between couples decreases as disparity in age increases.

Age disparity stands in a similar relationship to value consensus, although in the working class it is less clearly linear. Nevertheless, in this consensual area also age relations can act as a barrier to agreement about the most desirable characteristic for the fifth-grade child. When spouses are relatively close in age, they are more likely

Table VIII.5

Magnitude of Age Disparity Between Turinese Spouses and Role
Consensus, by Social Class

	Middle-Class Spouses				Working-Class Spouses			
Number of Restrictive Items Agreed Upon	0 to 4 Years %	5 to 9 Years %	10 to 14 Years %	15 or more Years %	0 to 4 Years %	5 to 9 Years %	10 to 14 Years %	15 or more Years %
3-4	49	41	33	20	39	38	30	25
2	30	38	42	50	42	42	39	25
0-1	21	21	25	30	19	20	31	50
Numbers	(33)	(66)	(24)	(10)	(41)	(58)	(23)	(12)

Significance of χ^2
(linear regression)   p $<$ .20   p $<$ .10

Table VIII.6

Magnitude of Age Disparity Between Turinese Spouses and Value Consensus, by Social Class

Husbands' Ranking of Wives' First-Ranked Parental Value	Middle-Class Spouses				Working-Class Spouses			
	0 to 4 Years %	5 to 9 Years %	10 to 14 Years %	15 or more Years %	0 to 4 Years %	5 to 9 Years %	10 to 14 Years %	15 or more Years %
First or second	32	24	25	18	36	35	34	27
Third or important	43	33	25	29	30	35	25	27
Unimportant	25	43	50	53	34	30	41	46
Numbers	(40)	(67)	(24)	(17)	(47)	(59)	(24)	(11)
Significance of χ^2 (linear regression)	$p < .05$				n.s.			

to share the same priorities; the same understandings do not form as readily where there is a wide age discrepancy. The exchanges that take place in marriage ordinarily result in a convergence of understanding. But should the structure of the marriage be such that the partners are set apart, communications become more difficult and are less likely to result in consensus.

The foregoing data support the observation that the forces that fuse perceptions and values in the larger society are those that also underlie consensus in marriage; the lines of demarcation that generally set people apart, also contribute to dissension in marriage. Status, religion and age may bind together those who share these characteristics by providing common vantage points and conditions from which judgments are made and by which precepts and practices are formed. But to the extent that such elements of social organization unite some people, they also separate them from others who are located elsewhere in the system, who experience different conditions and who possess different characteristics. It is not surprising, of course, to find a lack of consensus among strangers having neither similar locations in the social system nor opportunities to interact. It is surprising to find that these same social conditions also produce dissension among those who stand in the very closest and most durable relationship to one another. The potency of these divisive forces is a most remarkable phenomenon for they continue to operate in marriage against the flow of years of interaction. Husband-wife relations, however autonomous and self-generating they may appear, are not set apart from elements of the larger society. This is confirmed by an examination of marital companionship.

MARITAL COMPANIONSHIP

Companionship focuses on the interests and activities that husbands and wives have in common. More is implicated in companionship than merely doing the same things at the same time. It reflects the affinities that exist between the partners as persons and their use of each other as important reference figures and as sources of emotional support. These are some of the elements found in what Burgess and Locke have described as the companionship family, which they thought was characteristic of contemporary United States.[6] They saw the American family system marked by egalitarianism, joint decision making, affection and comradeship. Companionship as employed here is more narrow than the conception of Burgess and Locke; nevertheless, I shall continue to use the term.

---

[6]Ernest W. Burgess and Harvey J. Locke, *The Family, From Institution to Companionship* (New York: American Book Company, 1945).

We conceptualized two dimensions as reflecting on husband-wife companionship: the leisure time they spent together, and their use of each other as sources of support. Two questions specifically considered sharing leisure time. The first asked wives how frequently during the week their husbands had recreation outside the home by themselves or with other men, and the second inquired how frequently they and their husbands visited friends together. A third item dealt with supportiveness; it asked to whom the wife turned when she needed help or advice. The items were scored in a simple summary fashion, the highest score being three and the lowest zero. A wife received a score of three if she said her husband had no regular extra-familial recreation, if she also reported that together they visited with friends at least once a week and if she indicated that she was more likely to turn to her husband than to anyone else for help and advice. There are other aspects of companionship in marriage, but this measure is suitable for identifying some of the conditions that influence spouses to turn toward or away from each other and to use each other as supportive resources.

MARITAL COMPANIONSHIP AND MODERNITY. Companionship is probably a close correlate of modernizing trends in a society, for it is most likely to be found only under conditions generated by industrialized urban life. It is an element in marriage that is compatible with conjugal patterns of family relations where, Goode points out, "The small marital unit is the main place where the emotional input-output balance of the individual husband and wife is maintained, where their psychic wounds can be salved or healed."[7] The precise process by which modern social and economic conditions have brought about the present forms of the conjugal family and its marital companionship is, as Goode emphasizes, still an empirical mystery. It would be ideally desirable to relate specific social changes to the growth of companionship in marriage, but this cannot be done. To identify and trace changes and developments as they affect marital relations require a historical or longitudinal study of great duration. As a substitute for such a design, I shall bring into the analysis variables in which the passage of time is an inherent element: age and length of residence in Turin.

Although they all have fifth-grade children, the parents in the sample described a wide age range, extending from their late twenties into their sixties. The sample included those who were quite young after World War II and those who were adults before it. The younger parents, consequently, were born, socialized and married under social and economic conditions extensively different from and more ad-

7Goode, World Revolution, p. 9.

vanced than those experienced by the older. Do they differ also with regard to companionship? The answer is affirmative, though the relationship is not perfectly linear. The major differences are between those younger or older than 45 years of age. In a modal way this age distinguishes those whose adolescence was completed before Italy's involvement in World War II and those whose adolescence followed. The association between age and companionship is closest when the ages of husbands are used rather than those of their wives. This may reflect on the measure being used, where the companionship scores depend more on the dispositions and actions of husbands than on their wives. At any rate, since Table VIII.7 requires information from both husbands and wives, it can include only cases where there were paired interviews. In both age categories there is a greater proportion of middle- than working-class spouses in close companionship. Within each class, however, younger husbands are unquestionably more likely to be close companions than are the older. The net effect of class and age, consequently, is to produce the greatest difference in companionship between the younger middle class and older working class.

The point of Table VIII.7 is that age differences capture a myriad of conditions attendant upon increased urbanization and industrialization; early exposure to these conditions, in turn, shapes attitudes toward marriage. The younger husbands, socialized and married at a time of heightened material and social development, are more disposed toward companionship. In this way age is related to companionship in marriage, but the relationship is quite indirect.

The length of time a family has been exposed to the conditions of

Table VIII.7

Age of Turinese Husbands and Marital Companionship, by Social Class

Companionship Score	Middle-Class Spouses		Working-Class Spouses	
	Less Than 45 Years %	*45 Years and Over* %	*Less Than 45 Years* %	*45 Years and Over* %
2-3 (close)	68	49	48	29
1	25	37	40	52
0 (distant)	7	14	12	19
Numbers	(95)	(57)	(105)	(46)

Significance of χ^2 (linear regression)	$p < .05$	$p < .05$

an industrialized city may provide a more direct and clearer picture of the effects of modernity on marriage than does age. The vast majority of people moving to the city come from non-industrial areas, small towns or rural villages. It is very rare, for example, that a person comes to Turin from Milan, Florence or Rome unless, perhaps, he is a government functionary. Such cases notwithstanding, we can assume that those who moved to Turin during the 1960s are for the first time living under conditions completely urbanized and heavily industrialized. And, in fact, we find the least companionship in the families that have been in residence in Turin less than a decade. The class marginals in Table VIII.8 are also informative, for they indicate that relatively few middle-class couples have resided in Turin for less than 10 years while almost 50 per cent of the working-class couples have been in the city for less than a decade.

We might expect that age and length of residence in combination are additively related to marital companionship, and this is the case. If one is both young enough to have been socialized under modern conditions and has lived in an industrialized urban context for a decade or more, his marriage is most likely to be characterized by closeness. If he is a young, short-term resident or an older but long-term resident, there is still a good chance of close companionship. But when a person is both older and a short-term resident, his marital relationship is probably marked by greater distance. These additive associations are found in both classes.

In sum, the many processes and conditions found in the urban-industrial complex exert a force on the form of marital relations.

Table VIII.8

Length of Residence in Turin and Marital Companionship, by Social Class

Companion-ship Score	Middle-Class Spouses		Working-Class Spouses	
	Residents More Than 10 Years %	Residents Less Than 10 Years %	Residents More Than 10 Years %	Residents Less Than 10 Years %
2-3 (close)	64	46	51	31
1	27	39	37	51
0 (distant)	9	15	12	18
Numbers	(124)	(28)	(78)	(73)

Significance of χ^2
(linear regression) $p < .20$ $p < .05$

Table VIII.9

Age of Husband, Length of Residence in Turin, and Marital
Companionship, by Social Class

| | MIDDLE-CLASS SPOUSES | | | | WORKING-CLASS SPOUSES | | | |
| | Younger than 45 | | 45 and Older | | Younger than 45 | | 45 and Older | |
Companionship Score	More Than 10 Years Residence %	Less Than 10 Years Residence %	More Than 10 Years Residence %	Less Than 10 Years Residence %	More Than 10 Years Residence %	Less Than 10 Years Residence %	More Than 10 Years Residence %	Less Than 10 Years Residence %
2-3 (close)	72	50	51	33	56	39	41	13
1	22	36	35	50	35	45	42	64
0 (distant)	6	14	14	17	9	16	17	23
Numbers	(73)	(22)	(51)	(6)	(54)	(51)	(24)	(22)
Significance of χ^2 (linear regression)	p < .05		n.s.		p < .10		p < .10	

More study is required to delineate the particular processes and conditions that are implicated. But it seems likely that such factors as the romantic selection of mates, the physical separation of the household from the extended family, the segregation of work and family, the freeing of time from the logistical demands of home and the more equal participation of women in social institutions — education and politics — are among the concomitants of an urban-industrial setting that turn spouses toward each other for support and companionship. From indications brought together here, it appears that the more completely one is assimilated into these conditions, the more completely will his marriage be based on companionship.

It would be extremely misleading to assume that influences of modern life are in but one direction, that which results in marital companionship. The entrance of women into occupational life is a case in point. It could be argued, as Burgess and Locke have done, that occupational opportunities have elevated the status of women and this, supposedly, has brought them into closer comradeship with their husbands. Perhaps such opportunities do create more equality for women, but our evidence indicates that women's employment does not enhance marital closeness; on the contrary, it is inimical to it. We can demonstrate this by comparing families where the wife has outside employment with those where she is a housewife. Regardless of class, employed wives are *less* likely to have close companionship with husbands. There is a reasonable and simple explanation for such a relationship. Working wives spend less leisure with husbands because they have less leisure to spend; they do not turn to their husbands for support because they are together less.

Though reasonable, this explanation is incorrect. The reduction in companionship is for reasons other than a reduction in time and opportunities to be together. This can be asserted on the grounds that wives employed at occupations whose status is equal to or exceeds that of their husbands are more likely to be withdrawn from close companionship than those wives who are also employed, but at lesser jobs. This is indicated in Table VIII.10. Since this table contains information provided entirely by females, it includes all the women in the sample, regardless of whether their husbands were also interviewed. Essentially, the wives of both classes engaged in white-collar occupations are most distant from their husbands. In the middle-class, these women at least approach, if not actually equal or surpass, the status of their husbands. In the working-class the occupational status of white-collar wives clearly exceeds that of their husbands. Occupational opportunities for women, part of the picture of contemporary life in industrial settings, apparently can eventuate in competition between spouses — with divisive consequences for marriage.

Table VIII.10

Employment of Turinese Wives and Marital Companionship, by Social Class

Companionship Score	Middle-Class Wives			Working-Class Wives		
	White-Collar Employment %	Manual Employment %	Housewives %	White-Collar Employment %	Manual Employment %	Housewives %
2-3 (close)	45	58	65	29	40	49
1	41	26	27	42	40	41
0 (distant)	14	16	8	29	20	10
Numbers	(49)	(19)	(207)	(7)	(63)	(152)
Significance of χ^2 (linear regression)		p < .01			p < .05	

Perhaps these effects of women's employment are culturally distinctive of Italy. Employment in general, and that which indicates achievement in particular, contradicts the social definitions of female subordination. In the absence of data permitting cross-national comparisons, we cannot be sure that the consequences of occupational achievement by females are especially divisive in Italy, but I doubt it. Indeed they conform to Williams's observation of American society that the employment of women is least disruptive of marital solidarity when their jobs are not at status levels competitive with those of their husbands.[8] Of one thing we can be certain, however. The modern urban context is host both to conditions that draw spouses together and to those that are barriers to closeness.

DISCUSSION

Division and unity have been the themes of this chapter. These issues, I believe, are of critical importance to Italian men and women. The pervasive uncertainty of the surrounding world and its social institutions means that one's security system can be at stake in the cohesiveness and strains of marriage.

Both division and unity are influenced by circumstances residing outside marriage itself. There is, first, a context of laws and social norms bearing on marriage and the status of women that, at least in Turin, is a source of some resentment and conflict. Within this context, status and age relations, religiousness, assimilation into the circumstances of modern urban-industrial life and the occupational location of women are conditions that converge on marriage and the family, creating pressures and counter-pressures for accord and disaccord, for closeness and distance, for solidarity and division.

This analysis considered two criteria of unity: consensus and companionship. These are contemporary foundations of marital solidarity that have resulted from broad social and economic changes. The more traditional bases of marital solidarity seem to have given way to shared perceptions and values, friendship and support. Consensus and companionship appear to be now well-established features of Turinese marriage. It is unfortunate that there are no comparable data from other societies.[9] Impressionistically, however, Turinese spouses do not seem radically different from American husbands and

[8]Robin M. Williams, Jr., *American Society* (New York: Alfred A. Knopf, 1959), pp. 59 – 60.

[9]The lack of comparative data reflects, I believe, more on the methods of family research than on interests. Studies of marriage and family typically collect data only from wives and often only about wives. This precludes the examination of properties of the marriage itself, such as consensus.

wives in these respects. Considering that cultural norms militate against the sharing of precepts and practices in Italy, any similarity between the two societies is remarkable, indeed.

Judging by the criteria of consensus and companionship, it is clear that marital solidarity is sensitive to a variety of factors originating beyond marriage itself. If all the conditions affecting marriage could be seen together, we would undoubtedly find united families upon whom there are divisive pressures and many divided families upon whom there are unifying pressures. If there is a typical marriage in modern and changing society, it is one that enjoys harmony and is, at the same time, beset with conflict.

IX

Kinship Relations

Industrialization has shrunk the boundaries of family interaction. Several conditions intrinsic to modern social life suggest that the extended family has atrophied, leaving the nuclear unit as the remaining meaningful system. The highly specialized needs of industrialized societies produce an ever changing level of skills and training and occupations are no longer passed on from father to son. Each generation is different from the preceding and from the one to follow, and such discontinuity disrupts intergenerational family relations. Also, modern societies require a geographically mobile labor force; their populations are concentrated in urban areas where housing is spatially limited; and they create social mobility which contributes to status distance among relatives. These are among the circumstances that lead one logically to expect that only the most immediate family remains of appreciable importance.

In this instance the logic may be sound, but it is inconsistent with the findings of empirical investigations. Studies consistently show a continued attachment of nuclear units to the larger network. Although industrialization has produced a parent-child household, this small household is far from being isolated from its relatives. Strong bonds with the large kinship system are reflected in patterns of aid,[1] frequent face-to-face meetings with relatives,[2] and commitments to

[1]Marvin B. Sussman, "The Help Pattern in the Middle-class Family," *American Sociological Review*, 18 (1953), pp. 22-28; and Marvin B. Sussman, "The Isolated Nuclear Family: Fact or Fiction," *Social Problems*, 6 (1959), pp. 333-340.

[2]Several independent studies, both here and in other countries, show an overall high level of face-to-face interaction with relatives outside the nuclear family. For examples see: Eugene Litwak, "Occupational Mobility and Extended Family Cohesion," *American Sociological Review*, 25 (1960), pp. 9-21; Paul J. Reiss,

maintain extended ties.[3] In spite of the nucleation of the household, larger kin networks are still important to people, fulfill a number of functions in their lives, and are actively maintained by them. This is true even when geographic mobility has occurred.[4]

Such inquiries have enriched and enlivened knowledge of and interest in the family. They have also raised some important questions that await attention. One is whether kinship patterns found in the United States prevail in other societies. It is true that research has shown the extended family in this country to be more viable than might ordinarily be expected. But we do not know how the American family looks in comparison with other contemporary societies. Each country possesses a unique constellation of historical and contemporary conditions relevant to kinship behavior. There is reason to believe that conditions in this country generate a level of involvement with the larger family below that found in other societies, certainly Italy. We shall have the opportunity in this chapter to make some comparative observations of family relations in Turin and in American cities.[5]

Beyond these comparisons, the major part of this chapter is directed to two closely joined questions: With whom and with what intensity are kinship bonds maintained and what social conditions support or attenuate these bonds? It is absolutely essential that we answer the first question in order to pursue the second. The extended family is not an undifferentiated system; it is made up of distinct segments

---

"The Extended Kinship System: Correlates of and Attitudes on Frequency of Interaction," *Marriage and Family Living*, 24 (1962), pp. 333 – 339; Robert P. Stuckert, "Occupational Mobility and Family Relationships," *Social Forces*, 41 (1963), pp. 301 – 307. A most systematic and comprehensive study of kinship relations is presented in Bert N. Adams, *Kinship in an Urban Setting* (Chicago: Markham Publishing Company, 1968). For data drawn in an English community, see Michael Young and Peter Willmott, *Family and Kinship in East London* (London: Routledge and Kegan Paul, 1957). There is further evidence from Denmark in Jan Stehouwer, "Relations Between Generations and the Three-generation Household in Denmark," in Ethel Shanas and Gordon F. Streib (eds.), *Social Structure and the Family: Generational Relations* (Englewood Cliffs, N.J.: Prentice Hall, 1965), pp. 142 – 162.

[3]Cyrus M. Johnson and Alan C. Kerckhoff, "Family Norms, Social Position, and the Value of Change," *Social Forces*, 43 (1964), pp. 149 – 156.

[4]Eugene Litwak, "Geographic Mobility and Extended Cohesion," *American Sociological Review*, 25 (1960), pp. 385 – 394.

[5]Research into kinship relations, more than any other aspect of family life, approaches what Reubin Hill states is the major goal of family studies: to discover "propositions about marriage and the family that transcend the boundaries of nation and culture." Reuben Hill, "Cross-National Family Research: Attempts and Prospects," *International Social Science Journal*, 14 (1962), pp. 425 – 451.

and each one of them calls forth a different kind of interpersonal relationship. An individual, for example, does not interact with a cousin in the same way as he does with a grandparent. Thus, we can view the kinship affiliations of people as the result of a process of selection from a range of potential attachments, each selected affiliation entailing a distinct interactional process. These selections, in turn, may be influenced by social factors that lie outside the immediate kinship relations.

Among the social conditions this study examined in relation to kinship attachments are class and social mobility. The middle class and the upwardly mobile are of special interest, for these two groups have embraced and realized most fully the values and ethos of industrial society. Consequently, if modernization has erosive effects on family relations, they should be most sharply apparent among the members of these groups. Research in the United States, however, has found just the opposite and has shown that the most active kinship relations are maintained by the middle class and the upwardly mobile. First we will see that the same patterns prevail in Turin and then we will explore the reasons for these relationships.

We will also examine occupation for conditions influencing kinship relations. It provides a theoretically intriguing opportunity to examine empirically the contention that the structure of the modern family is an adaptation to the surrounding social and economic organization. The bureaucratization of work and authority are elements of occupation that I shall emphasize, for they appear to have a particularly interesting regulatory effect on the selection of kinship affiliations.

DIMENSIONS OF KINSHIP RELATIONS

Social anthropology has amassed a large body of materials describing different kinds of family organization. Their variety is truly profound and stands as testimony to the richness of social life, and to the ability of anthropology to conceptualize complex human organizations.[6] Sociological research in industrialized societies, by contrast, typically focuses on limited aspects of family organization. It attempts to account for variability in delineated dimensions of kinship rather than describe the entire system, its nuances, its nomenclature and its peripheral relations. The same is true here.

[6]Some of this complexity is reflected in the plethora of kinship labels a society puts to everyday use. For a discussion of those employed in the United States, see David M. Schneider and George C. Homans, "Kinship Terminology and the American Kinship System," *American Anthropologist*, 57 (1955), pp. 1194 – 1208.

This study was first interested in identifying the major kinship bonds that exist among the Turinese and second in assessing the viability or intensity of these bonds. The information bearing on these issues comes from questions asked only of women; consequently it is not possible to make any statements concerning the kinship behavior of men. It will be evident, nevertheless, that even their indirect role in kinship relations, which is exercised through the influence of their occupational statuses and experiences, is important.

The data examined come from answers to two questions. We first asked the mothers to designate the relative with whom they were closest. The answers are amenable to several classifications. They can be categorized according to whether the designated relative is on the spouse's side of the family or on the mother's; to whether the person is an older, transgenerational or collateral relative; or to whether or not he is a parent of the respondent. These classifications indicate different selective affiliations and, therefore, lend themselves to different purposes.

After asking the first question we asked the women how frequently they visited with the person they designated as their closest relative. This item corresponds to one used in several American studies, with an important difference. In Turin, we asked the frequency of face-to-face contact with the single relative with whom a woman was most close, while the American studies summate the frequency of contacts with all relatives outside the nuclear unit. Our frequency data do not embrace the full scope of contact with all relatives; they represent the minimum contact with the larger family that could occur. But this minimum focuses on those relations which are most actively maintained, most important, most emotionally charged and most enduring.

The bonds that exist between family members can come about through default as well as from positive selection. Attrition of relatives as a result of geographic movement or death necessarily affects kinship patterns. Some of our respondents had no relatives in Turin, and we omitted them from our analyses here. We also found, understandably, that the older our respondents the more likely their closest ties would be with a collateral relative rather than a transgenerational relative. Geographic movement and death, then, are limiting conditions on kinship relations. These conditions do not account, however, for the variations discovered between groups. When we controlled for place of birth and age of respondents, these group differences were still maintained; thus, we cannot explain these variations by geographic proximity or by the absence of relatives because of death.

SOCIAL CLASS AND THE INTENSITY
OF KINSHIP RELATIONS:
A CROSS-NATIONAL VIEW

Foreigners think of Italians as fiercely loyal to the extended family, enmeshed in its affairs, involved with its members. Compared to the United States, this is probably true. If historical conditions in America have tended to weaken family ties, others in Italy have intensified them. The sense of vulnerability to exploitation by the outside world that many Italians harbor has turned the family into a welcomed and needed sanctuary. But it is as difficult and inaccurate to speak of all Italians in this regard as to generalize for Americans. For one thing, we find for the Turinese, just as has already been discovered among Americans, that the higher the class, the more intense their kinship bonds.

Both the inter- and intra-national differences are revealed by comparing the frequency with which middle- and working-class Turinese and Americans visit with their relatives. Litwak's Buffalo, New York, findings provide the best basis for comparison, for his interviews were also with women.[7] Furthermore, there is a correspondence in the categorization of social class in the two samples: professional and managerial personnel, officials and proprietors, and clerical and sales workers are classified as "middle class" and all manual workers are "working class." Table IX.1 shows that, compared with the Buffalo respondents, a considerably greater proportion of Italians of both classes see relatives at least once a week. The magnitude of these

Table IX.1

Social Class and Mothers Having at Least One Family
Visit per Week, in Turin and Buffalo

	Turin		Buffalo[a]	
	%	N	%	N
Middle class	74	(232)	54	(331)
Working class	64	(195)	45	(317)
Significance of χ^2 (linear regression)	$p < .05$		$p < .05$	

[a] *Adapted from Eugene Litwak, "Occupational Mobility and Extended Family Cohesion," American Sociological Review, 25 (1960), Table II, p. 15.*

[7] Eugene Litwak, "Occupational Mobility and Extended Family Cohesion."

differences is all the more impressive when we realize that the figures for Turin represent visits only with the single relative with whom the women interviewed had the closest relationship, while in Buffalo the figures represent all visits with all relatives.

While these differences are interesting and undoubtedly reflect a variety of societal differences, they should not obscure the structural correspondence existing between the two nations. In each country the middle class is more actively engaged with family than is the working class, and in each country the magnitude of this class difference is about the same. The differences are not great, but their cross-national consistency corroborates their regularity. Above all, we must recognize that the greater family involvement of the middle class occurs despite its greater absorption of the experiences and values of industrialized society, presumably inimical to kinship bonds. We may say the same of the socially mobile.

Social mobility has been regarded as a prime deterrent to the continued viability of the extended family. On a priori grounds, it would seem that the location of members of the same family at different levels of the status system would limit interaction and have a divisive effect. Evidence from Litwak's studies, however, has shown that upward mobility does not result in the attenuation of family ties. Contrary to reasonable expectations, kin relations among mobile Americans are even more intense than relations in the groups from which they have originated. This is also the case for the Turinese. In Table IX.2 the Italian data are arranged in a way comparable to Litwak's. He excluded his stationary lower-middle-class respondents as well as those coming from farm backgrounds; for equivalence the same categories are not represented in the Italian sample. Both samples present only those having relatives in the same city. Both samples also judge women's mobility by comparing the occupational status of their fathers with that of their husband's current occupation. Mobility includes both intra- and inter-class movement. As in the case of the preceding class comparisons, we again find that in each category Turinese are more actively engaged with relatives than Americans, but that the intra-national differences are strikingly parallel.[8]

Neither a higher class position nor upward social mobility, then,

[8]These findings are different from Stuckert's. His results show less family contact by mobile than stationary groups. Comparisons are ambiguous here, however, as Stuckert employed the North-Hatt prestige scale, thus placing some categories of manual workers higher in occupational status than some white-collar workers. Robert P. Stuckert, "Occupational Mobility."

Table IX.2

Social Mobility and Percentage of Mothers Having at Least One Family Visit per Week, in Turin and Buffalo

	Turin		Buffalo[a]	
	%	N	%	N
Stationary upper class	81	(53)	59	(148)
Upwardly mobile class	74	(105)	51	(183)
Downwardly mobile class	61	(38)	51	(101)
Stationary manual class	68	(82)	43	(216)

$$\chi^2 = 5.5 \qquad \chi^2 = 8.9$$
$$3 \text{ d.f.} \qquad 3 \text{ d.f.}$$
$$p < .20 \qquad p < .05$$

[a]Adapted from Eugene Litwak, "Occupational Mobility and Extended Family Cohesion," American Sociological Review, 25 (1960), Table II, p. 15.

has erosive effects on kinship. Quite the contrary, their influence is enhancing. Why is this? To answer this question it is useful to consider the status-providing functions of the larger family.

SOURCES OF STATUS

An important function of the family is to confer an immediate social status on its children. Although it has many consequences for subsequent behavior, the status ascribed to a child is independent of his attributes or accomplishments. Ascribed status, however, usually attaches to an individual only through the period of socialization, except in families possessing considerable established wealth or recognized lineage. Especially in urban centers where family background can be buried in anonymity, the status of the grown child must eventually rest on his own achievements. The major institutional sources of adult status are education, occupation and, in the case of women, marriage. But, while the success or failure of status achievement is ultimately borne by the grown child, the family — especially parents — can play an important instrumental role. It appears that kinship bonds in part reflect the contribution the family has made to the child's adult status. This, I believe, helps to account for the more active engagement with kin by the middle class and by the socially mobile. The evidence for this contention is contained in Tables IX.3, IX.4, IX.5, IX.6 and IX.7. When these tables are pieced together, they consistently show that loyalties are most firmly anchored to those relatives who have had a part in the crystallization or enhancement of social position.

Table IX.3 identifies the relatives designated by the respondents when they were asked with whom they are most close. The table indicates considerable class difference. Middle-class women were more likely to be closest to a transgenerational relative, particularly a parent; working-class women were usually closest to a collateral relative, particularly a brother or sister. Both classes, however, strongly favored a relative from their own line, though we could not determine whether aunts, uncles and cousins were from the husband's or wife's side of the family.

The breadth of these class differences is revealed more completely when we observe the frequency of visits with the relative designated as closest. Table IX.4 distinguishes among women designating a transgenerational or collateral relative. This kinship division clearly differentiates the classes. The women are then sub-divided by those who visit their closest relative once a week or more and those who visit less than once a week. Now we see that middle-class women are more likely than working-class women to have their closest attachment in the transgenerational ranks (60 per cent vs. 31 per cent) and that they are more likely, also, to be in frequent contact with these relatives (51 per cent vs. 22 per cent). On the other hand, a greater proportion of working- than middle-class women have their closest ties to collateral relatives and, more specifically, proportionately more working-class women have intense ties to collateral kin.

Table IX.3

Relatives With Whom Turinese Mothers Are in Closest Contact, by Social Class

Closest Relative	Middle Class %	Working Class %
Parent	39	19
Parent-in-law	10	6
Aunts, uncles	9	6
Sibs	23	36
Sibs-in-law	11	21
Cousins	8	12
Numbers	(218)	(186)

Significance of χ^2
(linear regression) $p < .001$

Table IX.4
Generation of Closest Relative and Frequency of Visits
in Turin, by Social Class

Generation of Closest Relative and Frequency of Visits	Middle Class %	%	Working Class %	%
Transgenerational	60		31	
Once a week or more		51		22
Less than once a week		9		9
Collateral	40		69	
Once a week or more		25		45
Less than once a week		15		24
Numbers	(216)		(181)	

Significance of χ^2
(linear regression)
Class difference by closest relative only: p < .001

These findings need to be tied to my earlier suggestion that patterns of kinship attachment in part result from families' contributions to the status of the grown child. To pursue this argument, we must focus more directly on relations with parents rather than with all transgenerational relatives. How can parents contribute to the status of their adult children in a society that accords status on the basis of individual achievement? Parents and other senior relatives might exercise some control over occupational choice and mate selection, but the most institutionalized instrument of status stabilization or aggrandizement is advanced education. Education, in turn, is made available largely through the motivational and material support of parents. This is one way, at least, in which the family still plays an active part in influencing the future status of children in industrialized societies where attributes extrinsic to achievement are ignored in according social honor.

We should find, then, that devotion to parents increases with the extent of one's formal education, and this is what occurs. Table IX.5 shows that in the middle class attachment to parents increases as education increases. Those parents who have made an extended education available receive, in turn, the loyalty of their grown children. Because formal education is much more abbreviated in the working class we cannot see its role as fully in this group. For the middle class, however, we may state that class status by itself cannot ade-

Table IX.5

Education of Turinese Women, Their Closest Relative, and Frequency of Contact, by Social Class

Closest Relative and Frequency of Contact	Middle Class			Working Class	
	Secondary and University %	Technical %	Elementary %	Technical %	Elementary %
Parent	55	39	21	24	17
Once a week or more	54	36	14	14	16
Less than once a week	1	3	7	10	1
Other Relatives	45	61	79	76	83
Once a week or more	29	42	50	24	54
Less than once a week	16	19	29	52	29
Numbers	(89)	(64)	(58)	(21)	(159)

Significance of χ^2
(linear regression)
Education difference by
closest relative only: p < .001   n.s.

quately explain the intense affiliation with parents; what matters is *how* the class status has been attained and whether there has been parental participation in this process.

This interpretation is still highly speculative, of course. But it can be further substantiated by following its implications for the socially mobile. Women can achieve class mobility in two ways: by marrying into a higher class solely as a result of romantic attraction and in spite of the lack of educational achievement; or marrying into a higher class as a result — at least partly — of advanced education. In the first instance, marriage occurs without parents having a clear instrumental role; in the second, parents do have such a role. These different modes of mobility should be mirrored in the relations of women with their parents.

These relations are shown in Table IX.6, which cannot include working-class women since they have experienced neither upward inter-class mobility nor an advanced education. Two relevant comparisons can be made in this table. First, though their number is small, the highly educated who have been socially mobile are more likely to designate a parent as the relative with whom they are closest, and they also engage in more frequent interaction with them than do women with the same mobility history but without benefit of an advanced education. Second, the devotion to parents of the highly

Table IX.6

Mobility of Middle-Class Turinese Women, Their Education, and Attachment to Parents

Closest Relative and Frequency of Contact	Upwardly Mobile				Stationary			
	University		Less than University		University		Less than University	
	%	%	%	%	%	%	%	%
Parent	77		38		54		35	
Once a week or more		77		32		52		30
Less than once a week		–		6		2		5
Other Relatives	23		62		46		65	
Once a week or more		8		43		31		44
Less than once a week		15		19		15		21
Numbers	(13)		(53)		(71)		(45)	

Significance of χ^2
(linear regression)
Education level by
closest relative only: $p < .02$ $p < .05$

educated mobile women even exceeds that of stationary middle-class women with the same educational background.

A final piece of evidence further suggests that kinship bonds reflect a recognition of status contributions. If a woman marries a man of higher class status, it is reasonable to expect that she would be attracted to her spouse's side of the family. In a kinship network having an unequal distribution of material advantages and statuses, there would be a tendency to identify with the family line that is the more privileged.

Table IX.7 duplicates Table IX.6 except that it is now laterality that is of interest. The numbers here are somewhat smaller because this table excludes those whose relatives could not be identified as affinal or cognate (mainly aunts and uncles). But the differences are clear and entirely consistent with what we have already seen. Fully 92 per cent of the upwardly mobile women given a university education are attached to their own parents, their own brothers and sisters. While only a minority of all women favor their in-laws, the minority is smallest among those who have received a boost from their own family.

We interpret each of these several findings as resulting in part from the instrumental involvement of parents in the status of their children, their shared stake in the standing of their adult offspring. There is a possibility that what is being shared is more general and includes a host of values. I am suggesting, in other words, the possibility that the highly educated share many views and orientations with their parents, and it is this that might account for their close relations rather than parental involvement in status alone. Such is not the case, however. The women were asked to identify the people

Table IX.7

Mobility of Middle-Class Turinese Women, Their Education, and the Laterality of Kinship Attachments

| | Upwardly Mobile | | Stationary | |
| | University % | Less than University % | University % | Less than University % |
Laterality of Closest Relative				
Own family	92	70	80	70
Spouse's family	8	30	20	30
Numbers	(11)	(50)	(60)	(40)
Significance of χ^2 (linear regression)	p $<$ .20		p $<$ .30	

to whom their own general ideas and ways of thinking were most close. As could be expected, education tends to create a value gap between generations. The more limited the education of women, the more apt they were to indicate a parent or other older relative as most fully sharing their own thinking; the higher educated, on the other hand, were more likely to indicate someone entirely outside the family system, such as a friend, political figure or writer.

The close relations between highly educated children and their parents come about in spite of the absence of shared perspectives, therefore, and not because of them. The explanation most consistent with what we have seen is that filial devotion varies with the importance of parents as sources of status. When parents are able to provide their daughter with a university education and when this facilitates marriage to a man of higher occupational status than that of her own father, close and active bonds between the parent and the grown child are forged. Her status is tied most directly to her husband's occupation, but her parents perhaps helped make it all possible; at very least, her education serves to equilibrate her new status. For this she is indebted to her parents, though probably not consciously or calculatingly. Nor is the attachment unilateral, for parents, in turn, are proud of their own contribution to her station. Thus, feelings between them are reciprocal. These circumstances override whatever value differences might exist between them and lead to a potent relationship.

OCCUPATIONAL CONSTRAINTS
AND FACILITATIONS

Family relations assume some of their form and character from a process of adaptation to the constraints and imperatives of surrounding institutions. From this perspective, the occupational context, by structuring the experiences and orientations of its participants, should influence kinship behavior. Yet, other factors would seem to militate against such influence. In modern societies the temporal and spatial segregation of work from the extended family are even greater than from the nuclear unit. Furthermore, to the extent that women assume the most active role in interacting with relatives, husbands' occupational experiences should have little bearing on kinship patterns. Despite these structural separations, occupation does affect kinship relations.

Some of the effects are evident where individuals are at points of cross-pressure between bureaucratic and family authority. This was first suggested when several indicators of the bureaucratization of work were found to be related to the kin with whom women were most closely affiliated. Specifically, when men are employed in large work sections, having several layers of authority and requiring regular interaction with supervisors, their wives are more likely to have their closest relation with a collateral relative rather than a parent or other older relative. There is a hint in these findings that work embedded in a system of active bureaucratic controls results in an avoidance of relatives who possess an ascribed right to invoke authority — the family elders. If one must accept authority that is hierarchically and rationally organized, he will find it more difficult to accede to authority that by tradition is accorded entirely to parents. The magnitude and regularity of these relationships should not be exaggerated, however; they are neither large nor consistent. But they do suggest that it may be fruitful to examine more directly the concrete authority demands experienced by men in their occupations and the generational affiliations of their wives.

We can do this by considering the qualities that men say are required of them to do well at their work. Among these qualities, one, in particular, reflects both the presence of a hierarchically organized system of authority at work and the expectation that an individual be unquestioningly compliant to superordinates: "strict obedience to supervisors." The men were asked whether this was one of the three most important requirements of their work; important, but not among the top three; or unimportant to their jobs. Only four middle-class men ranked it as one of the three most important requirements of their jobs and, in Table IX.8, they are combined with those according it any degree of importance.

Keep in mind that this information pertains to an element of work experienced by men and that it is being observed in relation to the kinship behavior independently reported by their wives. This limits the analysis to cases where interviews were obtained with both spouses. But more important, perhaps, it mirrors the actual lines through which experiences in the occupational realm affect relations in the kinship system. At any rate, in each class the wives of men who must conform to bureaucratic authority were more likely to be most closely affiliated with collateral relatives, their generational peers with whom they are on equal footing. Brothers and sisters may make demands, but their demands are not legitimated by the ascribed authority that resides with family elders.

Several sharp contrasts subsumed by bureaucratic and traditional family authority may contribute to these selective affiliations.[9] Bureau-

[9]Litwak specifies a number of contrasts between the bureaucratic occupational setting and family and suggests structural adaptations of family to potentially conflicting requirements of the bureaucracy. Eugene Litwak, "Extended Kin Relations in an Industrial Democratic Society," in Shanas and Streib (eds.) Social Structure, pp. 291 – 323.

Table IX.8

The Importance of "Strict Obedience to Supervisors" as a Requirement
of Turinese Husbands' Work, and the Generational Attachments
of Their Wives, by Social Class

Generation of Closest Relative	Middle Class		Working Class		
	Obedience Important %	*Obedience Unimportant* %	*Obedience Most Important* %	*Obedience Important* %	*Obedience Unimportant* %
Transgenerational	44	58	20	34	40
Collateral	56	42	80	66	60
Numbers	(13)	(97)	(30)	(32)	(60)
Significance of χ^2 (linear regression)	n.s.		p < .10		

cratic authority is relatively free of emotion or expressiveness; it accords power and demands compliance according to the function of position rather than the personal qualities of individuals; it is directed toward the performance of specific tasks; and it is limited to the confines of the work situation. In short, it is highly impersonal. These qualities of bureaucratic authority are partially captured by another item from the same question of occupational requirements: "respect for the rules." Again we find that the wives of men whose work depends on observance of impersonal rules are more likely to establish their closest bonds with a family peer rather than with an elder. Those whose husbands work at jobs where this is unimportant or irrelevant, have a greater likelihood of entering into a close relationship with an older relative.

It is doubtful that these results reflect a competition between the occupational arena and the family. More likely, they exert contrasting and, perhaps, incompatible styles of authority. Work authority is wielded by an "expert" who by virtue of experience and knowledge has achieved his position; parental authority is legitimated through an ascribed status. In work, authority is calculated and anchored to concrete goals; in the family the functions of authority are less clear and more latent. In the occupational setting it is impersonal; in the family it is both personal and emotionally charged. The patterns of attachment, I believe, represent a selective avoidance of the cross-pressures that may result from exposure to these discontinuous modes of authority. This interpretation is speculative, of course, for we cannot know precisely the dynamics underlying these relationships. Basically, however, they suggest a process whereby the actions of individuals in one institution are selectively adapted to the demands and experiences in another.

I have been speaking of occupational requirements as though their only relation to kinship were that of forcing adjustments at points of potential conflict. However, some occupations, notably those stressing interpersonal skills, have a facilitative consequence for interaction with kin. Such work most directly implicates the frequency of interaction rather than the selection of particular relatives.

Facilitation can be seen, first, when we examine the principal components of husbands' jobs: whether they work primarily with ideas, things or people. Since only the frequency of visits is relevant, Table IX.10 has expanded the frequency categories to distinguish those who visit with their closest relative twice a week or more, once a week and less than once a week. The differences that appear, while not great, indicate that in both classes wives whose husbands are primarily engaged in working with people are most intensely involved with their kin.

Table IX.9

The Importance of "Respect for the Rules" as a Requirement
of Turinese Husbands' Work, and the Generational Attachments
of Their Wives, by Social Class

Generation of Closest Relative	Middle Class			Working Class		
	Respect Most Important %	*Respect Important* %	*Respect Unimportant* %	*Respect Most Important* %	*Respect Important* %	*Respect Unimportant* %
Transgenerational	42	61	57	23	34	39
Collateral	58	39	43	77	66	61
Numbers	(12)	(18)	(85)	(31)	(29)	(62)
Significance of χ^2 (linear regression)	n.s.			p < .20		

A second item gave results consistent with these. In the same fashion as they rated "strict obedience to supervisors," husbands were asked to indicate the importance of "being likeable" as a requirement of their work. Thus, they could designate this as one of the three most important demands of their occupation; as important, but not among the three most important; or as unimportant to their work. Wives of husbands whose jobs placed a premium on being likeable were more disposed to intense interaction with kin. This is especially clear in the middle class, where there is a 23 per cent difference at the most frequent level of visiting.

The set of relationships between work and kinship indicates a kind of congeniality or structural fit between the organization of important elements of occupational life and the selective organization of kinship patterns within the extended family. Where such a fit is lacking, the kinship patterns appear to yield to occupation. These institutional inter-connections are particularly intriguing when it is realized that they are established through the separate experiences and actions of husbands and wives.[10]

Table IX.10

The Principal Component of Turinese Husbands' Occupations and Frequency of Kinship Visiting by Their Wives, by Social Class

	MIDDLE CLASS Working Mainly With:			WORKING CLASS Working Mainly With:		
Frequency of Visits	*People* %	*Ideas* %	*Things* %	*People* %	*Ideas* %	*Things* %
More than weekly	28	25	20	29	24	21
Weekly	45	43	40	50	36	37
Less than weekly	27	32	40	21	40	42
Numbers	(56)	(47)	(16)	(24)	(25)	(79)

Significance of χ^2 (linear regression)	$p < .30$			$p < .20$		

[10] I cannot be sure that the occupational experiences of men affect their own kinship behavior in the same ways they influence that of their wives. There is some evidence that the maintenance of family relations falls primarily to the wife, particularly where her own mother is concerned. Sweetser presents evidence gathered in Finland that in an agrarian economy the most active bonds are between fathers and sons, while under industrial conditions they are between mothers and daughters. Willmott and Young also report a special attachment between mothers and their married daughters in England. Dorrian Apple Sweetser, "The Effect of Industrialization in Intergenerational Solidarity," *Rural So-*

Table IX.11

Importance of Being Likeable to Turinese Husbands' Occupations and
Frequency of Kinship Visiting by Their Wives, by Social Class

Frequency of Visits	Middle Class						Working Class					
	Most Important %		Important %		Unimportant %		Most Important %		Important %		Unimportant %	
More than weekly	42		26		19		25		22		23	
Weekly	37		39		44		50		45		42	
Less than weekly	21		35		37		25		33		35	
Numbers	(19)		(23)		(83)		(12)		(18)		(100)	
Significance of χ^2 (linear regression)	p < .10						n.s.					

DISCUSSION

Industrialization and its concomitants have not had a destructive effect on extended family relations among the Turinese and in this respect they are similar to Americans. The level of face-to-face interaction in the middle class and among the upwardly mobile is particularly notable in view of the fact that these groups would appear to be most vulnerable to any disruptive consequences of industrialization for family life. Middle-class and mobile women have notably close contact with relatives, especially with their parents. This is consistent with parental contributions to the status of their adult offspring, made primarily through the provision of advanced education. A joint interest in an important achievement is created that is powerful enough to override the value gulf that exists between highly educated children and their parents.

To say that modern industrial society and its occupational system have not destroyed the larger family system is not to suggest that they have had no impact on it. On the contrary, their impact in some ways is profound. It is best observed by going beyond class and mobility *per se* to examine other conditions, especially those connected to occupational circumstances. When the relevant aspects of both occupation and kinship relations are specified, it is possible to discern the institutional adjustments that occur. Authority is especially pertinent in this regard. Specifically, there appears to be a lack of structural congeniality between occupational authority bureaucratically organized and authority that is traditionally invested in parents and other family elders. A man whose occupational situation exposes him to considerable hierarchical authority and impersonal regulation tends to withdraw from close affiliation with transgenerational relatives. But some of the requirements of his work can lead him — or, more accurately, his wife — to intense family contacts. Work that demands interpersonal skills, for example, results in more frequent face-to-face contact with kin.

The kinship patterns of the working class deserve a special note. It is now more understandable that their relations, compared to the middle class, are more collateral and less intense. All the social and occupational conditions associated with close attachment to transgenerational relatives are concentrated in the middle class. Behind these statistical associations may lie a situation of considerable pathos.

ciology, 31 (1966), pp. 156 – 170; Peter Willmott and Michael Young, *Family and Class in a London Suburb* (London: Routledge and Kegan Paul, 1960), p. 74.

If it is true, as I observed in Chapter III, that continued family solidarity is most fiercely needed in the working class, then the disengagement of adult children from their parents must leave a residue of bitter disappointment and a deep sense of loss. Conditions exist to deprive this group, in particular, of the very thing they so desperately want: continued loyalty from their children.

Yet, working-class parents are probably unwitting partners to these conditions. Whatever potential conflict may exist between occupational and family authority, it is most likely to be brought to a head and exacerbated in working-class families. This statement can be made on the basis of what we have learned about working-class espousal of children's obedience to parental authority. The priorities they give to conformity and compliance to parental wishes may well contribute to the eventual withdrawal of children, particularly when they are confronted with demands from other institutions. Working-class parents may have an unconscious hand in alienating those with whom they want to be forever close.

Piecing together what has been learned in Turin with what has been discovered in the United States, it would seem that future studies of kinship in modern societies could benefit from a fresh conceptual approach. The major issue, I believe, is not whether relations within the family system have been weakened, but rather how they have been reshaped. Much of the material that could be brought together here really bespeaks a process of *selective* family bonds. The selection, of course, is not random; it is sensitive to many conditions external to the family. But in a real way these attachments come about because they reflect what people want, not what they feel compelled to accept. Kinship affiliations in contemporary societies, in other words, are based more on personal affinity than on social obligation.[11] What we need to know as sociologists is how these affinities are shaped by social structure and experience.

[11]This is essentially the same argument as presented by Firth. In discussing the effects of industrialization on family, he emphasizes that kinship ties once maintained formally can now be retained on a personal and selective basis, often making such ties more powerful. Raymond Firth, "Family and Kinship in Industrial Society," in Paul Halmos (ed.), *The Sociological Review, Monograph #8* (Keele, Eng.: University of Keele, 1964), pp. 65 – 87.

X

The Family in Society

This study was different from most studies set in foreign countries, for only infrequently has it highlighted that which is culturally distinctive of the country examined. It was also different from traditional textbook treatments of the family, which usually comprehensively treat the various stages of the family cycle, beginning with infancy and ending with old age. Instead of describing the culture of Turinese family life or looking at cyclical changes as maturation and aging occur, this work was organized around an interest in the penetrability of social structural forces into the family. This interest was best served by examining a variety of external structural conditions in relationship to different family patterns.

The social structural elements and family patterns selected for examination are not peculiar to Italian or Turinese culture, but generally prevail in industrially developed societies. Because the study avoided nation-bound variables it could maintain a transnational view of family and society. Where comparative data were available, they were analyzed in a manner fully in keeping with and instrumental to the major goals of the study: to identify the linkages between social conditions and family processes. Thus, social structures were not compared transnationally, nor were the family patterns of Turinese and Americans contrasted. Rather, *relationships* of social structural elements to features of family life were the units of cross-national comparison, just as they were the intra-national units of analysis. By comparing relationships across nations, an empirical basis was provided for judging the generality of the effects of social conditions on the family.

In addition to social class, which was the workhorse variable of the investigation, an assortment of structural conditions was brought into the analyses: various repetitive occupational experiences; social

187

aspects of both parents' and children's sex roles; vertical mobility; economic position; and husband-wife status discrepancies. The family patterns that were studied included relations between spouses and relations with the larger family. Most extensively considered were the relations between parents and children: the goals parents hold for children, expressed in their values and aspirations; and their mechanisms for regulating children's behavior, reflected in patterns of discipline and affection.

The bearing of social structural conditions on these aspects of the family is complex. Some are critically important to one dimension of family relations, but irrelevant to others. In one instance a condition has an independent impact; in a second instance it may be influential only in conjunction with other conditions. I shall not catalogue or summarize the many relationships that were arrayed throughout the chapters. It is more useful to draw selectively from the findings in a manner that will point up the complexity, the scope and the reach of the relationships of social structure to the inner life of the family. The most effective way to begin this is by centering on social class and then organizing around this basic context the description of the influence of other conditions on family relations.

Social class position is relevant to virtually every aspect of family life that was studied. Associated with the middle class is a parental valuation of self-control for children, high educational and occupational aspirations for them, a somewhat infrequent use of physical punishment, an active expression of affection toward children, greater marital companionship and an intense attachment to kin, especially to one's own parents. Working-class parents, conversely, stress obedience for children, have more modest aspirations, resort more frequently to corporal punishment, are more reserved in expressing affection, have less close marital relationships and are more detached from the extended family.

Occupation, which is related to class but conceptually distinct from it, is a second context whose influence on the family was examined. Its effects are far less encompassing than those of class, but they point up clearly how the experiences of a person in one social institution are related to his sentiments and actions in another. Occupational self-direction, for example, explains much of the class difference in parental values. Middle-class men are more likely to work at jobs that require self-direction, and this occupational condition is associated with high valuation of self-control for children. Working-class men, however, are more likely to be required to comply with the directives of others, and this is associated with valuing obedience for one's children. Social class is thus largely determinative of the extent of occupational self-direction, and this aspect of occupational experience, in turn, molds conceptions of good and proper behavior — not only for one's self within the occupational setting, but also for one's children in the family.

The relationship of occupational self-direction to parental values is beguilingly simple. Other aspects of occupation affect other dimensions of family relations in a somewhat less straightforward, although no less intriguing, fashion. For example, men who are occupationally frustrated are more reserved in the expression of affection toward sons than they are toward daughters. In contrast, men who are occupationally satisfied are more expressive toward sons than daughters. It would appear that fathers are best able to move into an affectionate relation with sons and function as socializing models for them only after they have mastered the goals and rewards of their work.

These kinds of relationships emphasize that occupation is a social system of considerable importance in shaping the actions and sentiments of people. The nature of the system and one's location in its network of roles, particularly his position of superordination and subordination in relation to others, are relevant to relations internal to the family. Eventually, the interpersonal relations and other realities that fathers repeatedly encounter at work come to serve as models on which relations are established with children and other kin in the family domain. In these ways, patterns of occupational experience contribute to the patterning of family relations.

Although social class and occupation are the main contexts from which analytic variables were drawn, several additional structural conditions were examined. Parents' and children's sex roles are relevant, for example, to the regulatory functions of discipline and affection. Thus sons are more frequently targets of severe punishment than are daughters. This is partly because socially defined expectations are somewhat higher for sons, making the fear that they will fail somewhat greater, and the discipline meted out to them commensurately more stringent, particularly with middle-class boys. At the same time, middle-class sons are also the recipients of most demonstrated affection, largely because mothers in this class use the expression of affection as a mechanism of control. Underlying these kinds of class and sex-role variations are differential social standards for sons and for daughters, and different instruments for enforcing these standards.

Social mobility was another variable in this study relevant to certain family issues. It influences such diverse aspects of family life as parental aspirations and kinship relations. Parents who have experienced the slightest upward movement are likely also to elevate their aspirations; even those of very limited economic resources who have had some modicum of mobility come to have relatively high hopes for their children. Mobility among women also strengthens their kinship bonds, but only if it results from advanced education. Women who have "married up" without benefit of educational opportunities and, correspondingly, without the direct help of their parents, tend to be more detached from their kin, orienting themselves now to their husbands' side of the family.

Husband-wife status discrepancies provide a final illustration of the penetration of social factors into family relations. When the wife is of a higher status background than her husband, these discrepancies, created by social definitions of prestige and honor, exert a considerable effect on parents' goals and aspirations. Although a wife is socially free to adopt her husband's status, the husband is not socially accorded his wife's. Consequently, disparities arising from the wife's higher status are resolved either by the wife accepting her husband's lower status or by long-range achievement striving in behalf of children. Disparities in status, moreover, militate against marital consensus. Although the respondents in this study had been married a minimum of eleven years, the status differentials they originally brought to their marriages remained a divisive force, blocking the acquisition of shared perceptions and values.

The totality of the findings from this study form a coherent, although certainly not complete, view of the family in society. All the relationships that are presented result from the very simple fact that individual family members also have multiple roles and statuses outside the family. From these roles and statuses they learn many things: different forms of interpersonal relations and their corresponding demands and expectations; the various types of goals that are available and a distinction between those that should be prized and those that should be eschewed; the norms for judging themselves and others; standards that indicate what is desirable; and imperatives that dictate what is necessary. These conceptions and norms, acquired from and reinforced by structured social experiences in the surrounding society, are expressed in the interactions and sentiments within family units. The network of family relations is thus inseparably interconnected with the larger society and is necessarily affected by its conditions.

It is amply clear that the underlying assumption of this study, persistently asserted, was that social structural conditions converge on various dimensions of the family to shape and mold its inner life. It is also clear that this overriding concern with structural factors leads us to ignore other forces influencing the family. Indeed, such an approach results in a highly selective picture of family and society. Every study, of course, must decide what to look at and what to ignore, and the selective emphasis given to structural conditions here requires little defense. The decisions underlying this study were based on the conviction that structural factors, despite their being the core matter of sociology, need to be specified more clearly and their effects on human affairs must be understood more thoroughly. At the same time, the great importance to the family of other considerations, especially personality factors, should be acknowledged.[1] Personality does not function independently of and apart from social structural conditions, of course. The major dimensions of personality are themselves integrated with larger social systems and are elements in the very processes through which structural effects on the family become exerted. What is ideally needed is not so much a study in which personality is substituted for social structure, in other words, but one in which personality is studied in conjunction with social structure as together they bear on the family.[2]

There are, in addition to aspects of personality, other calculated omissions, such as the size of families, birth order, and the age and sex distribution of siblings, to mention but a few conditions that may also affect family values and priorities. Designed omissions and inclusions represent but one kind of selective judgement. A second and more important kind of selection has been made involving the interpretation of findings. Deliberately and pointedly the effects of social conditions on the family were consistently asserted while the reverse, the possible effects of the family on society, was ignored with equal consistency. This is most crucial and must be discussed.

EFFECTS OF SOCIETY ON FAMILY:
THE DOMINANT FLOW OF INFLUENCE

It is easier to justify the purposive disregard of conditions other than structural than it is to defend the selective interpretation of relationships as reflecting the effects of structure on family. Such an inter-

[1] Information regarding personality should not be limited to parents but should be drawn from children as well. Bell has argued convincingly that data presumably showing the effects of parents on children could just as plausibly be interpreted as reflecting effects of children on their parents. Richard Q. Bell, "A Reinterpretation of the Direction of Effects in Studies of Socialization," *Psychological Review*, 75 (1968), pp. 81 – 95.

[2] For a most cogent statement of the inter-relationships of personality and social structure, see Alex Inkeles, "Personality and Social Structure," in Robert K. Merton, Leonard Broom and Leonard S. Cottrel, Jr. (eds.), *Sociology Today* (New York: Basic Books, 1959), pp. 249 – 276.

pretation involves more than judging the nature of the relationship between variables; it entails a major assumption concerning the predominant direction of influence between society and family. The assumption is not easy to support indisputably, yet it is close to the core of this study and, indeed, to sociological thinking about institutional arrangements in society.

Sociologists have long thought that the family in industrialized societies is not a dominant institution, one to which surrounding social institutions must make major adjustments. Instead, the structure and function of the family are typically seen as accommodations to other institutions. Despite this being a prevailing view in sociology, it has not been demonstrated empirically.[3] Furthermore, it is unlikely that it will be demonstrated, for our conceptual and methodological tools are poorly suited to "proving" the real nature of social processes. Most social research, and certainly this survey, present statistical associations. Only infrequently will anything intrinsic to an association reveal unquestionably whether one variable is a contributor to, a consequence of or a correlate of a second.[4] How, then, can I assert, as I do throughout this book, that social conditions influence the family when the same statistical associations would appear if an opposite flow of influence existed?

Two grounds exist for such an assertion. One is, simply, that it is an economical and plausible framework for explaining a wide array of data. It enables the analyst to see an orderliness among relationships that otherwise would appear as nebulous and disparate. It is an interpretive stance that provides a coherent view of the family in its social environment. It reveals a meaningful unity between the family's inner life and its external circumstances. In short, the explanation that family patterns result from social conditions is consistent with a variety of data and is theoretically meaningful.

But judgments about the flow of influence can be made on other grounds, too. By their very nature variables differ in what Rosenberg refers to as susceptibility to influence.[5] Two properties of variables, he points out, can be used to evaluate the probable direction of

[3]Goode has challenged sociologists to present evidence for assumptions concerning the place of the family in a hierarchy of dominance among social institutions. The challenge has not been met. William J. Goode, "The Sociology of the Family," ibid., pp. 180 – 181.

[4]Statistical procedures that deal with this problem are being tested, but it remains a major problem to establish the dominant direction of influence in a correlation or association. See H. M. Blalock, Jr., "Correlation and Causality: The Multivariate Case," Social Forces, 30 (1961), pp. 246 – 251.

[5]Morris Rosenberg, The Logic of Survey Analysis (New York: Basic Books, 1968), pp. 9 – 13.

influence: their alterability and their temporal order. Frequently one of the variables in an association can be seen as less amenable to alteration than other variables. Although one's position in a class order is not immutable, for example, it is relatively rigid in comparison to one's values for one's children. Since social class is the less easily altered, it is unlikely, therefore, that values will have as direct an influence on class as class on values.

The relevance of the temporal order of variables to a probable flow of influence may be exemplified by the relationship of education to kinship affiliation. Where this relationship appears, it is interpreted as resulting from an effect of education on kinship attachments. This is not unreasonable when we realize that the formal education of a woman is completed before she is a wife and mother with her own established patterns of affiliation with the larger kinship system. When this logic is applied to the entire array of data that are presented, we can see that the structural variables, rooted in the larger social order, are both relatively more rigid and temporally earlier than the values and behaviors encompassed by the family relations under examination. The properties of the variables thus support the interpretation that the relationships come about as a result of the influence of social conditions on dispositions in the family.

Some relationships, however, resist ready judgment about the direction of influence. One type of uncertainty concerns the actual temporal order of variables. Thus we discovered that family mobility is related to high aspirations, and we interpreted this as showing that concrete mobility experience stimulates striving for further mobility. But there is really no clearly discernible order of events behind such a relationship. Striving may follow actual mobility, or mobility may result from striving. We could reason, moreover, that this is a continual process that has no discrete beginning or end and, consequently, influence flows circularly. The perception of a temporal order in such a case may simply be a reflection of the point in the cycle at which the researcher happens to begin his exploration.

A fairly common problem regarding the direction of influence is that there may be no influence at all. An association can arise, that is, not because one variable is acting upon a second, but because both are being acted upon by a third. Thus we found Turinese fathers dissatisfied with the rewards of their work somewhat less expressive of affection than the satisfied. But might not occupational dissatisfaction and expressive reserve each come from the same source, perhaps a deep-seated personality characteristic that prevents a person from enjoying and being positively engaged with his surroundings? This is, of course, quite plausible. Furthermore, it is technically not difficult to determine; the analyst needs only to see if the original relationships persist while controlling on the relevant information. The problem is that pertinent information that may be used for such controls is often not available. Then other reasoning and other evidence must be brought in that will bear on the issue. In the case of occupational dissatisfaction and expressiveness, for example, it appears that the association between them is not a spurious result of their relationship to an extraneous variable. This reasoning is supported by the fact that the actual association is quite different among fathers in interacting with sons and daughters. Were the association due to extraneous factors, this kind of patterned variation would not occur. Thus problems in the interpretation of influence can often be arbitrated, although not solved, by introducing additional variables into the analysis.

Several specific interpretations in the array of data brought together in this study are open to challenge by alternate explanations. The overall weight and momentum of evidence, however, bespeak the influence of social conditions on the family. This does not mean that family transactions are wholly, or even primarily, explained by social conditions. It does not mean either that social conditions stand in a relationship of complete or unidirectional influence over the family. It means only that there is a dominant flow of influence to which the life of the family is apparently adapted.

Still, the family is much more than a plastic institution whose viability depends on its environment. On the contrary, the interpersonal relations within the family, the values and the actions of its members, probably influence the society in a forceful, although subtle, manner. This influence does not result from its being a powerfully dominant institution that pressures other institutions to accommodate to its functional requirements. Its influence, rather, is exercised through long-range reciprocal effects.

MECHANISMS OF RECIPROCAL EFFECTS
OF FAMILY ON SOCIETY

Every culture is made up of an enormous array of values, beliefs and practices that it espouses and idealizes. The more children internalize what society idealizes, the greater will be the stability and continuity of the society through time. Major responsibility for imparting cultural ideals usually rests with the family; this is an efficient arrangement since the young are likely to reside in the family until maturity. After maturity the children assume their full place in society, and they do much the same with their children as their parents did with them.

To view the family in this way is to treat it essentially as an instrument for the perpetuation of culture. Yet, however accurate this treatment may be, it is incomplete and one-sided. It regards the family as an irreversible production line, taking up the raw unsocialized material at one end and depositing a product finished in its own image at the other. But the family is more than a vehicle for the perpetuation of culture; even as it carries culture forth, the family may be modifying it. It does so, first, by "choosing" the social ideals that it transmits to its young, and, second, by endowing these ideals with particular meaning.

The family does not gather in all values, it does not indiscriminately embrace all ideals to pass on to its children. It picks and chooses, subjects to trial, and then rejects or accepts, condemns, proclaims, uses indifferently or altogether disregards. These selections are not made consciously, of course; but they are made actively. Families do not passively absorb cultural elements as a sponge soaks up water. It is more fitting to think of the family as a gatekeeper before whom the values of society must pass muster before they will be accepted as goals and values to which the family subscribes. What is allowed to pass through the gate depends on the location of the family in society and what it learns in that location. Although it may not be an innovative force, once it selects the values it will transmit to its young, it is having an effect upon society.

The second selective process pertains to the meaning that the family attaches to cultural elements. The conditions that arouse parents' values, the ways they express them and their styles of acting upon them all serve to stamp values with a particular sense or meaning that children learn. Parents do not simply foster obedience in children, by way of illustration; they are also imparting a broad evaluative context. Thus, as they attempt to inculcate this value, they may also be teaching that life is organized in such a way as to demand compliance, that this is the natural order of things and that it is morally right. The major point is that cultural ideals and social values are to a large extent interpreted and given their shades and nuances of meaning in the family domain. These interpretations and meanings will eventually pass beyond the boundaries of individual families to become elements in the expression of ideals and values in other institutions as well. In this fashion, the family is a critical link in the circumstances leading to social change.

The selective transmission and interpretation of values take place in an orderly way, regulated by conditions that are described throughout this book. That is, these selective processes essentially depend on the social and economic standing of families within the society and the experiences attendant upon these locations.[6] Once they are established by social circumstances, however, these selective patterns are then able to exert some influence over which values will be perpetuated and fostered, which will be treated with derision and which will eventually fade from view. Society thus influences families' selective treatment of values, and, through their selectiveness, families in turn influence society. In this way, the effect that society has on the family may underlie the effect of the family on society. The lack of family dominance relative to other institutions, therefore, should not be confused with a lack of importance to society. True, other institutions are not organized around it, and it is not a major lever for innovation and change. From a broad social perspective, nevertheless, the family has reciprocal consequences that have important facilitative or impeding consequences for the society, its continuities and changes.

SOCIAL STRUCTURE AND FAMILY IN TURIN: ISSUES OF GENERALITY

It is fitting that this study, with its cross-national perspective, should end with a discussion of the generality of its findings. This is an issue of concern to all research, not only that which is broadly comparative. It is an issue, though, that is likely to be especially salient to those who step out of their own societies to do their research. They, perhaps somewhat more than other researchers, are concerned lest that which they are observing is true only among people of a particular culture living in a given locale at a single point in time. It is amply evident that the data gathered among the Turinese are not hemmed in by these specificities. Nevertheless, it is difficult to discover and understand the extent to which patterns found in Turin may also prevail in other societies. Part of the difficulty stems from the presence of at least three levels of generality: descriptive, relational and developmental.

We can illustrate descriptive generality in several ways. We can state, for example, that Turinese parents want, above all else, that their children be honest. Also, they hope that their children will have

---

[6]Because these selective processes are tied to the social experiences of parents, they are subject to change as experiences change. Indeed, the ability of parents to change their allegiance to values and to modify their commitments is usually overlooked. It is this ability, however, which may help to reduce intergenerational conflict. This is pointed up by Inkeles in a study of pre- and post-revolution child-rearing values among Russian parents. Alex Inkeles, "Social Change and Social Character: The Role of Parental Mediation," *The Journal of Social Issues*, 11 (1955), pp. 12 – 23.

more formal education than they themselves were able to have. These statements, we discover, describe Americans as well as Turinese. Thus the generality of these simple descriptive statements is assured by the knowledge that they are applicable across nations.

Such information, regardless of its generality, still does not take us very far. This is because description deals with "what," "how much" and "where," but leaves unanswered the vital questions of "how" and "why." In dealing with these questions, we seek relational generality, and description, even if it has a wide generality, is but a first step toward this. In order to understand the circumstances under which described patterns arise, we must observe their relationships to other information. These relationships are of utmost importance, for they provide the basis for explaining and interpreting described phenomena. The generality of these explanatory relationships, in turn, depends on the extent to which they prevail in different societies.

Where descriptive generality asks if people are similar or different, relational generality asks under what conditions they are likely to be similar or different. Thus, we discovered obedience to be a prominent value of both Turinese and American parents. Instead of leaving the search for generality at this descriptive level, we compared the relationships of class and occupation to obedience and found them to be essentially similar for the two societies. As a consequence of these types of comparisons, we can state that the values of Turinese and Americans are likely to be affected in similar ways when faced with similar circumstances. This kind of statement is a far cry from one simply describing the prevalence of a value among Turinese and Americans. Rather, it helps the analyst assess the generality of antecedents and consequences and in this way directly contributes to the generality of sociological propositions explaining parents' values.[7]

It is obvious that we can seek the generality of relationships only among societies that possess all the elements entering into the relationships. Thus it would do no good to explore for the boundaries of generality in the relationships of occupation to parental values in non-industrialized societies. The non-comparability of their occupational systems would render such a search meaningless. From this perspective alone, Turin is an excellent research site, since many of its social conditions are comparable to those of urban America. At the same time, its culture is markedly different, providing an additional dimen-

---

[7]It was essentially the aim of Marsh to establish the generality of such propositions in his excellent secondary cross-national analyses. Robert M. Marsh, *Comparative Sociology: A Codification of Cross-Societal Analysis* (New York: Harcourt, Brace and World, 1967).

sion to relational generality. Specifically, using Turin enables us to be confident that the generality does not arise spuriously as a result of widespread, cross-national cultural conditions. When similar relationships appear in diverse cultural circumstances, generality can result only from elements intrinsic to the relationship. This is of critical importance to a study that aims to focus on relationships involving social structural conditions. In those instances where direct comparisons can be made, it is possible to gauge the penetration of such conditions into the flow of family life without concern that this occurs only in a limited cultural milieu.

The third level of generality, developmental, involves social change. Change is not considered directly in this study, but it is very much in the background of some of the analyses. Like relational generality, this, too, involves relationships, but relationships as they are evolving or will develop in the future. If it exists at all, it is a type of generality that results from nations sharing similar imperatives that emerge out of a course of industrialization and modernization. Do comparable value systems arise among societies engaged in a process of modernization; do people come to strive after similar life goals; do parallel institutional interrelationships emerge? In one form or another, these questions, because they are at the bedrock of social science, have been with us over many intellectual generations.

This study does not have data that deal directly with such questions. On an impressionistic basis, one presently sees much in Turin that, when projected into the near future, will emerge as patterns closely resembling those existing in American urban families today. Their city and their industry have given the Turinese a thrust and direction that has created many parallels between them and Americans. There are vast cultural differences between them that remain intact, but these do not obscure the basic similarities in the hopes and fears, the actions and attitudes of the two peoples. Indeed, it is no longer a serious challenge for Americans to do as Romans when in Rome.

Appendix

English and Italian Versions of the Interview Schedule

RESEARCH ON CONDITIONS OF FAMILY LIFE
AND WORK IN ITALY
*RISCERCA SULLE CONDIZIONI DELLA VITA FAMILIARE
E LAVORATIVA IN ITALIA*

In this research we hope to come to an understanding of your feelings and opinions regarding two aspects of life that are important to people all over the world: child-rearing and work. Many of the matters about which we would like to speak to you now have already been discussed with American families similar to yours who also have a child in the fifth grade of elementary school. This study will provide a way to compare opinions of Italian families with those of American families on these subjects.

Con questa ricerca desideriamo venire a conoscenza del Suo modo di sentire e delle Sue opinioni riguardo a due aspetti della vita che sono importanti per la gente di tutto il mondo: l'educazione dei figli e il lavoro. Molte delle cose di cui vorremmo ora parlare con Lei sono già state discusse con famiglie americane simili alla Sua e aventi un figlio in 5ª elementare. Questo studio ci darà modo di confrontare le opinioni delle famiglie italiane con quelle di famiglie americane su questi argomenti.

1. How old are your children? (Begin with the first born and continue in order of age.) (Listed by sex.)
   Che etá hanno i Suoi figli? (Cominciare dal primogenito e seguire in ordine di età.) (Figlio, figlia.)

   To interviewer: All subsequent questions concerning the fifth-grade child use an "X" to indicate his name. In asking the question, substitute his given name for the "X."

2. What type of school does X attend? (Religious or public.)
   Che tipo di scuola frequenta X? (Religiosa o pubblica.)
3. Would you tell me what are the best qualities of X?
   Vorrebbe parlami delle qualità migliori di Suo figlio (figlia)?

199

4. What are some of the things X does that please you?
   Quali sono alcune delle cose che X fa e che Le fanno piacere?
5. When X does something to please you, what is your response?
   (From the list of responses given below, place the number "1" next
   to the response most frequently used, and so on.)
   *Quando X compie qualcosa che Le fa piacere, come reagisce?
   (Se viene data più di una risposta, numerare con 1 ciò che viene
   fatto più di frequente, e così via.)*
   a. Never does anything that pleases me.
      Non fa mai niente che mi faccia piacere.
   b. Express praise, pride.
      Esprimo lode, fierezza.
   c. Take it as a matter of course.
      Considero la cosa come naturale.
   d. Hug and kiss.
      Abbraccio, bacio.
   e. Tell him I love him.
      Dico che gli (le) voglio bene.
   f. Don't know.
      Non so.
   g. Other (specify).
      Altro (specificare).
   What is the reaction of your spouse? (Use same categories as above.)
   *Che cosa fa Suo marito (moglie) quando X compie qualcosa che gli
   (le) fa piacere?*
6. Are you inclined to show much affection to X, or are you rather
   reserved in this regard?
   *E'incline a manifestare molto affetto verso X oppure è piuttosto
   riservato(a) in queste manifestazioni?*
7. Are you ever irritated by X?
   Le succede di essere irritato da X?

In the raising of children there are often problems that require the
intervention of parents. We would like to ask how you deal with these
situations. We are not interested in knowing what you would like to
do, but what you actually do in practice.
*Nell'educazione dei bambini sorgono spesso problemi che richiedono
l'intervento dei genitori. Vorremmo ora chiederLe come Ella si
comporta in queste situazioni. Ci interessa sapere non ciò che Ella
ritiene si dovrebbe fare, ma ciò che Ella fa in pratica.*

8. a. Does X ever play wildly? (If "no," go directly to questions 8.g
      and 8.h.)
      Accade che X giochi sfrenatamente?

   If he plays wildly:
   Se gioca sfrenatamente:

b. What does X do when he plays wildly?
   Che cosa fa X quando gioca sfrenatamente?
c. What do you generally do when he behaves himself in this manner?
   Che cosa fa Lei quando X si comporta così?
d. Do you find it necessary at times to use other means?
   Trova necessario a volte usare altri mezzi?

   If you use other means:
   Se usa altri mezzi:

e. What?
   Quali?
f. In which circumstances does this occur?
   In quali circostanze questo si verifica?

   If child does not play wildly:
   Se non gioca sfrenatamente:

g. What would you consider "wild play"?
   Che cosa sarebbe per Lei 'giocare sfrenatamente'?
h. What would you do if your child played wildly?
   Che cosa farebbe se X giocasse sfrenatamente?

To be asked only if the fifth-grader has brothers or sisters:
Questa pagina viene usata soltanto se il bambino ha fratelli o sorelle:

Consider now another very common situation:
Consideriamo ora un'altra situazione molto comune:

9. a. Does X exer fight with brothers and sisters? (If "no," go directly to questions 9.h and 9.i.)
   X litiga mai con i suoi fratelli o sorelle?

   If X does fight with brothers and sisters:
   Se litiga con i suoi fratelli o sorelle:

   b. What does he do when he fights?
      Che cosa fa quando litiga?
   c. Does he fight with older or younger brothers (sisters)?
      Litiga con i maggiori o con i minori?
   d. What do you generally do when X acts in this manner?
      Che cosa fa Lei, generalmente, quando X agisce così?
   e. Do you ever find it necessary to use other means?
      Trova necessario a volte usare altri mezzi?

      If other means are used:
      Se usa altri mezzi:

f. What?
Quali?

g. Under what circumstances?
In quali circostanze?

If the child does not fight with brothers and sisters:
Se non litiga con i suoi fratelli o sorelle:

h. What would you regard as "fighting"?
Che cosa sarebbe per Lei 'litigio'?

i. What would you do if X fought with brothers and sisters?
Che cosa farebbe se X litigasse con i suoi fratelli o sorelle?

10. a. Does your child ever fight with other children? (If "no," go directly to questions 10.h and 10.i.)
Succede che X litighi con altri bambini?

If child does fight with other children:
Se litiga con altri bambini:

b. What does he do when he fights with other children?
Che cosa fa X quando litiga con altri bambini?

c. Does X fight with children who are older, younger, or same age?
Litiga con bambini più grandi, più piccoli, o della stessa età?
(Indicare il sesso dei bambini.)

d. What do you do when X acts in this manner?
Che cosa fa Lei quando si comporta così?

e. Do you find it necessary at times to use other means?
Trova necessario a volte usare altri mezzi?

If other means are used:
Se usa altri mezzi:

f. What?
Quali?

g. Under what circumstances?
In quali circostanze?

If X does not fight with other children:
Se non litiga con altri bambini:

h. What would you consider "fighting with other children"?
Che cosa sarebbe per Lei 'litigare con altri bambini'?

i. What would you do if X fought with other children?
Che cosa farebbe Lei se X litigasse con altri bambini?

11. a. Does X ever really lose his temper? (If "no," go directly to questions 11.g and 11.h.)
Succede che X vada veramente in collera?

If child does lose temper:
Se va in collera:

b. What does X do when he loses his temper?
Che cosa fa X quando va in collera?
c. What do you do when he acts this manner?
Che cosa fa Lei quando X agisce così?
d. Do you find it necessary at times to do anything else?
Trova necessario a volte usare altri mezzi?

If you use other means:
Se usa altri mezzi:

e. What?
Quali?
f. Under what circumstances?
In quali circostanze?

If X does not lose his temper:
Se non va in collera:

g. What would you regard as "really losing his temper"?
Che cosa sarebbe per Lei 'andare veramente in collera'?
h. What would you do if X lost his temper?
Che cosa farebbe se X andasse in collera?

12. a. Does X ever *refuse* to do what you tell him to do? (If "no,"
go directly to questions 12.g and 12.h.)
Succede che X rifiuti di fare ciò che gli (le) dice?

If X refuses to do what you tell him to do:
Se rifiuta di fare ciò che gli (le) dice:

b. Could you tell me of a situation in which X has refused to do
what you had told him to do?
*Potrebbe indicarmi una situazione in cui X si è rifiutato di fare
ciò che gli (le) aveva detto?*
c. What do you do when X acts in this manner?
Che cosa fa Lei quando X si comporta così?
d. Do you find it necessary at times to use other means?
Trova necessario a volte usare altri mezzi?

If you use other means:
Se usa altri mezzi:

e. What?
Quali?
f. Under what circumstances?
In quali circostanze?

If X does not refuse to do what you tell him:
Se non rifiuta di fare ciò che gli (le) dice:

g. What would you consider a refusal to you?
Che cosa sarebbe per Lei un rifiuto?

h. What would you do if X refused to do what you told him to do?
Che cosa farebbe se X rifiutasse di fare ciò che gli (le) dice?

QUALITIES VALUED BY PARENTS
QUALITÀ APPREZZATE DAI GENITORI

13. On this card are listed various personal characteristics. (Hand card to respondent.) Keeping in mind X, which of them do you consider to be important for a child his age? From among these, which do you think is first, second, third in importance?
Su questo foglio sono elencate diverse caratteristiche personali. Tenendo presente X, quali ritiene siano le più importanti per un bambino della sua età? Tra esse, quali considera prima, seconda, terza in importanza?

  a. That he is popular with other children.
  Che sia simpatico agli altri bambini.
  b. That he has good manners.
  Che sia ben educato.
  c. That he is ambitious to succeed.
  Che sia ambizioso di riuscire.
  d. That he keeps himself clean and neat.
  Che si tenga pulito ed abbia buona presenza.
  e. That he is liked by adults.
  Che sia benvoluto dagli adulti.
  f. That he acts in a serious way.
  Che si comporti in modo serio.
  g. That he is able to defend himself.
  Che sappia difendersi.
  h. That he be able to control himself.
  Che sia capace di controllarsi.
  i. That he is affectionate.
  Che sia affettuoso.
  j. That he is happy.
  Che sia felice.
  k. That he is able to play by himself.
  Che sappia giocare da solo.
  l. That he obey his parents.
  Che obbedisca ai suoi genitori.
  m. That he is honest.
  Che sia onesto.
  n. That it is possible to count on his word.
  Che si possa contare su la sua parola.
  o. That he is considerate of others.
  Che abbia considerazione per gli altri.
  p. That he has a searching mind.
  Che abbia uno spirito indagatore.

q. That he is a good student.
   Che sia un buon scolaro.

14. Are there other important qualities not included in the list we have presented that you find desirable for X?
    Ci sono altre importanti qualità non indicate nella lista che Le abbiamo presentato che Lei trova desiderabili per X?

We are interested now in knowing how mothers and fathers might differ in the way they treat their children.
Vorremmo ora sentire delle differenze tra i padri e le madri nel modo di trattare i loro bambini di 5ª elementare.

15. With regard to X, would you say that you or your husband is more:
    Può dirci se nei riguardi di X Ella o Suo marito è più:
    a. Strict.
       Severo.
    b. Sure of self.
       Sicuro di sé.
    c. Easily irritated by the things X does.
       Facilmente irritato dalle azioni di X.
    d. Affectionate and loving toward X.
       Affettuoso e amorevole verso X.
    e. Likely to restrict X's freedom.
       Incline a limitare la libertà di X.
    f. Quicker to praise X for things done well.
       Incline a lodare X per ciò che fa bene.
    g. Likely to be very firm when X misbehaves.
       Propenso ad agire con assoluta fermezza quando X si comporta male.
    h. Likely to impose own will on X.
       Incline a imporre la propria volontà su X.
16. Do you or your spouse make the following decisions, or do you share in these decisions:
    Chi di voi prende:
    a. Every day decisions in the home (making sure that household tasks get done).
       Le decisioni di tutti i giorni riguardanti la casa? (prendere cura che le faccende domestiche vengano eseguite).
    b. Major decisions that affect the family (for example, changing residence or making a large expenditure).
       Le decisioni di maggiori importanza? (come ad esempio cambiare residenza o fare una spesa considerevole).
    c. Decisions directly concerning X (for example, giving him permission to do something).
       Le decisioni che riguardano direttamente X (come ad esempio dargli (le) il permesso di fare qualcosa).

17. With which of the two parents does X more easily talk about things in general?
Con quale dei due genitori X parla più facilmente delle cose in generale?

18. Speaking now of times when the child is feeling a little sad or finds himself in some difficulty: to which does he turn more easily?
Parlando ora di quando il bambino si sente un po' triste o si trova in qualche difficoltà: a chi si rivolge più facilmente?

19. Are there any ways in which you would like to behave differently toward X? If "yes": How?
Vorrebbe Ella stessa comportarsi in qualche modo diverso da come in realtà si comporta verso X? Se sì: Come?

20. Would you like your spouse to behave differently toward X? If "yes": How?
Vorrebbe che Suo marito (moglie) agisse diversamente nei riguardi di X? Se sì: Come?

21. As best as you can remember, when was the last time you physically punished X?
Quando fu l'ultima volta in cui, per quanto si ricorda, diede una punizione fisica a X?

22. During the past six months, how often has it been necessary to punish X in this way?
Nei sei mesi passati, Le è occorso sovente di punire in questo modo X?

23. Is X affectionate toward you?
E' X affettuoso con lei?

24. Are you proud of X?
E' fiero di X?

Let's turn now from your relations with X to talk about some of the things you would like for him in the future.
Passiamo ora dai Suoi rapporti con X a parlare di alcune cose che Ella vorrebbe per Suo figlio (figlia) nel futuro.

Consider first education:
Consideriamo prima la scuola:

25. a. What level of education would you like X to attain?
Che livello d'istruzione vorrebbe che X conseguisse?
b. What level of education do you think is probable for him to attain?
Che titolo di studio ritiene probabile che X consegua?
c. If there is a discrepancy between a and b: Why?
Se a e b discordano: Perché?

26. People have different ideas regarding what children should try to gain from school. Among those listed below, which do you personally think are important for X? Which is the very most important, second most important and third most important?

I genitori hanno idee diverse riguardo a ciò che i bambini dovrebbero trarre dalla scuola. Tra le cose qui elencate, quali sono quelle che Ella personalmente pensa siano importanti. Credo sia importante che la scuola di mio figlio (figlia) provveda a dargli (le):

a. Practical instruction that will help him earn a living.
   Una istruzione pratica che gli (le) serva per guadagnarsi da vivere.
b. Abilities to get along with different types of people.
   La capacità di trattare con tipi diversi di persone.
c. A general education and an appreciation of ideas.
   Una buona cultura generale e sensibilità sul piano delle idee.
d. A knowledge and interest in community and world problems.
   Conoscenza e interesse per i problemi mondiali e della propria comunità.
e. Moral capacities and good conduct.
   Valori morali e una buona condotta.
f. Preparation for marriage and a happy family life.
   La preparazione ad un matrimonio e una vita familiare felice.
   Are there other important things which school should provide that are not on this list?
   Ci sono altre cose importanti che la scuola dovrebbe provvedere e che non son qui elencate?

Let us now speak about the occupational future of X.
Passiamo ora a parlare del futuro professionale di Suo figlio (figlia).

27. If you could choose any occupation for X, which would you select?
    Se Lei potesse scegliere per X una qualsiasi occupazione, quale sceglierebbe?
28. What do you think are the realistic chances that X will achieve this goal?
    Quali sono le probabilità concrete che X faccia questo?
29. We have listed various qualities that an occupation may have. Which of these do you consider important for X to find in his future occupation? Among those that you think are important, which do you consider the very most important, second most important and third most important?
    Abbiamo elencato qui diverse qualità che una occupazione può avere. Quali di esse ritiene importante che X trovi nella sua futura occupazione? Quale la prima, la seconda e la terza in importanza?
    a. An opportunity to use his personal abilities or aptitudes.
       La possibilità di usare le sue personali attitudini e abilità.
    b. An opportunity to earn a lot of money.
       L'opportunità di guadagnare molti soldi.
    c. An opportunity to be creative and original.
       L'opportunità di essere originale e di usare la sua immaginazione.

d. An esteemed social position.
   Una stimata posizione sociale.
e. An opportunity to work with people rather than things.
   L'opportunità di lavorare con persone piuttosto che con cose.
f. A future that is stable and secure.
   Un futuro stabile e sicuro.
g. An opportunity to be relatively free of supervision of others.
   La possibilità di essere relativamente libero dalla supervisione di altri.
h. An opportunity to be a leader.
   L'opportunità di essere una guida per altri.
i. An opportunity to help his neighbor.
   L'opportunità di aiutare il prossimo.
   Are there any other opportunities that you think an occupation should provide for your child that are not on the above list?
   Vi sono altre qualità che l'occupazione di suo figlio (figlia) dovrebbe provvedere e che non è indicata nella lista qui sopra?

THIS SECTION ONLY FOR FATHERS
SOLO PER I PADRI

We have talked about what you would like occupationally for your child. Now we should like to ask about your own occupation.
Abbiamo finora parlato della carriera che Ella ritiene auspicabile per Suo figlio (figlia). Ora vorremmo chiederLe del Suo lavoro.

1. What do you do in your work?
   In che cosa consiste il Suo lavoro?
2. Do you work for others or yourself?
   Lavora Ella per altri o in proprio?

_____

If self-employed:
Se lavora in proprio:

3. What service or product does your company provide?
   Che servizio prodotto fornisce la Sua attività?
4. How many people work for you?
   Quante persone lavorano per Lei?
5. How long have you been in your present position?
   Da quanto tempo Ella ha ricoperto la Sua presente carica?
6. Have you occupied other positions before this? If "yes," what were they?
   Ha ricoperto altre cariche prima della Sua presente? Se sì: Quali?
7. Are you satisfied with your present work?
   E' Ella soddisfatto del Suo lavoro attuale?

_____

Questions 8 through 27 not to be asked of self-employed:

8. What service or product does your company provide?
   Che servizio o prodotto fornisce la Sua azienda?
9. How many people work in your company?
   Quanti dipendenti lavorano nell'azienda?
10. In which section or department do you work?
    In che sezione o reparto lavora Lei?
11. How many people work there?
    Quante persone vi lavorano?
12. What is the position or title of the head of your section or department?
    Che qualifica (posizione, titolo) ha il direttore della Sua sezione o reparto?
    a. Do you have every day contact with him?
       Ha con lui contatti quotidiani?
    b. Who is responsible after him?
       Chi è il responsabile dopo di lui?
    c. Do you have every day contact with him?
       Ha con lui contatti quotidiani?
    d. Who is responsible after him?
       Chi è il responsabile dopo di lui?

    Continue these questions until reaching the supervisor directly above respondent.
    Continuare finché si arriva alla posizione del superiore diretto e dell'intervistato.

13. Which of the above authorities has most responsibility for the direction of your work?
    Tra le persone in autorità chi dirige più direttamente il Suo lavoro? (se la risposta è 'io stesso': a domanda 14)

    To be asked only of those who answer "myself" to question 13:
    Per coloro che dirigono il proprio lavoro:

14. In which circumstances do you direct your own work?
    In quali circostanze dirige Ella il Suo lavoro?

    Go directly to question 20:
    A dom. 20:

    ---

15. Do you supervise others? (Indicate how many.)
    Ha Ella mansioni di supervisione su altre persone? (Indicare su quante persone.)
16. How much authority does your direct supervisor (the person indicated in response to question 13) have over you?
    Quanto controllo il Suo superiore diretto (persona indicata alla domanda 13) esercita sul Suo lavoro?

17. How often do you communicate to this person your ideas on how the work is getting along?
Accade sovente che Ella comunichi a questa persona le Sue idee su come svolgere il lavoro?

18. How do you get along with this person?
Como sono i Suoi rapporti con questa persona?

19. When your supervisor wants you to do something, how does he let you know what he wants?
Quando il Suo superiore vuole ottenere qualcosa da Lei, come fa a comunicarLe quello che vuole?

20. It is very important to you to be promoted to a higher position?
E' molto importante per Lei di venir promosso ad una posizione più elevata?

21. What are your realistic chances of being promoted in the near future?
Quali sono le Sue realistiche probabilità di avere un avanzamento nel prossimo futuro?

22. We should now like to know something about your past occupational experience.
Vorremmo ora sapere quali sono state finora le Sue esperienze di lavoro.

   a. Have you worked elsewhere before joining your present company?
   Ha lavorato altrove prima di entrare nella ditta dove è adesso?

   If yes:
   Se sì:

   b. What did your first work involve?
   In che cosa consisteva il Suo primo la voro?

   c. How long were you in that job?
   Quanto tempo è rimasto in quell'impiego?

   d. What did your second job consists of?
   In che cosa consisteva il Suo secondo lavoro?

   e. How long were you in that job?
   Quanto tempo è rimasto in quell'impiego?

   (Continue through the third, fourth, etc., until you get to present job.)
   (Continuare terzo, quarto, ecc., finchè si arriva all'impiego attuale.)

23. Considering now your present place of employment, did you have in the past jobs that were different from the one you now have?
Considerando ora il Suo attuale impiego, ha avuto in passato mansioni diverse da quelle che svolge attualmente?

   If yes:
   Se sì:

a. What?
Quali?
b. For how long?
Per quanto tempo?

(Start with the earliest full-time job and repeat these questions until you get to the present place in his organization.)
(Ripetere le domande a e b finché si arriva alle mansioni attuali.)

24. Do you do things in your work that you wouldn't do if it were up to you?
Accade spesso che Ella nel Suo lavoro faccia delle cose che non farebbe se dipendesse da Lei?

25. How much influence do you have on the way things are done at work?
Ha Ella molta influenza sul modo in cui viene svolto il lavoro?

26. How do you feel about the following statements?
E' d'accordo sulle seguenti affermazioni?
a. In my place of work, it is not important what one knows; it is who one knows that matters.
Nel mio ambiente di lavoro non ha importanza quello che uno sa, ma sono le raccomandazioni che contano.
b. I feel that I have the power to make decisions in the matters that are truly important to my work.
Sento di avere molto potere di decisione nelle cose che hanno veramente importanza nel mio lavoro.
c. In my work, I feel that I am master of my future.
Nel mio lavoro sento di essere padrone del mio futuro.

27. Are you satisfied with your present job?
E' Ella soddisfatto del Suo lavoro attuale?

For all men, including self-employed:
Per tutti:

28. Here is a list of personal qualities. Based on your experience, which of these are necessary for doing well at your work? (Of those considered important, which is first in importance, second, third?)
Le presento adesso una lista di qualità personali. In base alla Sua esperienza quali di queste sono necessarie per svolgere bene il Suo lavoro?
a. Strict obedience to superiors.
Stretta obbedienza ai superiori.
b. Understanding oneself.
Capire se stesso.
c. Intelligence.
Intelligenza.

d. Doing neither more nor less than is required.
Non fare né più né meno di quello che è richiesto.
e. Being likeable.
Essere simpatico.
f. Perseverence in work.
Perseveranza nel lavoro.
g. Being ambitious to improve one's position.
Essere ambizioso di migliorare la propria posizione.
h. Knowing how to work with others.
Sapere lavorare con gli altri.
i. Knowing how to avoid trouble.
Saper evitare le grane.
j. Being able to sacrifice today for tomorrow's results.
Essere capace di fare sacrifici oggi per ottenere risultati domani.
k. Respect for rules.
Rispetto dei regolamenti.
l. Bold imagination.
Ardita immaginazione.
m. Trust in oneself.
Fiducia in sé.
n. To be very honest.
Essere molto onesto.
o. To have genuine interest in one's work.
Avere un genuino interesse in ciò che si fa.
p. To be able to bear affronts.
Essere capace di sopportare gli affronti.
q. To have a sense of responsibility.
Avere senso di responsabilità.

Are there other qualities, not listed above, which you feel are important for doing a good job?
Ci sono altre qualità, non qui sopra elencate, che Ella ritiene importanti per svolgere bene il Suo lavoro?

29. How important is it to you to earn more money?
Che importanza ha per Lei il guadagnare di più?
30. What are the realistic chances that you will receive an increase in the near future?
Quali sono le Sue realistiche probabilità di avere un aumento nel prossimo futuro?
31. How important is it to you that a man's friends and acquaintances consider him a successful man?
Secondo Lei, quanta importanza ha per un uomo che i suoi amici e i suoi conoscenti lo considerino un uomo di successo?
32. In almost all occupations, it is necessary to work with things (like tools, instruments, machines), with people (conferences, negotiations, assisting), and with ideas (planning, calculating, writing), but occupations require these three types of activities in different proportions.

In quasi tutte le occupazioni è necessario lavorare con cose (come attrezzi, strumenti, macchine, ecc.), con persone (riunioni, contrattazioni, assistenza, ecc.), e con idee (programmare-calcolare-scrivere, ecc.), ma le varie occupazioni richiedono in proporzione diversa ognuno di questi tre tipi di attività.

a. Considering now your typical workday, how much of your time is spent with things, people, and ideas?

   Considerando ora una Sua tipica giornata di lavoro, in quale proporzione il Suo tempo viene dedicato alle seguenti: cose, persone, idee?

b. Which of these three aspects of work is most important in your occupation things, people, or ideas)?

   Quale di questi tre aspetti del lavoro è più importante nella Sua occupazione (cose, persone, idee)?

FOR MOTHERS ONLY
SOLO PER LE MADRI

1. Turning now to a discussion of how you were raised by your parents, do you feel that your way of bringing up your children is different?

   Passando ora a parlare del modo in cui Ella fu educata dai Suoi genitori, trova che il Suo modo di educare i figli è diverso?

   a. What are the differences?

      Quali le differenze?

   b. What are the similarities?

      Quali le somiglianze?

2. Let's speak for a moment of what mothers do for their children. Do you feel that your mother made sacrifices for you?

   Parliamo per un momento di quello che le madri fanno per i loro figli. Pensa che Sua madre si sia sacrificata per Lei?

3. Do you think your mother gave up part of her happiness for you?

   Pensa che Sua madre abbia persino sacrificato parte della sua felicità per il Suo bene?

4. Turning now to you, does it seem that you have given up part of your enjoyment of life for X?

   Passando ora a parlare di Lei, Le sembra di aver rinunciato a godere la vita a favore di X?

5. Do you feel you have given up part of your happiness for X?

   Le sembra di aver persino rinunciato a parte della Sua felicità per X?

6. We would like to ask now what you feel children's obligations are to their mothers.

   Ora vorremmo chiederLe che cosa Lei ritiene siano gli obblighi dei bambini verso le loro madri.

   a. Should a mother expect obedience to compensate her for what she does for him?

      Lei trova che una madre dovrebbe aspettarsi l'obbedienza di Suo figlio in compenso per ciò che Ella fa per lui?

b. Do you find that reminding a child of all that you do for him is a good way of keeping his affection?
   Trova che un buon modo per mantenere l'affetto di Suo figlio è di ricordargli di tanto in tanto ciò che Ella fa per lui?

c. Can a child be fond of his mother but yet often disobey her?
   E' possibile che un bambino provi affetto verso una madre ma nello stesso tempo la disobbedisca spesso?

d. Do you think a child should ask parental advice before coming to a decision about whom to marry?
   Pensa che un figlio (figlia) dovrebbe chiedere l'avviso dei suoi genitori prima di prendere una decisione su chi sta per sposare?

e. Do you feel children nowadays treat their parents as though they were servants?
   Le sembra che oggigiorno i figli trattano i genitori un po'come se fossero i loro servi?

f. Do you feel very lonely when your child is away from home?
   Prova Ella un senso di grande solitudine quando Suo figlio è lontano da casa?

g. Do you feel it is right that a mother do everything possible to prevent her adult child from living away from home?
   Trova giusto che una madre faccia tutto il possibile per impedire che suo figlio ormai grande, se ne vada a vivere lontano?

h. Would your feelings be hurt if your child stopped asking for advice after marriage?
   Si sentirebbe offesa se Suo figlio non continuasse a chiederLe consiglio quando sarà sposato?

i. Do you feel that a father and mother risk losing the respect of their children if they admit being wrong?
   Lei trova che un padre e una madre rischia di perdere il rispetto dei figli se ammette con loro di essere nel torto?

j. Do you think that men need protection and guidance from a strong woman?
   Trova che gli uomini hanno bisogno di protezioni e guida da parte di una donna forte?

k. According to you, what are the essential differences between being a man or woman in Italy?
   Quali sono, secondo Lei, le differenze essenziali tra l'essere un uomo o una donna in Italia?

7. We would like to ask now about your contacts with your relatives.
   Vorremmo ora chiederLe dei Suoi contatti con il parentado.

   a. Do relatives of yours or your husband's live with you?
      Con la Sua famiglia abitano anche parenti Suoi o della famiglia di Suo marito?

      If yes:
      Se sì:

b. Do they in some way take care of the children? (How?)
Prendono in qualche modo cura dei bambini? (Come?)

c. Does the relative take much initiative regarding the child or does he do only what you ask him to do?
Prende egli (ella) (parente) molte iniziative nei riguardi dei bambini o fa solo ciò che Lei chiede di fare?

d. Do you and the relative agree about how to raise the child?
Andate d'accordo con lui (lei) nel modo di educare i bambini?

8. Do you have relatives in Turin?
Ha parenti a Torino?

If yes:
Se sì:

a. With whom are you mostly in contact?
Con chi è più in contatto?

b. How often do you see each other?
Vi vedete spesso?

c. How often do you telephone each other?
Vi telefonate spesso?

d. Do you often speak to them of problems concerning your child?
Parla spesso con loro dei problemi dei Suoi bambini?

e. Is there someone in the family to whom you can easily turn when you need advice or help concerning your child?
C'è qualcuno nella famiglia a cui Ella si rivolge più facilmente quando ha bisogno di aiuto o consiglio per quanto riguarda i bambini?

9. How often does your husband have recreation with other men or by himself?
Ha Suo marito attività ricreative con altri uomini o da solo?

10. Do you and your husband often visit friends?
Lei e Suo marito si vedono spesso con amici?

11. Do your friends live in this area or in another part of the city?
I loro amici abitano nel rione o in altre parti della città?

12. This is a list of groups of people with whom we often share our ways of looking at things. With which of them do you feel most in agreement?
Questa è una lista di gruppi di persone con le quali spesso condividiamo il nostro modo di vedere le cose. Con quale di essi Ella si sente più in armonia?

a. parents (which)   *genitori (quale)*
b. other relatives (which) *altri parenti (quale)*
c. friends   *amici*
d. neighbors   *vicini di casa*
e. colleagues   *compagni di lavoro*
f. teachers   *educatori*

g. religious leaders   *religiosi*
h. writers (who)   *scrittori (chi)*
i. political party   *partito politico*
j. others   *altro*

BACKGROUND

We should like to ask some concluding questions that will help our statistical analysis.
Vorremmo ora terminare ponendoLe alcune altra domande che ci serviranno per la nostra analisi statistica.

1. What is your age?
   Qual'è la Sua età?
2. How far have you gone in your studies?
   Che studi ha compiuto?

For those who have gone beyond elementary:
Per coloro che hanno seguito studi superiori:

3. What kind of school did you attend?
   Che tipo di scuola (professionale, secondaria, università) ha Ella frequentato? (es. liceo classico o scientifico, ecc.)

4. Were you born in Turin?
   E' nativo di Torino?
5. In what province were your parents born?
   In che provincia sono nati i Suoi genitori?
6. What is (was) your father's occupation?
   Quale era (è) l'occupazione di Suo padre?
7. How long have you been living in this city?
   Da quanto tempo vive Ella in questa città?

For mothers only:
Soltanto per le madri:

8. What does your husband do?
   Che cosa fa Suo marito?
9. Where does he work?
   Dove lavora?
10. Do you work?
    Lei lavora?
11. What kind of work do you do?
    Che cosa fa?

12. If you were asked to indicate your social class using one of the following categories, which would you choose? (upper middle class, middle class, working class, lower working class.)

Se le fosse richiesto di classificare l'ambiente sociale a cui appartiene usando una delle seguenti categorie, quale indicherebbe? (borghesia agiata, media borghesia, ceto operaio, ceto sotto proletario.)

13. Approximately how much are the monthly earnings for your family?
    Può dirci a quanto ammonta approssimativamente il guadagno mensile della Sua famiglia?

14. Can you count on a stable income?
    Può Ella contare su uno stabile introito annuale?

15. What is your marital status?
    E' Ella sposato, separato, risposato, vedovo?

16. How long have you been married?
    Da quanto tempo è Ella sposato?

17. Do you consider yourself a believer?
    Si considera Ella un credente?

Index

Aberle, David F., 7
Adams, Bert N., 166 n. 2
Affection of parents: assessment of, 124; conceptualization of, 12; and control of children, 12, 43–44, 50, 128–133, 141; cross-national comparison of, 124–126, 136–138, 141; dimensions of, 123; expression of, 124; and family solidarity, 12; functions of, 12; importance of expressing, 140–142; and occupational experiences, 133–141; and occupational frustration, 134–140, 181; and parental discipline, 99, 124; and sex of children, 134–140; and sex roles, 125–133, 141, 189; and social class, 125–133, 141, 189; and socialization, 99, 123, 140–141, 189
Age: considerations of, in sampling, 20; at marriage in Italy, 23; of spouses and marital companionship, 148–160
Allinsmith, Wesley, 88 n. 9
Almond, Gabriel, A., 30, 34 n. 2
Anderson, R. Bruce W., 27 n. 9
Aspirations of parents: anticipated failure to realize, 109–111; assessment of, 74–75; behavioral consequences of, 11; class identification and, 84–87; cross-national comparison of, 11; of disprivileged strivers, 88, 97; and economic resources, 73, 76–77, 87–98; for education, 74, 76–77, 107–110; effects on, of husband-wife status differentials, 74, 78–83, 97, 190; meaning of, 73; and occupation, 7, 75; and parental discipline, 11, 100, 104–111, 121–122; and parental pressure, 93–94; and parent-child interaction, 11; and sex roles, 104–111; and social change, 37–38, 74; and social class, 75–98, 104–111; and social mobility, 83–87, 189–190; and socialization, 123

Babakat, Mohamed K., 27 n. 9
Bales, Robert F., 103, 127
Banfield, Edward C., 33, 34 n. 1
Banner, Robert T., 27 n. 9
Barber, Bernard, 6 n
Bass, Bernard M., 133 n. 8
Bayley, Nancy, 125 n. 4
Bell, Richard Q., 191 n. 1

Bendix, Reinhard, 29 n, 73 n, 76, 78, 79
Blalock, H. M., Jr., 192 n. 4
Blood, Robert O., 143 n. 2
Bonilla, Frank, 18 n
Bowers, William J., 89 n. 10
Bronfenbrenner, Urie, 103 n. 2, 125 n. 2, 125 n. 3, 125 n. 4, 133
Bronson, Wanda C., 103 n. 4
Broom, Leonard, 1, 191 n. 2
Brunetti, Pier, 19 n
Bureaucracy and socialization, 7. See also Occupational authority
Burgess, Ernest W., 143 n. 1, 157, 162
Burton, Roger V., 88 n. 8, 88 n. 9

Caranti, Elio, 23 n
Cartwright, Darwin, 143 n. 2
Cheating: effects on, of disprivileged striving, 88, 94–98; effects on, of parental pressure, 92–95; measurement of, 89–90; research into, 88–89
Christensen, Harold T., 25 n
Clausen, John A., 125 n. 2
Cochran, W. G., 58 n. 7
Companionship, marital, 12–13; age of spouses and, 148–160; assessment of, 157–162; husband-wife occupational competition and, 162–163; leisure time and, 157–158; meaning of, 157; modernity and, 158–162; social change and, 144, 158, 164–165; and social class, 159–160, 188; and urban residence, 159–160
Consensus, marital, 12–13, 144; husband-wife age relations and, 155–156; and husband-wife communication, 149; husband-wife religious differences and, 153–156; husband-wife status differences and, 152; meaning of, 149; social change and, 144, 164–165; and social differentiation, 151–157
Consideration, parental valuation of cross-national comparison of, 53–55
Control of children: and family solidarity, 41–46, 50; index of parental concern with, 129; and parental affection, 12, 43–44, 50, 128–133, 141; sacrifice as a means of, 44–47, 50; and sex roles, 130–133; and social class, 130–133; and social status, 49–50

219